Anti-Oppressive Social Work

Anti-Oppressive Social Work

A guide for developing cultural competence

Siobhan E. Laird

SAGE Publications
Los Angeles • London • New Delhi • Singapore

First published 2008

SAGE Publications Ltd
1 Oliver's Yard
55 City Road
London EC1Y 1SP

SAGE Publications Inc.
2455 Teller Road
Thousand Oaks, California 91320

SAGE Publications India Pvt Ltd
B 1/I 1 Mohan Cooperative Industrial Area
Mathura Road
New Delhi 110 044

SAGE Publications Asia-Pacific Pte Ltd
33 Pekin Street #02-01
Far East Square
Singapore 048763

Library of Congress Control Number: 2007932194

British Library Cataloguing in Publication data

A catalogue record for this book is available from the
British Library

ISBN 978-1-4129-1235-8
ISBN 978-1-4129-1236-5 (pbk)

Typeset by C&M Digitals (P) Ltd., Chennai, India
Printed in India at Replika Press Pvt. Ltd
Printed on paper from sustainable resources

Contents

Acknowledgements

I would like to thank my editors, Zoe Elliot-Fawcett and Anna Luker, for their total commitment to this project and their encouragement throughout its stages of working and reworking. I am also deeply grateful to the many practitioners in Sheffield who have willingly shared their experiences of working with people from ethnic minorities. Their discussions have helped to shape this book. Finally, I am entirely in the debt of Dorcas Boreland, my mother, who has given invaluable advice and support from the inception of this book.

Preface

About this Book

There are two experiences which have led me to write this book. The first was growing up in Northern Ireland, particularly during the 1970s. The conflict in that part of the United Kingdom cost the lives of over 3,500 people and injured around 45,000. Discrimination, predominantly against Catholics in the public and private sectors, was widespread. The sectarian divide was also articulated through separate provision for Protestant and Catholic children, most of whom attended different schools and, if brought into care, were looked after in different residential homes. It was in my native Northern Ireland that I qualified as a social worker and subsequently worked as a practitioner in Belfast.

The second experience was my move in 1997 to West Africa where I was appointed Co-ordinator of Social Work at the University of Ghana. During my years in Ghana I became aware of the tensions between different ethnic communities. Some tribal groupings wielded more economic and political power than others. Occasionally, frictions flared into violent confrontation resulting in fatalities, the destruction of property, and families made destitute as they fled their villages to escape danger.

These diverse experiences of violence and inequality have made me reflect on my own social-work training and the extent to which it prepared me to meet these challenges. I have found it woefully lacking. Since the 1980s there has been a strong emphasis within social-work training on anti-racist practice. That focus has been exclusively defined by discrimination against *black* service-users by *white* social workers. This concept of racism has failed to embrace the complexities of ethnicity and the cultural differences between people, which lie behind these catch-all terms of *black* and *white*.

My own experiences convince me that to combat racism requires a more comprehensive understanding of discrimination than an exclusive focus on the *black/white* dichotomy. This book forms part of a small, though growing, number of texts which endeavour to improve anti-racist practice by introducing students and practitioners to the cultural backgrounds of ethnic communities living in the United Kingdom. I believe that cultural competence is a necessary and indispensable component of anti-racist practice.

Structure of the Book

Chapter One explores the nature of discrimination against people from ethnic minorities. Chapter Two explores the concepts of anti-racist and anti-oppressive practice and critically examines the meaning of 'race' and 'ethnicity'. Chapter Three examines the concept of cultural competence and proposes a new framework for social-work practice with people from ethnic minorities. Chapters Four to Seven detail research conducted with the main minority groups in Britain, while Chapter Eight explores the cultural backgrounds of economic migrants and refugees living in the United Kingdom. The cultural values and lifestyles of each ethnic community are explored and consideration is given to how these differ from family to family, change over time and are often modified through contact with other communities in the United Kingdom.

At the end of Chapters Four to Eight there is a worked scenario, which explores how a culturally competent practitioner might intervene with service-users and carers from minority communities. They examine how cultural knowledge deployed through an open-minded engagement with service-users and carers can achieve culturally appropriate services. These scenarios are also designed to demonstrate the interconnections between cultural competence and anti-oppressive practice. Each chapter concludes with a short list of further reading to broaden cultural knowledge and deepen critical thinking.

The Conclusion sets out to reconcile cultural knowledge with the practitioner's own heritage and offers guidance on how to improve awareness of one's own cultural influences. This final section also details the major pitfalls practitioners need to avoid when addressing culture in social-work practice.

The Use of the Terms Black and White

It is my contention in this book that the use of *black* and *white* as all-inclusive terms for people disguises important aspects of ethnicity and cultural heritage. However, the first two chapters of this book do employ these catch-all terms. This is because a number of the research studies cited in Chapter One make distinctions between *black* and *white* groupings. I have also used the terms *black* and *white* in Chapter Two as I am critiquing their use in anti-racist theory. For the rest of the book these terms are not used and are replaced by references to people from different ethnic minorities.

The Choice of Ethnic Minorities for this Book

Much controversy has surrounded the categorisation of ethnicities. Different ways of conceptualising ethnic minorities produce different versions of their experiences.

Up until the 1980s national statistics identified ethnic minorities using very broad catch-all terms, typically dividing them into 'Asians' and 'West Indians'. Within these groupings there was no differentiation between those who immigrated to the United Kingdom and those born in the country. Nor were such statistics disaggregated for age or gender. Modood (1992) criticises this method of data collection and analysis because it creates a crude dichotomy between the circumstances of black and white citizens. This in turn disguises the divergent experiences of ethnic minority groups, which can be further subdivided on the basis of age, gender, language, religion, mixed parentage and ethnic self-identification.

Surveys such as the landmark *Fourth National Survey of Ethnic Minorities* in 1997, based around family origin, and the 2001 Census, based on self-identified ethnicity, chosen from a pre-specified list, have endeavoured to refine the process of categorisation. The methods used in these two instances are not above reproach. Recognising the unavoidable imperfections of classifying ethnic groups, this text devotes a chapter to each of the main ethnic communities appearing in the 2001 Census. It endeavours to counteract the homogenising tendency of categorisation in the 2001 Census by highlighting the cultural and religious diversity within each ethnic group. Attention is also given to the differing experiences of ethnicity and racism due to age, gender and disability. In addition, Chapter Eight focuses on white minorities from Eastern Europe and countries of the former Soviet Union alongside black minorities from the African continent.

There is a fine line between drawing on background knowledge of a particular ethnic community to inform practice and making perfunctory stereotypical assumptions about the values of individual families and service-users. Chapters Four to Eight are organised around the main ethnic minorities in the United Kingdom. They are not definitive accounts of different minority groups and only provide information about *some* of the cultural influences which *may* have a bearing on the perspectives and needs of *some* service-users and carers. Taken altogether the chapters are designed to alert practitioners to the range of issues which can bear on the needs of service-users and carers from minority communities.

1

Racism and Ethnic Minorities

A Brief History of Ethnic Minorities in the United Kingdom

Ethnic minorities have formed part of British society since the sixteenth century. In the wake of the slave trade, and later employment as seamen, those of African descent established small but notable communities in the port cities of Bristol, Liverpool, Cardiff and London. Not until the years immediately after the Second World War and the critical need for labour did the United Kingdom witness large-scale immigration from New Commonwealth countries in Africa, the Caribbean and the Indian subcontinent. The labour shortage was acute in unskilled manual employment and low-paid service-sector jobs. Then, as now, these were taken up by recently arrived immigrants while members of the majority white population moved to better paid employment and working conditions. Initially, government policy facilitated the wave of post-war migration under the British Nationality Act 1948, which granted citizens of Commonwealth countries the unfettered right to enter, work and settle with their families in the United Kingdom. Throughout the 1950s and 1960s migrants continued to arrive and establish themselves mainly in Greater London and the principal manufacturing cities of England.

The introduction of the Commonwealth Immigrants Act 1962, changed government policy and sought to limit the numbers of Commonwealth immigrants by establishing stricter controls on who could enter the United Kingdom to work or reside. Immigration legislation enacted during the 1960s and 1970s was chiefly aimed at reducing the numbers from visible ethnic-minority groups entering Britain as opposed to white migrants from Australia, Canada and South Africa (Mason, 2000: 27; Clayton, 2004: 6–7). By the 1960s immigration for visible minorities was largely confined to dependants joining a male family member already settled in the United Kingdom. These ever more restrictive immigration controls were driven by concerns over race relations.

As early as 1958 tensions between white working-class communities and first-generation immigrants in London resulted in the Notting Hill riots. Conservative members of parliament, most prominently Enoch Powell, began to make populist pronouncements on the dangers of permitting entry into the United Kingdom of large numbers of Black and Asian immigrants. It was alleged that they would take the jobs of the indigenous white population and obtain entitlement to public-sector housing and welfare benefits without contributing to the economy (Schoen, 1977). The Government White Paper *Immigration from the Commonwealth* (Home Office, 1965) gave expression to this concern. It declared that the presence in Britain 'of nearly one million immigrants from the Commonwealth with different social and cultural backgrounds raises a number of problems and creates various social tensions in those areas where they are concentrated'. Implicit in this assertion was the anxiety that large ethnic minority populations would retain their own identities, hindering their assimilation into mainstream British society. Control of immigration therefore became closely linked to good race relations.

These assumptions, widely held by both politicians and the general public, resulted in viewing immigration as a problem rather than as a contribution to the economy or cultural diversity. In response to this climate of opinion, legislation enacted during the 1970s and 1980s progressively limited migration from the New Commonwealth, including family reunion. By the 1990s concern over the growing ethnic-minority population in Britain emerged anew as anxiety over the large numbers seeking asylum. In fact, applications for asylum (excluding dependants) rose from around 33,000 per year in 1994 to 84,000 by 2002 (Home Office, 2004: 1). To put this into perspective, even the figures of 2002 represent less than one asylum seeker per 1,000 people who visit the United Kingdom each year, either on business, vacation or to work (CIH, 2003: 4).

The Geneva Convention relating to the Status of Refugees, 1951

This international accord is commonly known as the Refugee Convention and was originally drawn up after the Second World War to safeguard displaced peoples across Europe. It continues to provide the primary source of law worldwide for the protection of refugees. Article 33 places a legal duty on each signatory to the Convention to provide a safe haven for those forced to leave their own countries under the following circumstances.

No Contracting State shall expel or return a refugee in any manner whatsoever to the frontiers of territories where his life or freedom would be threatened on account of his race, religion, nationality, membership of a particular social group or political opinion. (Art. 33(1))

Nations, such as the United Kingdom, which have signed up to the Refugee Convention are obliged to grant asylum to refugees fleeing persecution in their own countries. Recent legislation has made the settlement of asylum seekers in the United Kingdom more difficult than previously. The Asylum and Immigration Act 1996 and the Immigration and Asylum Act 1999 limit asylum seekers' right of appeal against refusal of their application and reduce access to welfare benefits. They also increase the power of the Home Office to deport 'failed' applicants from the country. These statutes were the product of a public perception that the United Kingdom was being swamped by asylum seekers who were invariably making bogus applications, claiming welfare benefits and absconding before they could be removed from Britain (Clayton, 2004: 10–11). Since the attack on the Twin Towers in New York on 11 September 2001, according to Clayton (2004: 16), the prevention of terrorism has become a covert objective of legislation relating to refugees. This is achieved through the ever greater statutory powers of the state to control, detain and remove asylum seekers.

While the term 'ethnic minorities' has become synonymous with black and Asian minorities it must not be forgotten that there are numerous people from white minority groups living in the United Kingdom. Some of these are long established, for example people from Ireland have been migrating to Britain for many centuries. Others, such as Jews and gypsies fleeing persecution, came to settle in England during the nineteenth and early twentieth centuries. More recently, refugees from the Balkan wars of the 1990s and economic migrants from former Eastern Bloc countries, which are now members of the European Union, have increased the size of white ethnic communities in the United Kingdom. There is also increasing movement of people from countries of the former Soviet Union to member states of the European Union. Such individuals are not automatically protected from inequality by virtue of their colour. Many are confronted by the same prejudices, discrimination and immigration controls as are visible minorities.

The 2001 Census

The 2001 Census surveyed the whole of the United Kingdom population and obtained information on people's ethnic background. It established that out of a total population of approximately 59 million 7.9% were from ethnic minorities. Of those describing themselves as from an ethnic minority:

50% identified as Asian
25% identified as Black
15% identified as mixed (dual heritage)
5% identified as Chinese

Almost half of those belonging to ethnic minorities live in London while the rest are concentrated in the major cities of the Midlands and the north of England, reflecting historical patterns of settlement. But this disguises the fact that 78% of 'Black Africans' and 61% of 'Black Caribbeans' live in the capital. By contrast, only 19% of Pakistanis reside in London with 21% settled in the West Midlands and a further 20% in

Yorkshire and the Humber. Different minorities have contrasting settlement patterns which have been strongly influenced by the location of first-generation migrants. The distribution of ethnic-minority populations in the United Kingdom is not only a result of original migration and settlement patterns. The dispersal policy introduced under the Immigration and Asylum Act 1999 relocates asylum seekers from Greater London and the south east to the regions. The National Asylum Support Service arranges for refugees to be accommodated by private- and public-sector landlords in 'cluster areas' within each region on a 'no choice' basis. This has increased the presence of ethnic minorities in towns located away from their established communities and thus in areas which can leave them relatively isolated.

Race and Discrimination

The modern concept of race came to prominence during the nineteenth century. It was based on scientific claims that biological differences explained the diversity of peoples. Such ideas underpinned Social Darwinism which, based loosely on Darwin's theory of evolution, asserted that 'survival of the fittest' justified the dominance of some races over others. Conquest and domination was also rationalised through the belief that European peoples were mentally and physically superior to those of Africa and Asia. This same ideology was used to lend credence to the colonial exploits of European nations and the subjugation of peoples across the world (Miles & Brown, 2004: 37). Social Darwinism was again invoked by the Nazi regime during the twentieth century to legitimise the extermination of Jews in Europe. Public disquiet over colonialism and revulsion at the Holocaust discredited the biological concept of race (Miles & Brown, 2004: 59–60).

Social scientists and policy-makers have shifted attention away from *race* to the notion of *ethnicity*. In a frequently quoted definition, Smith (1986: 192) describes an ethnic group as 'a population whose members believe that in some sense they share common descent and a common cultural heritage or traditions, and who are so regarded by others'.

The Parekh Report

This was the report of a Commission consisting of 23 distinguished persons from different community backgrounds created in 1998 by the Runnymede Trust, an independent think-tank dedicated to advancing racial justice in Britain. The Commission was required to 'analyse the current state of multi-ethnic Britain and to propose ways of countering racial discrimination and disadvantage' (Parekh, 2000: viii). The Commission defined the nature of contemporary racism:

It may be based on colour and physical features or on culture, nationality and way of life; it may affirm equality of human worth but implicitly deny this by insisting on the absolute superiority of a particular culture; it may admit equality up to a point but impose a glass ceiling higher up. Whatever its subtle disguises and forms, it is deeply divisive, intolerant of differences, source of much human suffering and inimical to the common sense of belonging lying at the basis of every stable political community. (Parekh, 2000: ix)

Contemporary racism has also kept pace with changing concepts. Discarding racial prejudice grounded in biology, the 'new racism' which emerged in the late twentieth century relies on the idea of cultural incompatibility (Barker, 1981). Instead of an appeal to 'race', the beliefs and customs of different ethnic groups are characterised as irreconcilable with those of the majority white British population. In other words, those using cultural incompatibility as a justification for curbing immigration have made their language neutral, when in fact their target is still visible minorities (Miles & Brown, 2004: 112). On closer inspection it is arguable that the 'new racism' is simply camouflage for the crudity of biological racism. The preface to Parekh (2000) captures the multifaceted nature of present-day racism

Parekh (2000) distinguishes between street racism and institutional racism. The first consists of overt racism such as abusive language, criminal damage and physical assault – acts usually perpetrated in public spaces. Modood et al. (1997) found in a survey of over 5,000 people from ethnic-minority households that 12% of them had suffered racial abuse within the previous year. For 1% of all those questioned this consisted of a physical assault, while for 2% their property was damaged in a racist attack. In the same survey one in five white people admitted to being racially prejudiced against those of Caribbean origin and one in four against those of Asian descent. Addressing the police force, a report by Her Majesty's Inspectorate of Constabulary stressed that '…to be a victim because of skin colour multiplies the emotional and psychological hurt well beyond that of the physical pain' (Blakey & Crompton, 2000: 45). According to Parekh (2000: 128), this is because racism is an attack upon 'the values, loyalties and commitments central to a person's sense of identity and self-worth – their family, honour, friends, culture, heritage, religion, community, history'. This is particularly true for Asian Muslims who, after the destruction of the Twin Towers in 2001 and the suicide bombings in London during 2005, are increasingly subject to Islamophobia. This form of racism is based on colour, religion and the belief that the Muslim community supports terrorism. Police recorded over 1,200 suspected Islamophobic incidents nationwide in the first three weeks after the bombings on London's transport system on 7 July 2005. These consisted of verbal abuse, arson attacks on mosques and physical assaults on people suspected of being Muslim (*Observer*, 2005; *Guardian*, 2005). The Muslim Safety Forum reported a 500% increase in 'faith-based' attacks across London during July 2005 as compared with the same period in the previous year (BBC, 2005a). More wide reaching than the racist acts perpetrated by individuals is institutional racism, which received unprecedented public attention during the Stephen Lawrence Inquiry.

The Stephen Lawrence Inquiry

Stephen Lawrence, a black youth, was stabbed to death in the street on 22 April 1993 by a group of five white youths in an unprovoked racist attack. The ensuing police investigation produced just a single witness and no one was publicly prosecuted for the murder. Stephen's parents made a number of complaints because of the slow progress of the case. As a result of media attention, a public inquiry was opened in 1997 to examine the failure of the police to properly investigate the racially motivated murder of Stephen Lawrence. The Inquiry concluded that racist attitudes within the Metropolitan Police Service had obstructed an efficient investigation. It also produced a comprehensive and oft-quoted definition of institutional racism:

> The collective failure of an organisation to provide an appropriate and professional service to people because of their colour, culture, or ethnic origin. It can be seen or detected in processes, attitudes and behaviours which amount to discrimination through unwitting prejudice, ignorance, thoughtlessness and racist stereotyping which disadvantage minority ethnic people. (Macpherson, 1999: para. 6.34)

Institutional racism can take many forms. It includes negative stereotyping of people from ethnic minorities, patronising language or actions due to ignorance of a person's culture, the inequitable treatment of people from ethnic minorities and the failure to take into consideration an individual's cultural background. Institutional racism can be inferred from the overwhelming evidence revealed by national statistics and research studies on the experience of ethnic minorities in relation to education, employment, housing, health and criminal-justice.

Education and Ethnic Minorities

It is important to recognise that table 1.1 below does not present a simple picture of underachievement by black and Asian students relative to their white peer group. There is plainly divergence between the genders and various ethnic minorities in terms of academic accomplishment. Overall, students with Indian and Chinese backgrounds are higher academic achievers that those who are White British. Within these ethnic groups, females tend to obtain better results compared with males. Black Caribbean males do particularly badly academically. Those with mixed white and Caribbean heritage also do poorly, compared with white pupils. Although these statistics indicate that discrimination contributes to the underachievement of students from ethnic minorities, there are evidently other processes at work.

Initially, government policy addressed poor academic results among ethnic minorities by assuming that these were the consequence of cultural deficits such as family structure

Table 1.1   2004 GCSE results for ethnic minorities

Ethnic Group and Gender	Percentage of 15-year-olds in England achieving five or more GCSEs at grades A–C in 2004
Chinese females	79
Indian females	72
Chinese males	70
Indian males	62
White British females	57
Pakistani females	52
White British males	47
White & Black Caribbean females	45
Black Caribbean females	44
Pakistani males	39
White & Black Caribbean males	34
Black Caribbean males	27

Source: Department for Education and Skills (2005a: Table 3)

and customs. The official response was to assimilate pupils into the education system by insisting that they adjust. This strategy was part of a wider agenda to absorb ethnic minorities into mainstream society and ensure that they did not remain distinctive from the majority white population (Gillborn, 1990: 142–6). The failure of this policy to improve the academic performance of ethnic-minority pupils led to the adoption of multicultural education which explicitly acknowledges and values diverse cultural backgrounds.

However, evidence suggests that students from ethnic minorities are still treated differently on the basis of stereotypes, which many teachers from the white majority hold. For example, African-Caribbean boys are assumed to be trouble-makers or thought only able to excel on the sports field, while Asian girls are supposed to be passive and compliant. These stereotypes alter the behaviour of teachers in ways which reinforce underachievement for African-Caribbean boys and Pakistani or Bangladeshi girls (Gillborn, 1990: 113–14; Troyna & Carrington, 1990: 50–5). Labelling of black males as disruptive also explains the disproportionate numbers of black pupils who are excluded from schools.

School exclusions

Figures produced by the Social Exclusion Unit show that:

    0.58% of African-Caribbean pupils were excluded
    0.15% of White pupils were excluded
    0.04% of Indian pupils were excluded
    0.03% of Chinese pupils were excluded

(SEU, 2000a: Table 2)

A greater percentage of African-Caribbean pupils are excluded than are white pupils. It is also important to note that children from other ethnic minorities, such as those of Indian or Chinese heritage, were actually less likely to be excluded than white children. Clearly there are differences in the experiences of pupils from ethnic minorities in terms of academic achievement and school exclusions. They cannot simply be lumped in together and assumed to be subject to the same kinds of discrimination.

Despite evidence of racism in schools (Gillborn, 1990; Mirza, 1992), Asian and black students in the 18–24 years age range are actually over-represented in universities as a proportion of their numbers in the population. Overall, those from ethnic minorities are 50% more likely to obtain a university place than applicants from the majority white community. This reflects the perseverance of individual students from ethnic-minority backgrounds to achieve university-entry requirements. It also hides the fact that the vast majority of ethnic-minority students are concentrated in the 'new universities' rather than the more prestigious 'red brick' universities which can in turn reduce their career prospects (Modood, 2003: 61). In terms of achievement in higher education, 14% of those identifying as Chinese obtained a higher degree while only 5.1% of the white population held such a qualification. The proportion of the working population who were black, Asian or of mixed heritage holding a higher degree was similar to that of the white majority (Department for Education and Skills, 2005b: Table 1).

Employment and Ethnic Minorities

The first generation of post-war immigrant workers from South Asia and the Caribbean were predominantly from rural backgrounds and tended to be concentrated in low-paid jobs in transport, the textile industries and the health service. Their adult children, although born and educated in Britain, continue to be over-represented in unskilled and semi-skilled work. During the 1970s 'African-Asian' refugees expelled from the newly independent states of East Africa also arrived in Britain. Many of these refugees were highly educated professionals and came to Britain with substantial economic means at their disposal. Often they set up their own successful business enterprises. Highly qualified asylum seekers and economic migrants continue to settle in the United Kingdom, bringing with them considerable experience. Despite the advantages of many people from ethnic minorities, given their educational and professional qualifications, they experience higher unemployment rates and lower-paid occupations than the majority white population. Analysis of Labour Force Survey figures by SEU (2000b: 92) show that while less than 4% of the white population with a degree were out of work, this rose to 6% of Asian graduates and around 12% of African Caribbeans.

The Parekh Report

The Commission identified the disadvantaged position of ethnic minorities in the work-force and summarised their position as:

...over-represented in low-paid and insecure jobs; [they] have lower wages than the national average; and often work antisocial hours in unhealthy or dangerous environments. Many are not working at all. The underlying causes include industrial restructuring and a range of discriminatory practices by employers. Among individuals who are in work, many have good or excellent qualifications. They nevertheless have greater difficulty than white people with the same qualifications in gaining the most sought-after jobs – the top 10 per cent of jobs are denied to them by various subtle glass ceilings. (Parekh, 2000: 192–3)

As revealed in Table 1.2, there are substantial differences in unemployment rates as between ethnic groups and the majority white population. These figures also disguise the higher levels of part-time employment among some ethnic groups. Part-time work among men from the Bangladeshi, Pakistani and Black African communities is two to three times higher than among white males. For women, part-time employment is much more evenly distributed across ethnic groups, with around one-third of all women undertaking work on this basis. Doubtless this reflects their greater domestic and child-care responsibilities (Heath & Cheung, 2006: 13). It is also significant that 23% of those identifying as ethnically Chinese and 25% of those identifying as Pakistani are self-employed as compared with just under 7% of white people. This substantially reduces potential unemployment among these ethnic groups and thus it being reflected in official statistics. Furthermore, as compared with white people, unemployment rates among ethnic minorities are 'hyper-cyclical', meaning that in times of recession jobs are lost to those from ethnic minorities at a much faster rate than to those from the majority white population. This is because they are over-represented in casual and unskilled or semi-skilled jobs which tend to be lost first in times of recession (Jones, 1993: 112–23).

There are a number of explanations as to why people from ethnic minorities do less well in the job market. There is evidence that, for some, poorer language skills in English are an obstacle to employment (Gray et al., 1993; Modood et al., 1997: 87). Though this fails to explain the finding that there is no appreciable difference in the employment prospects of first- and second-generation immigrants, despite the fact that those growing up in Britain will almost certainly have fluency in English (Heath & McMahon, 1997; Heath & Cheung, 2006: 2). Nor does it explain why those from Indian and Chinese minorities are better qualified than those from the majority white community and yet are not proportionately represented in higher-paid occupations (Parekh, 2000: 194).

Explaining these contradictions, an important study by Brown and Gray (1985) found that, despite the Race Relations Act 1976 outlawing racial discrimination, many

Table 1.2 Unemployment 2001–2004

Ethnicity	Men (%)	Women (%)
White	5	4
Indian	6	7
Bangladeshi	17	13
Pakistani	13	15
Chinese	4	6
Black Caribbean	15	11
Black African	14	12

Source: Heath & Cheung (2006)

employers continued to treat those from ethnic minorities less favourably than white people. The research surveyed employer replies to job applications and found that 90% of white applicants received a positive response as compared with only 63% of Asians and African Caribbeans. A later study by Simpson and Stevenson (1994) revealed that the probability of a white applicant being called to a job interview was twice that of an Asian or African-Caribbean applicant.

Housing and Ethnic Minorities

Household size together with the tenure, location and condition of housing are closely linked to the wealth and health of family members. Large household size combined with low income may create problems of overcrowding. For example, the average Bangladeshi and Pakistani household is twice as large as that for African Caribbeans and members of the majority white population (GHS, 2003). While cultural factors and personal preference may account in part for larger family groupings, it is not coincidental that 60% of Bangladeshi and Pakistani households are on low income. This compares with just 20% of white people (National Statistics Online, 2005). Tenure is also significant given that a substantial amount of money can be locked up in the capital value of an owner-occupied home in contrast to rented accommodation.

The rates of owner occupation are highest among the majority white and Indian populations. This contrasts with African Caribbeans, only half of whom own their homes with under half renting from the council or a housing association. This compares to just one-fifth of the British white population who rent from the council or a housing association. It is notable that just one-tenth of those from Indian communities rent from the social sector, that is to say half the proportion of the white population. It is important to note from Table 1.3 that there is considerable variation in the housing-tenure patterns of different ethnic groups. For example, there is a much higher level of owner-occupation and a lower level of social housing among the Indian community than among other ethnic-minority groups. At the other end of the scale,

Table 1.3   Housing tenure by ethnic group

Tenure ethnic group	Owner-occupied (%)	Rented from council/housing association (%)	Privately rented (%)
White British	71	20	9
Indian	78	10	12
Pakistani & Bangladeshi	62	20	18
Black Caribbean	48	45	6
Black African	26	51	23

Source: GHS (2003)

one-quarter of those from black African communities own their own homes with half renting from the local authority or a housing association.

Owner-occupation among the white population is strongly associated with greater wealth secured through the capital value of a home. Historically, for many ethnic-minority families owner-occupation has been a response to discrimination in both the public and private rental sectors. Extended families have clubbed together to purchase their own dwelling or utilised wider social networks within their ethnic community to obtain finance and contacts. Much of this housing is located in impoverished inner-city areas and is in disrepair. Low income among many ethnic minorities may further contribute to the poor maintenance of such dwellings. Owner-occupation for substantial numbers of ethnic-minority families actually results in more overcrowding and poorer housing conditions than renting from the local authority or a housing association (Mason, 2000: 81). Conversely, many households, particularly those from Indian and African-Asian groups, have been able to purchase detached and semi-detached properties and move to the suburbs (Modood et al., 1997: 222). Despite this progress, 56% of people from ethnic minorities live in the 44 most deprived local authority areas in the United Kingdom (SEU, 2000a: 17).

Typically, ethnic minorities are concentrated in particular inner-city areas. These have been popularly portrayed as segregated communities and ghettos of disadvantage. In these localities overcrowding, poor housing, unemployment, lack of amenity and high crime rates intersect. More recent research paints a different picture. In a comprehensive study, Modood et al. (1997) found that while there was evidence of segregation, this was not extreme. Pakistanis and Bangladeshis resided in local-authority wards where the average proportion of inhabitants from ethnic minorities was around one-third. For those of African-Caribbean descent the comparable figure was one-quarter. By contrast, Chinese households tended to live in wards where on average just one-seventh of the population was from ethnic minorities (Modood et al., 1997: 187). Discrimination by estate agents and public and private landlords in conjunction with low incomes have undoubtedly combined to restrict the housing options for people from ethnic minorities.

However, as Modood et al. (1997: 221) discovered, households also made active choices to reside close to kin or members of their own community. This is often to ensure mutual material and social support and for the reassurance of living in close proximity to others who share common linguistic, cultural and religious traditions.

Indeed, one of the reasons why homelessness tends to be a hidden problem among ethnic minorities is that many individuals and families depend on relations and wider social networks to provide accommodation in times of need (Chahal, 1999). The housing patterns of ethnic minorities are thus determined by interaction between the constraints posed by racism and low income, on the one hand, and positive choices to reside near members of one's own community, on the other hand.

The Benefits System and Ethnic Minorities

Craig and Rai (1996: 132–4), in their collation of the research, concluded that institutional racism, the failure of social-security agencies to translate information into minority-community languages or understand other cultures, and claimants' fear of the authorities explained the lower take-up of benefits by ethnic minorities. The Social Security Act 1986, which granted much greater discretion to staff in deciding claims, increased the potential for racial discrimination (Craig & Rai, 1996: 132). On the other side of the equation, people speaking English as a second or third language, or who could not speak it at all, were reliant on receiving information from relatives and friends (Craig & Rai, 1996: 135). Increasingly stringent immigration and residency rules regarding entitlement and anxiety over the action of immigration officers also reduce benefit claims from ethnic minorities (Craig & Rai, 1996: 132).

Difficult encounters with welfare agencies are one aspect of the low take-up of benefits by people from ethnic minorities. Another factor is the reluctance of some members of ethnic communities to claim benefits from the state. For example, many people among the Chinese community prefer to rely on kin support if at all possible rather than resorting to state benefits. Indeed, some may even feel ashamed to have to rely on the state rather than their family. For a number of individuals of Pakistani and Bangladeshi descent claiming benefit is associated with charity for the poor and therefore perceived as being only for those in extreme need. Some individuals felt stigmatised by other members of their ethnic community for claiming benefit. In particular, their relatives could come in for criticism for failing to adequately support them. But, where individuals had made national-insurance contributions, there is often a sense of entitlement to benefit. In these circumstances, the complexity of claiming benefits, the patronising attitudes of staff and a lack of interpreters dissuaded a number of people from applying (Law et al., 1994). Those unused to making their own financial decisions or interacting with people outside their kin group or community (most often women) are likely to feel distressed and possibly overwhelmed (Barnard & Pettigrew, 2003: 4).

Pensions are problematical for many individuals from ethnic-minority groups for a number of reasons. First, the high rates of unemployment among some minority communities relative to the majority white population means that many do not have a personal pension, nor will they have contributed towards a state pension. Secondly, the nature of low-paid and casual work which most first-generation immigrants had to accept regardless of their qualifications also means that a substantial proportion were

Table 1.4   Pension coverage among ethnic minorities

Ethnic minority	Pension coverage* for men (%)	Pension coverage* for women (%)
White	61	37
Indian	46	26
Black	35	30
Chinese/Other	33	23
Pakistani	17	6
Bangladeshi	9	3

*Includes those contributing to private or occupational pensions
Source: Adapted from Ginn & Arber (2001: 528)

not able to contribute to a pension scheme. Thirdly, self-employment or employment in family-owned businesses may also disadvantage older people in pension terms. This is because many will have made no pension provision, while others have not been able to depend on an employer's contribution to an occupational pension topping up their own payments. Consequently, older people from ethnic minorities have less income available from personal or occupational pension schemes and therefore are more reliant on means-tested benefits than are those from the white majority community (Ginn & Arber, 2001: 522). The large-scale analysis of pension coverage among men and women aged 20–59 years conducted by Ginn and Arber (2001) discovered differences between genders and ethnic groups.

It is evident from Table 1.4 that men in all ethnic groups are more likely than women to be in a pension scheme. However, there are substantial differences in the proportions of people from ethnic minorities contributing to a pension. For example, 35% of men and 30% of women among the African and African-Caribbean communities are in a pension scheme compared with only 9% of Bangladeshi men and just 3% of Bangladeshi women. These revealing statistics reflect the different employment profiles of the various minority communities. They also demonstrate that older people among the Pakistani and Bangladeshi communities, particularly women, are likely to be the most financially disadvantaged in retirement.

Health and Ethnic Minorities

Research has consistently revealed positive correlations between ill-health, unemployment, poverty and poor housing conditions (Mason, 2000: 92). It is therefore not surprising to find that ethnic minorities are at greater risk of illness than the population as a whole. Table 1.5 presents results from a national survey as to the risk of a person from a given ethnic minority suffering ill-health.

Most striking is the much higher risk of ill-health among Pakistani and Bangladeshi communities as compared with the rest of the population. Both men and women in these minority groups are three to four times more likely to rate their health as bad or very bad

Table 1.5   Self-assessed health among ethnic minorities

Ethnic groups	Standardised risk ratio for males	Standardised risk ratio for females
General population	1.0	1.0
Indian	1.6	2.6
Pakistani	2.9	3.6
Bangladeshi	3.9	3.3
Black Caribbean	1.2	1.8
Chinese	1.1	0.9

Source: Department of Health (2001a)

compared with the general population. These same two ethnic minorities experience the highest rates of unemployment and the lowest incomes. Indeed, all those from ethnic-minority groups (with the exception of Chinese communities) are at greater risk of sickness than the general population. Nazroo (1997), in his analysis of a national survey, found that if adjustment was made for social class, housing and standard of living, then the disparity in the chances of becoming ill between the white population and ethnic minorities was substantially reduced. Aside from a correlation with poverty, research studies reveal a linkage between racial harassment, increased levels of stress and a higher incidence of ill-health (Nazroo, 2003: 100–1). A comprehensive review of research on ethnic-minority health was conducted by Smaje (1995), who found that most studies failed to take into account institutional racism and wider socio-economic inequalities when examining referral rates and service provision for ethnic minorities. These studies challenge the dominant view that there is a race factor determining the health outcomes for different ethnic communities. Only in very few cases, for example the higher incidence of sickle-cell anaemia among African and Caribbean peoples, has incontrovertible evidence established that a disease has a purely genetic cause.

Most studies on the incidence of mental illness in ethnic groups have relied on admission rates to hospitals. By contrast, the EMPIRIC (Ethnic Minority Psychiatric Illness Rates in the Community) survey investigated prevalence rates of psychiatric illness among a random sample of those living in the community. No statistically significant differences in the incidence of psychotic illnesses among ethnic minorities compared with the white majority population were found. Nor were there any marked differences in the prevalence of common mental disorders (i.e. depression, anxiety and obsessive-compulsive disorder) among different minorities or between them and the white population (Sproston & Nazroo, 2002). Yet, ethnic minorities are over-represented among those diagnosed with a mental disorder or admitted to psychiatric wards. For example, African-Caribbean men are five times more likely to be diagnosed with schizophrenia than are white males. Asian men are three times more likely than white males to be so diagnosed. Similar findings have been collated for women (Mason, 2000: 98). Proportionately, more individuals from ethnic minorities are compulsorily subject to detainment and treatment under the Mental Health Act 1983 than are white people (NIMHE, 2003: 19).

The explanation for the marked differences between the diagnosis and treatment of those from ethnic minorities in contrast to the majority white population is now a matter of considerable controversy. Diagnosis of a mental disorder is dependent on the observation of the behaviour and the self-report of the person being assessed. Therefore, it is argued that racial stereotypes play a substantial role in the assessment of mental health among ethnic minorities (Knowles, 1991; Sashidharan & Francis, 1993). The pervasive labelling of African-Caribbean men as 'aggressive' would explain why they are three times more likely to be compulsorily detained under the Mental Health Act 1983. Once detained, there is a higher probability that they will be identified as violent, kept in secure units or special hospitals and receive invasive treatments such as major tranquillisers and electro-convulsive therapy (Smaje, 1995: 66).

The Criminal-Justice System and Ethnic Minorities

People from ethnic minorities are over-represented in the criminal-justice system. Drawing together research findings and Home Office statistics, Mason (2000: 105–9) reveals the inequitable treatment of white suspects and offenders compared with those from ethnic minorities. Under the 'stop-and-search' powers of the Police and Criminal Evidence Act 1984, black people are five times more likely to be stopped by police than white people. A breakdown of more recent figures from the Criminal Justice System Race Unit (CJS, 2006: v) found that under s. 1 and s. 60 of the 1984 Act, black people are respectively six and fourteen times more likely to be stopped and searched compared to white people. Statistics for those of Asian origin reveal that they are twice as likely to be stopped and searched under s. 1 and six times as likely to be so under s. 60 compared with white people. Around one in ten people are arrested in these circumstances, but these are disproportionately from ethnic-minority populations. Aside from arrests under 'stop-and-search', black people are on average five times, and Asians three times, more likely than members of the white population to be arrested in other circumstances.

Once under arrest a person can be informally dealt with, cautioned or detained. Home Office figures show that black people are less likely to be cautioned as opposed to being charged than white people or Asians. If brought before the court, a black person has between a 5% and 7.6% greater chance of receiving a custodial sentence than a white offender. Those of Asian descent are actually less likely to be sent to prison than are white people, although this finding varies across the country. If a black or Asian offender is sentenced to prison, the length of their term is likely to be longer than that for a white individual (Mason, 2000: 105–9). Home Office figures show that this general pattern is the same for both men and women. People from ethnic minorities account for 18% of males in prison and 24% of females even though they comprise only 7.9% of the population as a whole (SEU, 2000a: 34; National Statistics, 2003). Drawing together national statistics, Parekh (2000: 130) noted that black people were six times more likely to be in prison than white people. Given this overall picture, it is not surprising to discover that in regular national surveys around one-third of people from ethnic-minority groups express the view that they would be treated less favourably by the criminal-justice system than those who are white (CJS, 2006: vi). Mason (2000: 108) characterises these instances of discrimination as a 'process of cumulative disadvantage in which differences of treatment at successive stages of the criminal justice system mount up to generate significant differences between ethnic groups in their representation in the prison population'.

A number of explanations account for the over-representation of ethnic minorities at every level in the criminal-justice system. The Report of the Stephen Lawrence Inquiry made detailed examination of police attitudes towards people from ethnic minority communities. It concluded that the disparity in stop-and-search figures across different ethnic communities was due to racist stereotyping. Such stereotyping within the police force went unchallenged through lack of training on race relations or cultural awareness (Macpherson, 1999: para. 6.45). By pooling the research on discrimination within the criminal-justice system Mason (2000: 110–16) identifies a number of other factors. These include the role of the media in caricaturing people from ethnic minorities in ways which produce moral panics. For example, young black men are consistently portrayed on television and in the newspapers as aggressive and responsible for a large proportion of rapes, muggings and violent crime. In fact, more people from the majority white community commit these crimes. Negative stereotypes of this kind pressure the police to act while at the same time shaping police attitudes. The end result is a self-fulfilling prophecy in which more black men are suspected of criminal activity, stopped and searched or arrested.

Social Care and Ethnic Minorities

In their overview of the literature, Butt and Mirza (1996: 31) conclude that there is no convincing evidence of a higher incidence of abuse or neglect of children among black families. Conversely, using evidence from government statistics, Thoburn et al. (2005: 49) discovered that in 2003 of all children in need 20% were from ethnic minorities even though they made up just 13% of the total child population. When these figures were further broken down it was found that:

- children of Chinese or Indian heritage were less likely to be receiving an 'in need' service than would be expected from their numbers in the child population
- Bangladeshi children were in receipt of an 'in need' service in the same proportions as they appear in the child population as a whole
- children who had an African or African-Caribbean parent and a white parent were twice as likely to be receiving an 'in need' service as would be expected from their numbers in the child population.

This disparity is similar in relation to child protection, with 17% of ethnic-minority children receiving a formal service when they make up just 13% of the total child population. When this figure is broken down it again shows that those of mixed heritage are over-represented and those of Asian heritage are under-represented within the child-protection system as against their proportions in the entire child population (Thoburn et al., 2005: 75). Yet again, the pattern is repeated for 'looked after children', with 18.5% of them from ethnic minorities. Those children having mixed heritage or both parents of Caribbean or African descent were twice as likely to be 'looked after' as their proportions in the child population would indicate. By contrast, children of Asian heritage are only half as likely to be 'looked after', as would be expected from their proportion in the child population.

In an overview of the quality of social services provided to ethnic-minority children and families, O'Neale (2000: 1–4) concluded that most local authorities did not offer services appropriate to, or sensitive to, the needs of ethnic minorities; families often experienced difficulty accessing social services; ethnicity was not fully addressed in social-work assessments; and practitioners had varying levels of understanding of ethnic minority issues. A more recent review of the research by Thoburn et al. (2005) came to similar conclusions. Surveys of young people continue to reveal that their religious and cultural backgrounds were often ignored by residential staff and foster carers. In some instances this left them isolated from their own ethnic community after leaving care (Barn et al., 2005). Studies on young carers among ethnic-minority families found that professionals use cultural stereotyping, presume that young carers receive assistance from their extended families, disregard the positive aspects of a child's caring role, and fail to appreciate parental mistrust of social services. These appear to be major obstacles for ethnic-minority families in obtaining appropriate services (Shah & Hatton, 1999; Jones et al., 2002).

A study by Chamba et al. (1999) which surveyed 600 ethnic-minority families caring for a severely disabled child found that ethnic-minority respondents reported higher levels of unmet need than did white families. In a report commissioned by the Department of Health to review the literature on ethnic-minority experiences of services for people with learning difficulties, Mir et al. (2001: 47–8) found that social-care agencies failed to pay sufficient attention to cultural background, most particularly the importance of religious faith and contact with other members of a service-user's own ethnic community. This made it difficult for many service-users to preserve a robust and meaningful sense of cultural identity. Stereotyping by professionals of ethnic-minority people with learning difficulties and their carers was another obstacle to quality in service provision identified in the report. Commenting on ethnic-minority carers, Butt and Mirza (1996: 101) noted the scarcity of studies in this area. On the basis of incomplete research, they mention that carers from the white majority, like those from ethnic minorities, can be both 'unsupported and isolated'. However, for carers from ethnic groups, 'this is often exacerbated by communication difficulties and the lack of sensitive and appropriate services. Service provision continues to remain ethnocentric, geared to meeting the needs of the white majority' (Butt & Mirza, 1996: 101).

Studies of service provision for people from ethnic minorities with sensory impairments reveal similar concerns. This is a particularly pressing issue for people with hearing impairments who find that deaf culture is dominated by the viewpoint of the white- majority community. As a result, many deaf people from ethnic minorities feel their spirituality or cultural outlook is not reflected in day-to-day activity with other deaf people. They often experience a contradiction between their heritage, which it can be difficult for them to access because they use British Sign Language, and deaf culture. Both social-care workers and their managers appear reluctant to engage with the dilemmas posed for such individuals. Either agencies fail to act due to other budgetary priorities or staff from the white-majority population abdicate responsibility for meeting the cultural needs of service-users (Ahmad et al., 1998; Flynn, 2002). Physically disabled service-users from Asian minorities have identified a lack of cultural knowledge among social workers as a major factor in their low confidence in either them or the services they offer (Vernon, 2002).

Mental-health services for people from ethnic minorities are the subject of mounting criticism. Some minorities, for example those from the African-Caribbean community, are subject to higher levels of compulsory detainment under the Mental Health Act 1983 and higher dosages of psychotropic drugs than are members of the white majority population (Mclean et al., 2003: 658). Those from Asian backgrounds are under-represented in the mental-health-care system. In part this is due to stereotypical assumptions on the part of professionals that they are more 'psychologically robust' and are cared for by their families. The failure of services to acknowledge the impact of racism on mental health or adapt to the cultural and religious needs of people from Asian minorities is another reason for low take-up of provision (Wilson, 2001).

Referring to mental-health provision for older people from ethnic minorities, the government acknowledged that 'services may be neither readily accessible nor fully appropriate. Assessments may be culturally biased, making it difficult for needs to be properly identified, or assumptions may be made about the capacity and willingness of families to act as primary carers for their older relatives' (Department of Health, 2001b: para. 7.3). This confirmed the findings of an earlier collation of the research by Butt and Mirza (1996: 54) which states that social-care agencies 'are not in a position to meet the social care needs of black elders. There are various barriers, ranging from a lack of knowledge of services to racism, or to inappropriate services.' This con-clusion accords with the findings of the government's own investigation into service provision for ethnic-minority elders. The inspection revealed that 'the ethnocentric nature of service provision meant that many black elders had difficulty in having their needs met' (Department of Health & Social Services Inspectorate, 1998: 5). Butt and Mirza (1996: 94–9) come to the overall conclusion that, regardless of age, people with disabilities from ethnic minorities are confronted with services which, due to language barriers, cultural insensitivity and racism, simply fail to meet their needs.

📖 Further Reading

Butt, J. & Mirza, K. (1996) *Social Care and Black Communities*. London: HMSO. This report provides an overview of research studies examining the experiences of ethnic-minority service-users and carers. It covers a wide range of service provision, from children to adults and older people, in relation to both mental and physical health.

Department of Health & Social Services Inspectorate (1998) *'They Look After Their Own, Don't They?': Inspection of Community Care Services for Black and Ethnic Minority Older People*. London: HMSO. This government inspection examines the extent to which Social Services Departments are meeting the needs of older people from ethnic minorities. It makes recommendations for improvement to service delivery.

Modood, T., Berthoud, R., Lakey, J., Nazroo, J., Smith, P., Virdee, S. & Beishon, S. (eds) (1997) *Ethnic Minorities in Britain: Diversity and Disadvantage,* The Fourth National Survey of Ethnic Minorities. London: Policy Studies Institute. This is a comprehensive overview of social and economic conditions of the major ethnic minorities in the United Kingdom.

Thoburn, J., Chand, A. & Proctor, J. (2005) *Child Welfare Services for Minority Ethnic Families*. London: Jessica Kingsley. This book presents an overview of the research literature on the delivery and outcomes of child-welfare services for families from ethnic minorities. It also details the implications of the findings for policy and social-work intervention.

2

Anti-Racist and Anti-Oppressive Practice

Case Study 2.1

Mr and Mrs Chowdhury both came originally from Bangladesh and settled in Britain during the 1960s. They live in the same locality as their adult son, Hanif, who is married to Razia, whose parents also come from the same village as Hanif's. Nazneen, aged 16 years, is the eldest of their four children and has two sisters and one brother aged 14, 10 and 8 years. They all live together in the same three-bedroom terraced house. Hanif's elder brother, who is also married and has a young family, lives just a few doors away in the same street.

Nazneen is presently undertaking her GCSEs at school and is expected to achieve 'A' and 'B' grades in her up-coming examinations. Two weeks ago she complained to her best friend at school, Andrea, that her parents are planning an arranged marriage for her with a cousin from Bangladesh, whom she has not yet met. Nazneen tearfully tells Andrea that she does not want to marry and is worried that her parents are going to make her. She thinks her parents are already negotiating the dowry. That evening Andrea informs her mother, who is white and English, that Nazneen is being pressured to marry. Within a few days Andrea's mother telephones Children's Services to express concern at the prospect of Nazneen being forced into a marriage she does not want. Andrea's mother insists that Social Services should intervene to prevent it.

- What would be an anti-racist position in this situation?
- To what extent does anti-oppressive social work provide sufficient guidance for good practice?
- How would an awareness of the cultural heritage of Nazneen's family help intervention?
- What would culturally competent practice look like if Children's Services were to intervene?

There is disagreement within the social-work profession between advocates of an anti-racist approach and those who promote cultural competence as strategies to eradicate racial discrimination from social-work practice. Those supporting dominant anti-racist approaches argue that focusing on the cultural aspects of ethnic-minority experience will undermine endeavours by social workers to challenge racism. They also believe that cultural sensitivity will result in practitioners stereotyping service-users and carers from ethnic communities by assuming that they all hold the same values and abide by the same norms of behaviour. This chapter both explores these perspectives and demonstrates that understanding different cultures, through acquiring cultural knowledge, is a vital component of effective anti-racist practice.

Anti-Racist Practice

Concern with racism first emerged in the social-work profession in the 1970s and during the 1980s major social-work texts appeared to guide practice (Payne, 2005: 277). By 1990 the introduction of the new Diploma in Social Work made anti-racist practice a compulsory element of the curriculum for professional training. This was underpinned by *One Small Step Towards Racial Justice* (CCETSW, 1991), which focused on anti-racist approaches in social-work education. Major social-work texts published throughout the 1980s concentrated on the oppression of black service-users by white social workers alongside the broader issues of discrimination in Social Services provision.

Lena Dominelli

Lena Dominelli has been one of the most influential figures in the development of anti-racist practice within the social-work profession. In particular, her book *Anti-Racist Social Work*, which originally appeared in 1988 and has since been republished several times, has become a central text for students and practitioners alike. She identifies three planes on which racism operates.

Individual level – this consists of personal attitudes which negatively evaluate or prejudge those who are black. It also includes behaviours based on those attitudes which discriminate against black people.
Institutional level – this includes all policies, procedures, practices and outputs of an organisation which create inequality in the treatment of black people as compared with white people.
Cultural level – this refers to values, beliefs or ideologies which affirm the superiority of an Anglo-Saxon way of life.

Since individuals work in institutions and both are products of the dominant culture, each level is interdependent. Thus racism is constantly reinforced across the individual, institutional and cultural dimensions.

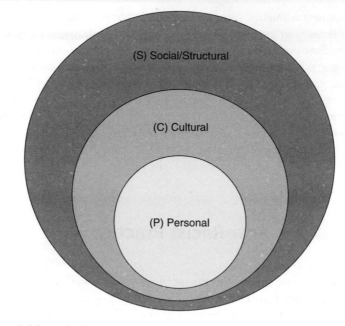

Figure 2.1   PCS analysis
Source: Thomson (2006: 27)

During the 1990s the focus shifted from anti-racist practice to anti-oppressive practice and the development of a generic approach to different forms of discrimination. The shift towards anti-oppressive practice meant that other forms of discrimination on the grounds of class, disability, age, sexuality and gender were identified, together with that of racism. This meant that the interaction of different oppressions could be explored rather than only focusing on racism. Thompson (1998, 2006) advanced 'PCS analysis', which refers to the personal, cultural and structural levels at which discrimination can occur, as a means of identifying and combating oppression, including that against black service-users (see Figure 2.1).

The personal level, shown in the first circle, is embedded in a cultural context, represented by the second concentric circle, which heavily influences individual attitudes, perception and behaviour. The combination of personal and cultural predispositions can create an ethnocentric outlook. Ethnocentrism results in judging other distinctive groups of people according to the norms of one's own group. Any differences observed between one's own group and that of others are at best misunderstood, at worst negatively evaluated. This in turn underpins racist attitudes and behaviour. The third and last concentric circle in Figure 2.1, referred to as the social/structural, encompasses both the personal and cultural levels. This structural level includes social divisions, such as those of gender, race and class. It also embraces political and economic forces which determine the distribution of power and material resources. These factors are collectively termed 'structured inequality'. As in Dominelli's (1997) model, the three dimensions of oppression set out in Figure 2.1 interact with one another to reinforce racism at the personal, cultural and structural level. All of these dimensions profoundly affect the interactions between white social workers and black service-users during intervention.

Dominelli (2002) criticises treating racism separately from other forms of oppression on the grounds that many people are simultaneously subjected to several forms of discrimination. For example, a woman who is both black and disabled will experience oppression due to her gender, race and disability. These oppressions will interact and reinforce one another to produce a distinctive experience of discrimination. It also follows that a social worker can be oppressed while still behaving oppressively towards a service-user. A white female practitioner, for instance, may be oppressed on the basis of gender while oppressing a service-user who is a woman and black on the grounds of race. Dominelli (2002: 46) argues that this double experience, of being both the oppressed and oppressor, opens up an empathetic space enabling social workers to engage in effective anti-oppressive practice. Unlike anti-racist practice, the anti-oppressive approach focuses holistically on each individual and addresses the multiple oppressions to which he or she is subject.

Definitions of Black and White in Anti-Racist Theory

Despite the change of emphasis from anti-racist to anti-oppressive practice, principal exponents of the latter have not reassessed the use of the terms 'white' and 'black' nor the use of 'race'. Dominelli (1997: 9), commenting on her text *Anti-Racist Social Work*, acknowledges that 'this book is conducted largely in terms of black and white. I focus on this division because the groups currently being subjected to the most vicious and intractable expressions of racism are black people, of Asian, African and Caribbean descent.' She asserts that 'since white social workers benefit from the existence of racism, they lack the material base from which to extend empathy to black people' (1997: 46). Consequently, 'the failure of white social workers to appreciate the power and privileges they enjoy because they live in a racist society, and their fundamental misunderstanding of black people's experiences, facilitates the fostering of racist stereotypes in their practice' (1997: 46).

Dominelli (1997) does not address white-on-white or black-on-black racial discrimination. Nor does her theory permit any differentiation in the experience of racism as between different ethnic groups. All are homogenised into one category 'black', which is portrayed as experiencing prejudice in the same manner and to the same degree. This erases important differences in how racism operates to the disadvantage of diverse ethnic minorities. It also downplays the variety of ways in which racial discrimination affects the lives of people from those different ethnic communities. Finally, it tends to reduce the identity of black people to one solely determined by racism.

Thompson (2006: 82) admits that 'there is a danger that assessment will be based on dominant white norms without adequate attention being paid to cultural differences.

Failure to take such differences into account will not only distort, and thereby invalidate, the basis of the assessment but will also serve to alienate clients by devaluing their culture'. He stresses that 'what social work assessment also needs to take into account is what black communities have in common – their experience of *racism*' (2006: 83). Thompson (2006: 84) also highlights his apprehension that attending to the cultural backgrounds of black service-users will distract social workers from challenging the racism which constitutes a formative experience for people from ethnic minorities.

Essentialising Blackness

Essentialism is the idea that different groups have essences resulting in fixed and unchanging characteristics. Werbner (1997: 228) defines the process of essentialising as attributing 'a fundamental, basic, absolutely necessary constitutive quality to a person, social category, ethnic group, religious community, or nation'. Essentialism, because it assigns specific qualities to whole groups of people, is a worldview which plays a major role in negative stereotyping and the rationalisation of inequality between different 'races'. Anti-racism is a set of principles applied through a range of strategies to combat racial prejudice and discrimination. In seeking to promote anti-racist practice, Dominelli (1997) and Thompson (2006) tend to essentialise 'black' and 'white' people, ascribing to them fixed characteristics normally associated with the concept of 'race'. An increasing number of social scientists are now challenging these conceptions of 'blackness' and 'whiteness'.

While all minorities experience racial discrimination to some degree, this is not uniform. Different stereotypes and discriminatory practices have different effects on people across ethnic groups. Without this acknowledgement it is impossible to explain the evidence of major studies such as the *Fourth National Survey of Ethnic Minorities* (Modood et al., 1997), which clearly show dissimilar levels of disadvantage across different ethnic minorities. A further issue surrounding emphasis on the black–white dichotomy is the degree to which people from diverse ethnic groups identify with the label 'black'. Since the 1960s anti-racists have employed the term 'black' as a political term to describe the common experience of racial discrimination among people from visible ethnic minorities. It also implies that ethnic groups in Britain 'ought to embrace a common identity as a basis for effective mobilization and resistance' (Mason, 2000: 17). This is problematic because there has been a growing tension between some Asian minorities and other ethnic groups.

Gilroy (1993) acknowledges the importance of the interaction between the cultures and ideas of African Americans, the peoples of Africa and those of African descent living in Europe in forging a black cross-Atlantic identity. Referring to black communities in Europe, Gilroy (1993: 19) observes that 'modern black political culture has always been more interested in the relationship of identity to roots and rootedness than in seeing identity as a process of movement'. Speaking more personally of his own experiences as a black man growing up in London, he recounts that 'the Caribbean, Africa, Latin America, and above all black America contributed to our lived sense of a racial self' (1993: 109). The linkages between 'black' and the experiences of Africans and those of African descent are so pervasive that they marginalise Asian cultures (Modood, 1988). It is therefore not surprising to find that in a major study of the attitudes of Asian minorities, out of approximately 3,500 respondents only a quarter of those having Indian descent, and around one-fifth of those from Pakistani or Bangladeshi backgrounds, self-identified as 'black' (Modood et al., 1997: 295).

The 2001 Census

The 2001 Census (National Statistics, 2003) revealed considerable religious diversity among ethnic populations:

   The White community is 75% Christian, 15% no religious affiliation
   The African-Caribbean community is 75% Christian, 10% of no religion
   The Black African community is 70% Christian, 20% Muslim
   The Indian community is 45% Hindu, 29% Sikh and 13% Muslim
   The Pakistani and Bangladeshi communities are 92% Muslim
   Those of mixed heritage are 52% Christian, 25% no religious affiliation

The religious differences recorded by the 2001 Census (National Statistics, 2003) are particularly important as British Muslims have from the 1990s onwards been subject to a form of racial prejudice linked to their religion rather than skin colour. Members of many Asian minorities are subject to a particularly virulent form of racism encapsulated in the term 'Islamophobia'. The attacks on the Twin Towers in New York in 2001 and the London bombings on public transport during 2005 perpetrated by suicide bombers who justified their actions by reference to a fundamentalist version of Islam has resulted in Islam being ever more closely associated with fanaticism by the mass media. This has served to further alienate Muslims in Britain and other European countries in ways not true for other ethnic communities (Miles & Brown, 2004: 166–7). Indeed, it has resulted in members of the Bangladeshi and Pakistani communities being redefined in terms of their religion rather than their ethnic origins (Anthias & Yuval-Davis, 1992). Increasingly, Muslims are being stigmatised as 'self-chosen outsiders' (Mason, 2000: 141). Consequently, forms of racism directed at British Muslims are diverging from those against other ethnic communities in ways which can no longer be satisfactorily comprehended under a single dimension of black–white relations.

Islamophobia: A Challenge for Us All

Produced by the Runnymede Trust in 1997, *Islamophobia: A Challenge for Us All* was the first major study of anti-Muslim hostility in Britain. It received considerable media attention

(Continued)

(Continued)

on its publication and brought to public attention the increasing violence and racist abuse confronting Muslims in the United Kingdom. The Runnymede Trust (1997: 5) describes Islamophobia as occurring when people instantly reject the criticisms Muslims make of the West while perceiving Islam as:

- a single monolithic bloc
- not having values in common with other cultures
- inferior to Western values
- violent and supportive of terrorism
- a political ideology

The usage of 'black' is also under attack from social scientists who argue that it fails to reflect the fluid nature of ethnic-minority cultures in contemporary Britain. Back (2002), Gilroy (1987, 1993) and Hall (1992a) observe that the culture among communities of African descent in Britain is heavily influenced by global networks and international cultural exchanges. At the same time minority cultures interact with that of the majority white population and influence what it means to be British. Hall (1992b) makes a case for dispensing with the idea of an 'essential black subject' who is defined by the oppression of white people and portrayed as having an identity dominated by the experience of racism. Hall (1992b: 254) asserts that there is an 'extraordinary diversity of subjective positions, social experiences and cultural identities which compose the category "black"'. Some of these identities are vibrant, self-defined and self-assertive representations of what it means to share an African heritage.

According to Gilroy (1987) and Back (2002), these identities draw inspiration from association with the African diaspora and are expressed through the medium of black music (rap, reggae, hip hop and soul) and other forms of popular culture. Their contention is that being black in Britain is not merely an identification constructed in reaction to white racism, it is a self-chosen identity, which incorporates a self-regarding expression of African heritage. Transnational and transcultural identity formation is facilitated by the processes of globalisation which, through low-cost travel, the World Wide Web and mass media, overcome the disconnections caused by geographic distance. Essentially, Gilroy (1987: 197) and his colleagues are arguing that black people should be treated not merely as victims of white oppression, but 'as actors capable of making complex choices in the furtherance of their own liberation'.

Gilroy (1987) and Back (2002) also argue that black cultural forms are influencing the lifestyles of white youth. Both sociologists observe that in the major cities of Britain urban white youth are copying black styles of fashion, music and idioms of speech. Alexander (2002: 558) comments that broadly 'African-Caribbean youth cultures are seen as moving outwards, into mainstream cultures, transforming and transgressing ideas of integral British cultural identity'. This is reflected in the new alliances observed between white and African-Caribbean youth in the generation of cross-cultural identities based on locality. While this 'neighbourhood nationalism' acted as a vehicle for common identifications between white and black youths, it did not entirely eliminate racism (Back, 2002: 240–1). Furthermore, it created a bounded sense of community which, while extending to those of African heritage, excluded other ethnicities such as Vietnamese youth (2002: 240–1). This finding of Back's (2002) study of urban youth reiterates the divergent experiences of African-Caribbean groups and those of Asian heritage. Conversely, Baumann (1997: 218–19) refers to a 'community of culture' which is being created by many Asian youths from the Indian sub-continent who are discovering new group identities based around shared traditions and interests, for example Bhangra as an Asian music form.

Both Gilroy (1987) and Back (2002) acknowledge the pervasive racism experienced by people of Asian and African descent, but they question its predominance in the construction of black–white relations and what it means to be 'black' in Britain. For Gilroy (1987: 201), this cross-cultural trend illustrates 'the richness of cultural struggle in and around 'race' and demonstrates also the dimensions of black oppositional practice which are not reducible to the narrow idea of anti-racism'.

Essentialising Whiteness

The Burnage Report

The Burnage Report was commissioned by Manchester City Council into the circumstances surrounding the death of 13-year-old Ahmed Iqbal Ullah in 1986. Ahmed, a British Asian pupil, was murdered by a white youth in the playground of Burnage High School. The Burnage Report received extensive media coverage on its publication and made a controversial attack on the anti-racist policies in place at the school. In particular, the report criticised the school's policies because they characterised all white pupils, by virtue of being white, as prejudiced against ethnic minorities. Labelling white working-class youths attending the school as racist contributed to resentment against ethnic-minority pupils which ultimately worsened rather than improved relationships between both groups. The report concluded:

> The operation of the anti-racist polices almost inevitably results in white students (and their parents) feeling 'attacked' and all being seen as 'racist', whether they are ferret-eyed fascists or committed anti-racists or simply children with a great store of human feeling and warmth who are ready to listen and learn and to explore their feeling towards one another. … Racism is placed in some kind of moral vacuum and is totally divorced from the more complex reality of human relations in the classroom. (Macdonald et al., 1989: 347)

Racism is constructed by Dominelli (1997) and Thompson (2006) in ways which tend to essentialise white people, slotting them into the same category without differentiation. There are a number of problems with this standpoint. The white population of Britain is not homogeneous. The 2001 Census figures show that approximately 1,300,000 people identified themselves as 'other white' (this figure excludes those identifying as 'white Irish') (National Statistics, 2003). This population is supplemented annually by economic migrants from other member states of the European Union who, under the Treaty of Rome, have the right of free movement within the Union. Given the continued expansion of the European Union to include former Eastern Bloc countries, there is potential for growing numbers of migrants from continental Europe to work and reside in the United Kingdom. To this must be added refugees from the Balkan Wars of the 1990s, many of whom have opted to remain in Britain.

Increasingly, the United Kingdom is a destination for asylum seekers and migrants from the countries of the former Soviet Union. Between 1995 and 2000 the number of asylum applications from the successor states of the Soviet Union and European countries outside the EU rose from around 7,000 to 23,000 (Home Office, 2004: Table 2.1). These exclude the large numbers of refugees from Kosovo who were settled in the United Kingdom during the crisis of 1999 when Serbian troops started to clear the province of its population. Many families from Kosovo still remain in Britain.

In the 2001 Census 625,000 respondents described themselves as 'white Irish' (National Statistics, 2003). Despite being commonly treated as homogeneous with the white population of Britain, Irish people actually suffer more ill-health than the general population, are more likely than those from Asian ethnic minorities to be compulsorily detained under the Mental Health Act 1983 and are over-represented in the prison system (Parehk, 2000: xvii, xix; O'Hagan, 2001: 123). British Jews, reckoned to be around 300,000 in number, have also tended to be subsumed within the white British population despite having a distinctive heritage associated with religious observance, a history of persecution culminating in the Holocaust and, for many, a special relationship with the state of Israel. Members of the Jewish community, unlike those belonging to the white majority population, are exposed to anti-Semitism. Apart from the Irish and Jewish populations, there are estimated to be 150,000 travelling people in Britain who regularly face prejudice, eviction and poor amenities because of their traditional lifestyle, which is to roam rather than settle (Parehk, 2000: 34).

The discriminatory experiences of many Irish people, white immigrants and asylum seekers from Eastern Bloc countries, and those belonging to the Jewish and travelling communities have much in common with the experiences of black people. The strict black–white dichotomy at the centre of anti-racist worldviews de-racialises these groups by subsuming them with a single racial category labelled 'white'. By treating such groups within anti-racist theory and practice as if they were collectively similar to the majority white population, the unique difficulties confronting each of these 'invisible' ethnic groups is overlooked. There is no acknowledgement within dominant conceptualisations of anti-racist theory that white people are not a homogeneous group, but composed of a plurality of ethnic identities.

A major problem with the version of anti-racism promoted by Dominelli (1997) and Thompson (2006) is that it ignores variation in the relationships between white people and members of ethnic minorities. If all white people are racist by definition, then this essentialises whiteness. Bonnett (2000: 128) criticises this approach to anti-racism on the grounds that 'whiteness is defined as referring to a racial group characterised by its moral failings'. It denies the possibility of personal change over time and obscures the real differences between individuals in their attitudes and treatment of people from ethnic minorities. If almost all the actions of white people are interpreted as perpetuating political, economic and cultural structures which subordinate black people, then racism becomes a catch-all term for white behaviour.

Furthermore, by assuming that all white people are uniformly racist and the majority of their actions are discriminatory, no account is taken of motivation. The white person who inadvertently discriminates through a misunderstanding of another's cultural background would be grouped together with the intentional street racism of a right-wing extremist. Such an approach is morally objectionable as it undermines the connection between deliberation, responsibility and guilt. It cannot be correct to judge a white person who inadvertently discriminates against a black person as morally blameworthy as someone who maliciously intends racial discrimination. The distinction between intentional and unintentional acts of racism is also important as these require different intervention strategies to reduce their persistence.

The Concept of Ethnicity

The concept of a tribal group, which is closely associated with ideas of race and ethnicity, was first developed by anthropologists during the early twentieth century. Barth (1969: 10–11) summarises the five main elements of this original conceptualisation of large social groups: biologically self-perpetuating; characterised by bounded group interactions; comprising of people who identify themselves as belonging to the tribal group; identified by others as belonging to that tribe; and share common cultural values. Plainly this is an essentialist interpretation of social groupings. People of a particular tribe are viewed as possessing fixed cultural values and traditions which they are assumed to pass on to their offspring unmodified. These traditions are also presumed to be observable and can be used to categorise people into distinct tribal groupings. Since the mid-twentieth century this conception of large social groupings has been vigorously challenged.

Everett Hughes

The sociologist Everett Hughes was one of the first to question the predominant view among anthropologists of unchanging and distinctive cultural traits. He argued:

An ethnic group is not one because of the degree of measurable or observable difference from other groups: it is an ethnic group, on the contrary, because the people in it and the people out of it know that it is one; because both the ins and the outs talk, feel, and act as if it were a separate group. This is possible only if there are ways of telling who belongs to the group and who does not, and if a person learns early, deeply, and usually irrevocably to what group he belongs. If it is easy to resign from the group, it is not truly an ethnic group. (Hughes, 1994: 91)

The most important aspect of Hughes' definition of ethnicity is that it moves away from notions of unchanging cultural practices to social interaction between groups of people in the creation of group identification. What causes ethnicity (i.e. what makes one group become distinctive from another) is the interaction between social groups over time (Jenkins, 1997: 11). Barth (1969) takes this development a step further, observing that cultural differences and social groupings do not necessarily coincide. He asserts that:

> we can assume no simple one-to-one relationship between ethnic units and cultural similarities and differences. The features that are taken into account are not the sum of 'objective' differences, but only those which the actors themselves regard as significant … some cultural features are used by the actors as signals and emblems of differences, others are ignored, and in some relationships radical differences are played down and denied. (Barth, 1969: 14)

Barth's conceptualisation of ethnicity is fluid and introduces an anti-essentialist flexibility in which the actors decide what aspects of culture matter in determining group membership. His focus is not on an anthropological examination of cultural practices, but on the social processes which generate distinctive groupings and how these distinctions are maintained over time. If ethnic groups are created by social processes (i.e. through their interactions with other social groups), then a shared culture is only one aspect of group membership. From this perspective, culture is not a collection of unvarying values and traditions. Instead it comprises a set of beliefs and practices, some of which become important to signifying membership of a particular ethnic group. Which beliefs or practices become important arises out of the interaction between social groups. Wallman (1979: 3) succinctly makes this point: '[E]thnicity is the process by which "their" difference is used to enhance the sense of "us" for purposes of organisation or identification. … Because it takes two, ethnicity can only happen at the boundary of "us", in contact or confrontation or by contrast with "them".'

The work of both Barth and Wallman explicitly acknowledges that ethnicity can be deployed as a means of social organisation to obtain economic and political objectives or as a source of mutual support. In other words, ethnicity can be manipulated and used as a strategy to create a sense of collective identity which in turn is used to mobilise people to make political demands for their group. Ethnicity can be a proactive self-identity which deliberately creates boundaries between 'us' and 'them' in an effort to achieve specific objectives or gain rights for group members.

There are weaknesses in Barth's and Wallman's theory of social groups as self-defined ethnicities. This ignores power imbalances between different ethnic groups and the degree to which ethnicity can be a coerced identity, forced on one social group by another. Jenkins (1997: 22–3) addresses this problem by referring to processes of *group identification* and *social categorisation. Group identification* is a process of self-ascription, meaning people elect to belong to a social group on the basis of shared roots, culture and interests. They experience a sense of belongingness to that social group and identify themselves as members of it. Self-definition is a crucial aspect of the processes involved in group identification. Conversely, *social categorisation* is a social process which imposes group membership from without and usually from a position of power. During the process of *social categorisation*, a dominant group imposes its own definitions upon the subordinate group and determines who belongs to that subordinate social group.

There is a direct connection between the concepts of *group identification* and *social categorisation* on the one hand and notions of ethnicity and race on the other. *Group identification*, like ethnicity, tends to be self-defined and is concerned with describing 'us' and producing boundaries or markers to differentiate 'us' from 'them'. *Social categorisation,* by contrast, is closely related to processes of racialisation during which negative or inferior traits are attributed to members of subordinated social groups and used to justify discrimination (Banton, 1983: 106). This type of hostile categorisation operates to impose an identity upon another social group which characterises it as inferior. There is also a presumption of unalterable differences between members of the subordinate group and that of the dominant group. These differences could refer to cultural aspects or to assumed biological differences, such as physical appearance or mental ability. In essence, processes of *social categorisation* are employed to define 'them', generally negatively and generally from a position of power. By contrast, *group identification* refers to a voluntary association with an ethnic group based on a shared sense of being 'us'.

For the individual, primary socialisation during infancy and childhood encompasses language, religion, gender identity and other aspects of culture. These underpin the development of a social identity which includes a sense of ethnic membership. If ethnic differences are emphasised during social interactions, then children will internalise the self-image they encounter through group identification and social categorisation. In a society structured by power relations between different ethnic groups, the negative evaluation by the dominant group of the cultural values, physical appearance or capabilities of members of the subordinate group will be incorporated into personal identity at an early age. The result will be a damaged self-image and sense of inferiority. However, processes of group identification, if these are based on positive evaluations of the ethnic community, can counteract the detrimental effects of social categorisation. Neither individual nor group identity is determined solely by the dominant or majority community. Members of an ethnic community also engage in processes which powerfully influence which values, beliefs and practices are recognised as expressions of their group.

Hybrid Ethnic Identities

Culture, and what it means to belong to a particular social group, changes over time. Influences which modify the common values and practices of an ethnic community have multiplied due to advances in telecommunications and the mass media combined with globalisation. Ethnic identities are increasingly transnational and transcultural, drawing their inspiration from a variety of traditions and sources. For communities which grew out of historical or recent migration, these tend to incorporate aspects of the host population. For example, in their national survey Modood et al. (1997: 332–7) found that second-generation immigrants tended to adapt lifestyles and practices taken from wider British society. This did not prevent them from also embracing values inherited from their families and more traditional perspectives held by people within their own ethnic group. Indeed, the survey findings highlight the strong ethnic identifications which persist among the second generation despite the adoption of less traditional cultural practices.

The *Fourth National Survey of Ethnic Minorities* investigated the extent to which people identified themselves as members of a particular community. It also examined what it means to belong to an ethnic community. Respondents were asked to what degree they thought of themselves as British and/or as a member of a distinctive ethnic group. Generally, around 60–65% of those across all ethnic groups identified themselves as British, while approximately 85–90% identified themselves as belonging to a particular ethnic group. This is an important finding as it demonstrates that the majority of people from ethnic minorities participating in the survey did not experience a contradiction between being British and having a strong ethnic identity (Modood et al., 1997: Table 9.32). Some respondents did express difficulty with the term 'British' because members of the white-majority population refused to recognise members of ethnic minorities as equally British (1997: 330).

Nimmi Hutnik

Hutnik theory builds around people's experience of their group identity and where, potentially, they belong to more than one group. This is particularly significant when a person feels conflict between different group identifications. Hutnik (1991: 134) details her theory in *Ethnic Minority Identity: A Social Psychological Perspective*, which sets out the strategies adopted by individuals faced with membership of several different social groups.

The dissociative strategy – self-identification is with a person's ethnic group but not the majority group of which he or she is also a member.
The assimilative strategy – self-identification emphasises membership of the majority group and downplays or denies an ethnic minority heritage.
The acculturative strategy – self-identification is equally strong with the majority group and that of the ethnic minority to which the person belongs.
The marginal strategy – self-identification relies on more individualist aspects of social life, such as a person's profession or club membership and largely ignores wider identifications with ethnic or majority groups.

The survey conducted by Modood et al. (1997) investigates how respondents formulated their self-identity and builds on the work of Hutnik (1991). Modood et al. (1997: Table 9.33) found that roughly 60–70% of respondents across all ethnic groups employed an *acculturative strategy*. This contrasts with the much lower figure of 20–30% of those who adopted a *dissociative strategy*. It is also notable that despite widespread stereotyping of the Pakistani and Bangladeshi communities as separatist in outlook, in this survey they are as likely as any other ethnic group to use *acculturative strategies*. These draw on the social and cultural heritage of the white-majority population in Britain, other minorities and that of a person's own ethnic community.

Investigating what it means to be a member of an ethnic group, Modood et al. (1997) next examined the participation of people in the cultural practices associated with their ethnic community. The survey found that what determines self-identification with a particular ethnic community is a general sense of belonging to that group rather than regular participation in cultural activities or adopting a range of cultural practices. For example, people under 35 years of age were observed to be less likely than those over 35 years to dress in garments traditionally worn by members of their ethnic group (1997: 326–8). But this did not weaken their sense of identification with their ethnic origins and heritage. Modood et al. (1997: 332) describe this as an 'associational or community identity'. The survey concludes that 'it is possible for people to have a sense, even a strong sense, of an associational minority identity without participation in many distinctive cultural practices'. The findings from the survey explicitly link this associational identity with experiences of racism and the need to develop 'a group pride' in response. Modood et al. (1997: 290) go so far as to frame this in terms of a political project:

> There is an ethnic assertiveness, arising out of the feelings of not being respected or of lacking access to public space, consisting of counterposing 'positive' images against traditional or dominant stereotypes. It is a politics of projecting identities in order to challenge existing power relations; of seeking not just toleration for ethnic difference but also public acknowledgement, resources and representation.

Modood et al. (1997: 337) speculate that ethnic-minority-identity formation has shifted away from a focus on the observance of specific cultural practices towards new solidarities which draw on a range of heritages. Gilroy (1987) describes the development of a common group identity among people of African descent based around a sense of shared roots and expressions of youth culture through music and dance. Modood et al. (1997: 291) also refer to the increasingly hybrid nature of Asian group affiliations which may revolve around a broad youth culture rather than specific cultural practices or activities.

The emergence of media specifically aimed at an Asian audience, such as the BBC's Asian Network, which broadcasts news, cultural events and music, and *Q-News*, a leading Muslim magazine publishing articles of interest to the British Muslim community, act to create a broader sense of group membership. The Muslim religion, particularly in response to Islamophobia, is also providing a focus for group identification which crosses the boundaries of ethnic communities. A sense of solidarity with the *ummah*, the worldwide Islamic community, is for many British Muslims an important aspect of their ethnic identification (Runnymede Trust, 1997: 16). The establishment in 1997 of the Muslim Council of Britain, an umbrella body for Muslim organisations, is both an expression of and a contribution to a faith-based focus for ethnic identification. Endorsing this view, Jacobson's (1997) qualitative study of Pakistani youth in London found that their religious affiliation as Muslims was more important for self-identification than belonging to a social group defined by being 'Asian' or 'Pakistani'. Religious identity was perceived by these young people to be more inclusive than attachment to family origins or cultural practices specific to a particular ethnic community.

The concept of ethnicity which emerges from the *Fourth National Survey of Ethnic Minorities* is one of changeability and variableness. The nature of ethnic identity revealed is not primarily determined by racist structures in society, although these certainly play a major role in shaping group membership. Ethnicity is to a considerable extent a self-chosen identification which may change over time as communities are affected by other social groups and make adjustments to new circumstances. The self-chosen assertion of ethnic identity has the potential to act as a political force designed to advance the interests of a particular group. In a similar way to the feminist and gay-rights movements, a person's ethnicity, like gender and sexuality, can become the focus of political activity. This agitation can be aimed at countering prejudice and discrimination, changing oppressive societal structures and/or obtaining rights and access to resources.

Ethnic communities may also exert pressure on members to conform to certain norms. For example, Baumann (1997) reports an incident in Southall during the 1980s when the Southall Black Sisters, an organisation set up and run by ethnic-minority women, publicised and challenged domestic violence and arranged marriages within the South Asian community. Their assertions drew condemnation from 'community leaders', who accused the Southall Black Sisters of acting against the traditions of the community and behaving in ways unacceptable to their ethnic group. This incident raises the question as to who determines the values and cultural practices of an ethnic group, who decides which individuals belong to it and who represents it. These are matters of contention, often involving power struggles within local ethnic communities. At times prominent figures or organisations within a community may attempt to define it in ways which project an essentialist self-image of that ethnic minority, a self-image based on assumptions of what constitute traditional values and practices. The fact that such struggles take place in the political arena highlights the negotiable nature of ethnicity.

📖 Further Reading

Dominelli, L. (1997) *Anti-Racist Social Work*. Basingstoke: Macmillan. This volume focuses on racism by white social workers against black service-users. It examines the discriminatory processes within Social Services and the social-work profession.

Dominelli, L. (2002) *Anti-Oppressive Social Work Theory and Practice*. Basingstoke: Palgrave Macmillan. This book considers the different levels at which oppression takes place and the groups which are most affected.

Thompson, N. (2006) *Anti-Discriminatory Practice*. Basingstoke: Palgrave Macmillan. This book sets out a conceptual framework for considering the nature of discrimination on the grounds of race, gender, sexuality, religion, age and disability.

3

Cultural Competence in Social Work

Policy Frameworks and Practice Guidance on Services to Ethnic Minorities

Government policy explicitly acknowledges the necessity of addressing the particular needs of individuals and families from diverse ethnic communities. The *National Service Framework for Older People* sets out a ten-year programme for delivering integrated health-and social-care provision to older people. It requires that 'all services should be culturally appropriate, reflecting the diversity of the population that they serve' (Department of Health, 2001b: para. 12). The *National Service Framework for Mental Health* explicitly recognises 'that black and minority ethnic communities lack confidence in mental health services' (Department of Health, 1999b: 17). *Delivering Race Equality in Mental Health Care,* produced by the Department of Health (2005), acknowledges that people from ethnic minorities have greater difficulties accessing services and experience lower satisfaction than those from the majority-white community, are subject to incomplete assessments in relation to culture and language, and are subject to disproportionate detainment under mental health legislation. *Delivering Race Equality* is an action plan designed to redress discrimination in mental-health services. It provides for the introduction of a broader range of culturally appropriate services, to include peer support and psychotherapy alongside medication.

The importance of acknowledging and actively attending to the cultural diversity of carers is recognised in the government's *National Strategy for Carers* (Department of Health, 1999c: 45). Concern over the disproportionate number of 'children in need' from ethnic minorities led to their specific mention in *The Government's Objectives for Children's Social Services,* which states that 'the needs of black and ethnic minority children and families must be identified and met through services which are culturally sensitive' (Department of Health, 1999a: para.16). The *National Service Framework for Children,*

Young People and Maternity Services, which sets standards for delivery in both health- and social-care settings, highlights the requirement for culturally appropriate provision for users, carers and parents from minority communities (Department of Health, 2004: 32, 115).

Successive governments have backed up policy initiatives with more detailed instructions to frontline professionals. Practice guidance issued by the government requires incorporation of the cultural background of service-users and families into needs assessment and service provision. The Department of Health's (1991: 58–9) *Care Management and Assessment: Practitioners' Guide* sets out the Comprehensive Assessment Guideline which obliges care managers to include consideration of a person's 'race and culture' within the assessment of need. The Department of Health's (2000) *Assessing Children in Need and Their Families: Practice Guidance* devotes a full chapter to guiding social workers in assessing children and families from ethnic minorities.

As regards service providers, the Commission for Social Care Inspection (CSCI) is responsible for registering and inspecting care services, including domiciliary provision, residential and nursing homes, together with fostering and adoption services. Registration is dependent upon service providers meeting the national minimum standards issued by the Department of Health for each type of service provider. These standards require sensitivity to the cultural background of users and for this to be reflected in service delivery (CSCI, 2005: 25). The CSCI also evaluates the quality of Social Services for which the local council has responsibility. The performance assessment used by the CSCI is based on a star-rating system which takes account of 'race equality'. It includes an appraisal of the extent to which local government has tackled discrimination and worked in partnership with ethnic-minority organisations to improve services (CSCI, 2005: 28).

Problems Caused by a Lack of Cultural Competence among Practitioners

Government policy documents and independent surveys increasingly recognise the multicultural reality of Britain and emphasise the need for training in cultural sensitivity for social-care professionals. Parekh (2000: 306), at the end of a long consultation process and extensive deliberation on the circumstances of minorities in the United Kingdom, concludes that 'all those employed in the health and social welfare services should be trained in cultural awareness and sensitivity'. Barn et al. (1997: 50) attributes the over-representation of ethnic-minority children in the care system in part to social workers' lack of an 'adequate understanding of cultural backgrounds'. In the area of child protection, research continues to stress the need for social-work professionals to be aware of child-rearing practices in parents' countries of origin or which may form part of their heritage. There is an explicit insistence that cultural competence is a necessary component of effective child-protection work among families from ethnic minorities (Brophy et al., 2003). For those in the care system or leaving care, a Department of Health report found that for a quarter of ethnic-minority children surveyed, their 'cultural needs were not recognised and dealt with appropriately' (O'Neale, 2000: 16). Among social work staff, 'poor levels of understanding about cultural and religious issues impacted negatively on assessments and placement choice for children' (O'Neale, 2000: 26). The Department of Health report concluded that 'cultural knowledge is also important' in social-work training (O'Neale, 2000: 34). Responding to these findings, the Department of Health's strategy document, *The Government's Objectives for Children's Social Services* (1999a: para.16), which frames work with 'children in need', insists that 'the needs of black and ethnic minority children and families must be identified and met through services which are culturally sensitive and which recognise and value diversity'.

In terms of work with people who have learning difficulties, a major report (Mir et al., 2001: 55) commissioned by the Department of Health revealed that 'many professionals currently feel ill-equipped to respond to people from a different culture'. The report concludes that 'training for all staff is needed to improve competence in cultural awareness and prevent the marginalisation of minority needs' (Mir et al., 2001: 3). The National Health Service's own report (NIMHE, 2003: 20) both highlighted the existence of institutional racism in the delivery of mental-health services and the necessity of 'developing a culturally capable service'. Based on their compilation of recent research around mental-health-service delivery, Malek and Joughin (2004: 20) recommend that 'training in cultural competence is incorporated into the personal development plans of clinicians and administrative staff', and furthermore that 'professional bodies develop explicit frameworks for providing and evaluating cultural competence'.

A review by the Race Equality Unit of research studies on social-care delivery to ethnic minorities revealed that carers found that 'service provision continues to remain ethnocentric, geared to meeting the needs of the white majority community' (Butt & Mirza, 1996: 114). Indeed, organisations such as the National Black Carers Workers Network (2002: 17), which represents black carers, criticises the failure of mainstream services to cater for ethnic minorities and insist that 'all service providers should ensure their staff receives appropriate cultural awareness training'. Despite the clear promotion of cultural sensitivity in these reports and policy documents social-work training continues to be focused around a narrow anti-racist approach. This concentrates on power relations between white social workers and black service-users rather than the encounter between people of different cultural backgrounds.

The consequences of continuing with an anti-racist training programme for social workers which excludes consideration of cross-cultural issues beyond a black/white divide are evident from a number of studies. Research into social care for older people from ethnic minorities conducted by Bowes and Dar (2000: 309–10) found that white social workers 'revealed a lack of knowledge of the minority ethnic communities and difficulties were expressed by these white staff about approaching work with minorities; they spoke of being afraid to do the work, of not knowing how to approach it, and of their fear of offending'. Endorsing this finding, a major study of community care services for older people from ethnic minorities observed 'without the training, knowledge and skills, some white staff did not have the confidence to make judgements of the contributions of relation and culture in the assessment of older people' (Department of Health & Social Services Inspectorate, 1998: 8). It concluded that social work staff 'required skills in anti-discriminatory practice and cultural sensitivity' (1998: 8). Similar findings emerge from a study of social workers intervening with South Asian families in the area of child protection (Qureshi et al., 2000). The anxiety of white social-work staff meant that in many areas of service provision they tended to withdraw from work with ethnic-minority service-users. Instead, they over-relied on black colleagues, who in turn resented the allocation of service-users on the basis of their ethnicity and the assumption of racialised experiences (O'Neale, 2000: 3; Goldstein, 2002: 771–2).

Another study by Burman et al. (2004) explores the impact of professional anxiety on service delivery to minority communities. The fear of engaging with culture meant that many women of African-Caribbean and Asian heritage found themselves unable to obtain effective help in situations of domestic violence. Service providers often failed to challenge the prevalence of domestic violence in the local ethnic community for fear of offending community leaders or those providing funding. As a result, survivors of domestic abuse often felt there was no public forum through which they could articulate their experience. Justifying their position, service providers relied on notions of 'cultural privacy' and respect. Agencies also admitted to a fear of involvement 'out of fear of being labelled as racist' (Burman et al., 2004: 347). Staff in the statutory sector described themselves as 'not feeling qualified to know what to ask – both in terms of minority cultural practices *and* domestic violence' (Burman et al., 2004: 348). Service-users acknowledged that many members of their ethnic community would resist and object to issues, such as domestic violence, being publicised. But, as the researchers comment, 'this respect for women's (and others') 'cultural privacy' seems, then, to play into the ways women are silenced in their communities, while the unwillingness of organizations to challenge cultural norms works to bolster patriarchal and class-based relations within minoritised communities to make domestic violence more invisible' (Burman et al., 2004: 348). Similar evidence has emerged from the way in which social workers deal with domestic abuse against women of Asian descent. Many practitioners appear to assume that arranged and forced marriages are synonymous and therefore retreat from any intervention for fear of being accused of racism or being disrespectful towards another's culture (*Community Care*, 2006: 29). Adoption of a position of cultural relativity by white social workers through fear of behaving in a racist manner also affected statutory provision to children and families. Barn et al. (1997) discovered that some social workers are reluctant to intervene to protect children because they believe that abusive behaviour towards them is sanctioned by their culture.

Changing Professional Attitudes to Cultural Competence

O'Hagan (2001: 122) criticises advocates of anti-racist practice for caricaturing cultural competence as creating an 'exotic' understanding of people from ethnic minorities whose behaviours provide a source of fascination. Social workers practising cultural sensitivity are subsequently deemed to be so immersed in this exotic profiling that they are rendered incapable of recognising practice issues of social inequality or racial discrimination. O'Hagan (2001: 124) observes that the continuous attack on cultural competence from social-work academics has hindered practitioners in taking proper account of carers' and service-users' cultural backgrounds or delivering culturally sensitive services. This may explain why research consistently highlights the failure of social-care professionals to provide culturally appropriate services (Butt & Mirza, 1999; Chamba et al., 1999; O'Neale, 2000; Mir et al., 2001; Thoburn et al., 2005).

The prevailing view within social work contrasts with that of the health-care professions in the United Kingdom, which from the 1980s onwards have been concerned to introduce cultural sensitivity into practice. Texts such as those by Henley (1982, 1983a & 1983b), Karmi (1996) and Sheikh and Gatrad (2000) were designed to provide health-care professionals with a basic knowledge of other ethnic groups in order to ensure more culturally appropriate patient care. It could be argued that some of these texts fail to highlight the range of difference in beliefs and norms to be found in any single ethnic group. They have been criticised from within the health-care profession for over-simplified accounts of ethnic communities and presenting checklists of cultural norms, which amount to stereotyping (Gunaratnam, 1997). More sophisticated cross-cultural approaches have been developed, as epitomised in Mares et al.'s *Health Care in Multi-racial Britain* (1985) and in a more recent publication by Holland and Hogg entitled *Cultural Awareness in Nursing and Health Care* (2001). Rather than setting out the specific religious or cultural norms of a particular ethnic community, Holland and Hogg (2001) identifies the diversity of family structures, religious observances and conceptions of illness.

It is also important to appreciate that social work in the United States has historically been more open to integrating culturally sensitive approaches into social-work training. For instance, Lynch and Hanson (1994), Lum (1996) and Devore and Schlesinger (1999) are fairly typical of texts available to American social-work students which make available both a knowledge base and techniques to develop cultural competence. These texts detail some of the beliefs and values which influence family dynamics and health-care practices among ethnic minorities in the United States. In many instances they set out a bank of questions and considerations for practitioners to address as they prepare for and then undertake intervention. With the recent publication in the United States of Sue's *Multicultural Social Work Practice* (2005), it is obvious that American social-work educators will continue to teach cultural competence as an integral part of anti-oppressive practice.

Those advocating anti-racist practice base their approach on a narrow understanding of how it can be achieved. Social workers will continue to engage in unintended racism and preside over racially discriminatory services until such times as they learn about other cultures. Cultural sensitivity is in fact a vital component of anti-racist practice. It is not possible to be anti-racist without knowledge of another's cultural values and norms. Such a position neither necessitates essentialising other cultures nor demands the abandonment of challenging racism. Indeed, recognising one's own racism depends to a large extent upon recognising the cultural differences between self and others while endeavouring to accept the norms of other people. O'Hagan (2001: 262) also makes the same point, commenting that 'cultural competence emerges from rigorous self-exploration; it expands the professional's empathic repertoire, ensuring there is no culturally biased instant response, on learning of actions or behaviour which might otherwise be incomprehensible or alarming'.

Models of Cultural Competence

A number of models for cultural competence have been elaborated since the early 1990s. The vast majority of these were developed by educators and practitioners in the United States of America where cultural competence has become a required standard for members of the American Psychological Association and the National Association of Social Workers (NASW). The American nursing profession, in conjunction with the US Department of Health and Human Services, has also actively advanced workable models of cultural competence in health care (HRSA, 2001; Shen, 2004). This chapter utilises many of these models and draws on the cultural competencies set out by the NASW to explain the underlying principles of competent practice with ethnically diverse populations (NASW, 2001).

Practitioner Cross-Cultural Attitudes

Carballeira (1996: 4) identifies a range of cross-cultural attitudes which providers and practitioners can hold towards people from minority communities.

Superiority – the practitioner believes that the service-user's culture is inferior and attempts to impose his or her values and worldview.
Incapacity – the practitioner recognises that there are cultural differences, but has no skills to address them and therefore offers a standard intervention based on the dominant culture.
Universality – the practitioner believes that all human beings share the same fundamental values and therefore treats all service-users and carers alike.
Sensitivity – the practitioner recognises cultural differences, particularly around language, and makes an effort to address these within an essentially standard intervention.
Competence – the practitioner identifies, respects and incorporates the values of the service-user in the design and delivery of the service.

Confronted by attitudes and behaviours exhibiting *superiority, incapacity, universality,* or a limited form of *sensitivity*, service-users and carers from minority groups are likely to react in one of two ways. They may feel hostile and refuse to participate in the intervention or they may try to please the practitioner by accommodating the values of the dominant culture, even though these conflict with their own worldview. Due to the power differential between service-users and social workers (because practitioners control access to resources through assessments and have statutory powers), people from minority groups usually feel compelled to choose accommodation with culturally inappropriate interventions rather than resistance to them (Carballeira, 1996: 4–5). To reduce attitudes and behaviours which hinder the development of culturally appropriate practice, social workers need to adopt a number of strategies.

LIVE and LEARN Model

Developed by Carballeira (1996) this model identifies a series of activities which practitioners need to engage in if they are committed to fostering positive and culturally appropriate interactions with people from other ethnic groups.

Practitioners need to:

Like – develop a keenness and liking for work with people from minority communities.
Inquire – commit to finding out about the history, beliefs, social norms and family structures of other ethnic groups.
Visit – adopt the position of a respectful and observant visitor when working with people from other ethnic groups.
Experience – deliberately seek out social interactions with people from other ethnic groups and establish peer relationships to better understand their cultural background and worldview.
Listen – observe the style used by people from different minority communities in their interactions and endeavour to adopt preferred styles of communication.
Evaluate – recognise that everyone integrates culture and personality in distinctively individual ways and avoid stereotyping by identifying the attitudes, beliefs and values particular to each service-user or carer.
Acknowledge – identify the similarities and differences in attitudes, beliefs and values between different family members and any areas of potential conflict with statutory requirements and inform the service-user.
Recommend – offer service-users and carers a range of intervention approaches and consult on which are most culturally acceptable.
Negotiate – openly discuss areas of conflict which appear to have a cultural dimension and work towards acceptable compromises.

What emerges from the LIVE and LEARN Model is that cultural competence is an ongoing process and not an endpoint which can be achieved at a particular point in time. It demands a sustained, consistent and enduring commitment to learning about and respecting the cultural influences affecting the lives of people from different ethnic backgrounds. Campinha-Bacote (2002) takes this a step further and defines the elements which comprise cultural competence.

ASKED – A process model of cultural competence

Campinha-Bacote (2002: 182–3) identifies five interdependent dimensions of cultural competence. All five of these have to be worked on simultaneously by the practitioner seeking to become culturally competent. The model uses the shorthand acronym ASKED.

Cultural awareness – in-depth self-examination of the practitioner's own cultural and professional background and recognition of the practitioner's own biases, prejudices and assumptions about people from minority communities.
Cultural skill – ability to collect cultural data relevant to the service-user's problems and needs as part of the assessment process.
Cultural knowledge – searching for and acquiring detailed information about other cultures and ethnic groups.
Cultural encounter – engagement in cross-cultural interactions with service-users and carers from culturally diverse backgrounds which modify the practitioner's existing beliefs about a cultural group and dispels stereotypes.
Cultural desire – the practitioner's motivation to *want* to, rather than *have* to, engage in the above four processes. It includes a real willingness to accept differences, build on similarities and learn from people as cultural informants.

Diversity within Ethnic Groups and Individual Differences

Cultural encounter is a crucial aspect of recognising not just differences in values, beliefs and attitudes between practitioner and service-user, but between different service-users and carers with the same ethnic background. In his Multidimensional Model of Cultural Competence, Sue (2001: 793–4) sets culture within a three-tier framework of universal, group and individual levels of personal identity.

At the universal level, *all human beings are alike* – they have a similar physiological make-up, are self-aware, and are able to use symbols and share life experiences in common, such as love, anger and sadness.

At the group level, *all individuals are, in some respects, like some other individuals* – each person is born into a set of beliefs, values and social practices and his or her experience is mediated by membership of different reference groups on the basis of:

- gender
- socio-economic status
- age
- geographic location
- ethnicity

- disability
- culture
- religious preference
- marital status
- sexual orientation

At the individual level, *all individuals are in some respects like no other individual* – each person has a unique genetic endowment and a collection of life experiences which are different from everyone else's.

Sue (2001) sets culture within a system of three interdependent and interlocking relationships. First, each person shares common characteristics with everyone else as they experience major life-cycle events, consciousness and emotion. Practitioners need to bear this in mind and not suppose that because a service-user or carer comes from a different ethnic background from themselves that they are somehow alien or incomprehensible. Secondly, everyone belongs to reference groups of one kind or another which both influences their outlook and how they are regarded by others. For this reason, a married, middle-class, able-bodied 50-year-old woman of Pakistani descent will have different experiences and a different worldview from a 20-year-old unemployed gay male wheelchair user of Pakistani descent. Both these people are likely to also share many experiences, such as Islamophobia, because of their common ethnicity. As service-users or carers their reference group statuses plainly shape their experiences, circumstances, outlook and needs. Thirdly, each person is unique and even two people in their twenties who are disabled, gay, unemployed and of Pakistani heritage will not experience their situation in exactly the same way. They will be subject to alternative family influences, experience varying degrees of acculturation and have different temperaments which in turn result in a diversity of reactions to the world around them.

Working towards cultural competence is difficult because it requires social-care professionals from the majority white population and other ethnic groups to step outside their own cultural context and relate to service-users and carers within the frame of their cultural contexts. It also requires practitioners not to stereotype or essentialise people from other ethnic groups. Any assumption by a social worker that individuals from a particular ethnic background have fixed characteristics is necessarily racist. This is regardless of whether those attributes are viewed positively or negatively. The major difficulty for any professional endeavouring to use information about a person's cultural heritage to enhance service provision is the tendency to stereotype. Once an assumption is made that all people from the Indian community are practising Hindus or that all those identifying as Hindu do not eat meat, then racial stereotyping has already taken place. The result is likely to be a perpetuation of misunderstanding between people of different cultural heritages and ultimately inadequate or discriminatory service provision. The most critical requirement of culturally sensitive social work is to keep open the dialogue between people of different ethnic backgrounds and to ensure that each individual and family emerges as a unique composite of values, beliefs and aspirations. Cultural competence is not about presumption or the deployment of specific information about each ethnic group. Cultural competence is founded on a comprehensive understanding of the broad nature of potential differences between people of diverse ethnic backgrounds.

The Practitioner's Cultural Heritage

All cross-cultural encounters between social workers and service-users bring into play not only the heritage of the service-user, but also that of the practitioner. Each person, whether they are a member of the white-majority population in Britain or belong to a ethnic-minority group, grows up within a family or community context which socialises them through a set of beliefs, values and norms. For this reason, social workers cannot simply focus on the cultural background of service-users and carers. They need to discover and reflect upon their own value system and traditions. Most social workers in the United Kingdom are from the majority-white community. They bring into their practice, often unknowingly, a whole set of presumptions drawn from their own cultural heritage. These values, beliefs and social norms are then superimposed by social workers on individuals from other ethnic communities. This happens without the practitioner from the white-majority community necessarily realising the extent to which their interpretation of a person's circumstances and best interests is heavily influenced by the practitioner's own worldview. This obliviousness to another's heritage, combined with professional power, results in cultural imposition. Leininger and McFarland (2002: 51) note that care professionals often seem unaware of their own cultural ignorance, ethnocentric biases and racism. Practitioners tend to be equally unmindful of the cultural imposition which occurs when they impose their own beliefs, values and patterns of behaviour on those from ethnic minorities. This is most likely to happen where professionals perceive the views of service-users and carers as peculiar or when they are trying to accomplish tasks in a hurry (2002: 52).

Social workers from ethnic-minority communities may find that their professional training and subsequent employment means an accommodation with many of the prevailing social norms in British society. The result is that they too may find themselves engaging in cultural imposition as they implement standard interventions with ethnic minority service-users and carers. While ethnic-minority social workers are likely to be better attuned to the affects of racism than their white British counterparts, they are not necessarily better positioned to understand and respond to the cultural background of someone from a different ethnic group. For ethnic-minority practitioners who were born in the United Kingdom or who have spent a substantial part of their lives residing in the country, the process of acculturation means that they too will have adopted some of the attitudes and norms of the majority white community. Therefore, regardless of the ethnic background of the social worker, each person needs to reflect on their own cultural heritage and how this shapes their worldview.

Anglo-Centric Values

Dwivedi (2004a: 19), Lau (2004: 94) and Leininger and McFarland (2002: 109) identify a number of values which underpin social expectations and lifestyles in Western countries and are evident in the dominant norms of British society:

- Separation and individuation
- Independence
- Autonomy
- Self-sufficiency
- Competitiveness

- Self-expression
- Assertiveness
- Achievement oriented
- Immediate action
- Technological dependency
- Reliance on positivist science
- Materialism

As will become evident from Chapters 4–8, which explore important values and norms among different ethnic minorities in the United Kingdom, many Anglo-centric values are at odds with those of other cultures. Since Anglo-centric values underpin the development and principles of social work both in the United States and in Britain, professional intervention of itself can result in confusion and conflict where ethnic-minority service-users and carers are involved.

Professional Culture and Norms

Social work makes a number of Anglo-centric assumptions as to the goals and methods of practice. Generally, though not always, the social-work encounter is characterised by the following:

- A one-to-one relationship
- A professional and formal relationship as opposed to a personal one
- Direct communication by the practitioner often within a specific timeframe
- Interaction which follows established procedures
- The personal life of the practitioner is not disclosed
- A prohibition on practitioners accepting gifts from service-users and carers
- Responsibility for change is with the service-user or carer
- Service-user insight is valued as a primary means of change
- Service-users and carers are asked to disclose intimate details about their lives
- The expression of emotion by service-users and carers is encouraged
- Interventions are secular rather than spiritual
- Intervention strategies promote independence and independent living.

As will become clear from later chapters, in a number of cultural traditions gift exchange and collective approaches to problem-solving are key aspects of a helping relationship. While direct verbal communication and articulating feelings are promoted by social workers, for some people living in Britain with roots in South and East Asian societies direct communication and emotional expressiveness may take second place to family harmony (Dwivedi, 2004b: 53–5). When social workers assert that they are assisting service-users and carers while simultaneously engaging in behaviours which from the perspective of a different cultural tradition appear to contradict this, the credibility of the practitioner is at stake. Furthermore, the diverse values and beliefs which are influential among various minority groups may mean that some service-users have a different conception of normality and healthy development from the social worker. For example, theories of human development which underpin social work perspectives emphasise individuation and increasing independence as part of normal adolescence. But among a number of cultural traditions interdependency is considered the norm and is actively fostered in children as they grow into adulthood (Dwivedi, 2004b: 52). For other ethnic-minority families there may not be a clearly recognised distinction between childhood and adulthood, and consequently relatively young children may be expected to take on what, in British society, are regarded as adult responsibilities (Maitra & Miller, 2004: 117–19). Confusion and conflict will inevitably arise if ethnic-minority service-users or carers are on the receiving end of procedures which take no account of their value system and interfere with religious practices or social norms. Social workers need to develop not just an insight into their own cultural heritage, but also into the culture-bound theories and processes which characterise their interventions.

Multidimensional Model of Cultural Competence (MMCC)

Sue (2001) developed the MMCC to take account not just of individual practitioners, but of the professional contexts in which they work. Obviously, a culturally competent social worker cannot function effectively in a mono-cultural agency. Sue (2001: 802) observes that cultural competence in service delivery requires the removal of barriers at four different levels:

Individual level – prejudices and misinformation.
Professional level – culture-bound theories and methods.
Organisational level – mono-cultural policies, procedures and practices.
Societal level – invisibility of Anglo-centric mono-culturalism.

Cultural Negotiation

The encounter between social worker and service-user involves not just their own respective cultural heritages, but the values, beliefs and attitudes which underpin professional and organisational practices and perspectives. Consequently, practitioners may need to act as culture brokers in an endeavour to negotiate between the service-users' or carers' cultural norms on the one hand and agency goals and methods of intervention on the other. Making time to fully explore a person's cultural background and worldview is crucial to opening up a negotiating space between provider and service-user. This can be used, first, to identify the lack of fit between care provision and the cultural requirements of the service-user. Secondly, it permits an interactive process during which the service-user's values and beliefs shape the practitioner's understanding of the problem and his or her response. However, such brokerage may be of limited effectiveness where providers are mono-cultural or if cultural practices, for example female genital mutilation, violate basic human rights and contravene legal protections.

Speaking of nursing, but equally relevant to social work, Leininger and McFarland (2002: 12) assert that 'culturally congruent care refers to the use of sensitive, creative, and meaningful care practices to fit with the general values, beliefs, and lifeways of clients for beneficial and satisfying health care, or to help them with difficult life situations, disabilities or death'. It is important to appreciate that where culturally congruent social or health care does not take place, service-users and carers are likely to experience cultural conflict in the form of moral dilemmas around religious practices or social norms. Where service-users and carers from minority communities are presented with forced choices which are detrimental to their value systems, they will become distressed and either opt for non-compliance or reluctant acceptance of an unsuitable service.

Standards for Cultural Competence

The National Association of Social Workers (NASW), which is the professional body for social workers in the United States, defines cultural competence as 'the process by which individuals and systems respond respectfully and effectively to people of all cultures, languages, classes, races, ethnic backgrounds, religions, and other diversity factors in a manner that recognizes, affirms, and values the worth of individuals, families and communities and protects and preserves the dignity of each' (NASW, 2001: 11). In 2001 the NASW formally adopted a set of ten standards for cultural competence in social-work practice.

NASW Standards for Cultural Competence

Standard 1: Ethics and values – social workers shall function in accordance with the values, ethics, and standards of the profession, recognizing how personal and professional values may conflict with or accommodate the needs of diverse clients.

Standard 2: Self-awareness – social workers shall seek to develop an understanding of their own personal, cultural values and beliefs as one way of appreciating the importance of multicultural identities in the lives of people.

Standard 3: Cross-cultural knowledge – social workers shall have and continue to develop specialized knowledge and understanding about the history, traditions, values, family systems, and artistic expressions of/major client groups that they serve.

(Continued)

(Continued)

Standard 4: Cross-cultural skills – social workers shall use appropriate methodological approaches, skills, and techniques that reflect the workers' understanding of the role of culture in the helping process.

Standard 5: Service delivery – social workers shall be knowledgeable about and skillful in the use of services available in the community and broader society and be able to make appropriate referrals for their diverse clients.

Standard 6: Empowerment and advocacy – social workers shall be aware of the effect of social policies and programs on diverse client populations, advocating for and with clients whenever appropriate.

Standard 7: Diverse workforce – social workers shall support and advocate for recruitment, admissions and hiring, and retention efforts in social work programs and agencies that ensure diversity within the profession.

Standard 8: Professional education – social workers shall advocate for and participate in educational and training programs that help advance cultural competence within the profession.

Standard 9: Language diversity – social workers shall seek to provide or advocate for the provision of information, referrals and services in the language appropriate to the client, which may include/use of interpreters.

Standard 10: Cross-cultural leadership – social workers shall be able to communicate information about diverse client groups to other professionals.

Source: NASW, 2001: 4–5

Cultural Competence and Anti-Oppressive Practice

Each person is a member of different reference groups on the basis of gender, age, sexuality, disability, marital status, socio-economic status, religious belief, ethnicity and culture which shape their identity. The experience of being a member of a reference group includes both positive and negative reactions from others. For example, a person who has a disability may encounter disablism as well as acceptance among the able-bodied. A person of Bangladeshi ethnicity may be subject to racism by people of a different ethnic background, but experience security and a shared value base among many people who are of Bangladeshi descent. However, a single, unmarried Bangladeshi mother might find that her status attracts censure from a section of her own ethnic community while being unremarkable among some of her own Asian and white British contemporaries at the university she attends. In other words, each person is simultaneously a member of a number of reference groups which attract different reactions from others. These reactions shape a person's self-concept and in turn their interactions with the people around them.

Social context often determines which reference group identity is paramount. For instance a 76-year-old African-Caribbean woman experiencing the early stages of Alzheimer's disease may find that she is at risk of disablism and ageism from some members of her own ethnic community. But as a black woman in a predominantly white luncheon club for older people she is exposed to racial abuse. In the first situation disability cuts across ethnic solidarity, while in the second ethnicity cuts across the shared experience of being an older person. In other words, ethnicity is but one aspect of social identity and its significance is likely to be influenced by the situational context. Similarly, the beliefs, values and social norms which comprise a person's culture may be unremarkable aspects of daily life within their household. However, they can become grounds for conflict when, for example, Romany parents recently arrived in Britain from Romanian refuse to send their young daughter to school because they are preparing her for marriage and want to protect her virginity. Plainly, culture and gender are the paramount reference groups in these circumstances as the parents collide with the local education authority on school attendance for their daughter.

Assessment and intervention have to address not just culture and the experience of racial prejudice, but how these interrelate with other aspects of social identity. Ethnicity and culture cannot be treated separately from age, gender, sexuality, etc. Furthermore, ethnic solidarity should not be assumed. Some people can experience prejudice and rejection from members of their own ethnic community because of being divorced, homosexual or disabled, just as they can from white British people due to racism. Over-focusing on culture without appreciating how it intersects with other aspects of identity or without exploring the potential for black-on-black and white-on-white oppression as well as white-on-black racism will result in inadequate assessments and services which fail to meet needs.

As the anti-oppressive and anti-discriminatory perspectives mapped out by Dominelli (2002) and Thompson (2006) clearly demonstrate, social identity within the context of reference groups is not neutral. Each reference group is composed of dominant and subordinate relationships which result in oppressive ideologies and practices at the individual, organisational and societal level. Thompson (2006) details the oppressive relationships between men and women, the able-bodied and disabled, younger and older people, heterosexuals and homosexuals, and black and white people. These oppressive relationships are sustained and perpetuated through the beliefs and attitudes associated with patriarchy, disablism, ageism, homophobia and racism. Dominelli (2002) explores how these multiple oppressions can combine to fundamentally disadvantage those who are female, disabled, aged, homosexual or black. The exploration of a service-user's cultural background must be undertaken in this wider context. Not only do beliefs, values, attitudes and practices differ between individuals of the same ethnic background, but their experience of oppression will also differ depending on the social group to which they are perceived to belong.

There are clear parallels between elements of Sue's (2001) Multidimensional Model of Cultural Competence and the conceptual frameworks of Dominelli (1997) and Thompson (2006). All three authorities highlight the different levels on which prejudice operates. In Sue's (2001) model, Anglo-centric values, attitudes and norms at the individual, professional, organisational and societal levels result in widespread cultural imposition, which produces inferior and discriminatory services for many people from ethnic minorities. Dominelli (1997) and Thompson (2006) also stress how racial discrimination takes place at these different levels, which then become mutually reinforcing.

Advocates of cultural competence in the caring professions identify mono-culturalism as a major contributory factor in racial discrimination. They argue that without cultural self-awareness, complemented by a knowledge of the cultural influences in the lives of other people, social workers and health professionals will invariably impose their own worldviews on their clients. This will occur whether or not the practitioner actually thinks his or her value system is superior. It is the failure to explore and examine culture which results in the obliviousness of many professionals to the imposition of Anglo-centric values. Like Dominelli (1997) and Thompson (2006), those advancing cultural competence in social work, such as Lynch and Hanson (1994), Green (1995), Lum (1996), Devore and Schlesinger (1999), O'Hagan (2001) and Sue (2005), are acutely aware of the dangers of stereotyping and reinforcing racist assumptions when encouraging students and practitioners to focus on cultural influences. But, as so many American social-work scholars have already concluded (and indeed the NASW), this danger is not sufficient reason for steering clear of the cultural context of professional practice.

📖 Further Reading

Holland, K. & Hogg, C. (2001) *Cultural Awareness in Nursing and Health Care*. London: Arnold. Although addressed predominantly to health-care professionals in the United Kingdom, this book is very relevant to social workers. It describes the diversity of health beliefs and health-seeking behaviours of individuals from different cultural backgrounds, including the white-majority community. The text also explores a range of approaches to people with different views of health and illness.

O'Hagan, K. (2001) *Cultural Competence in the Caring Professions*. London: Jessica Kingsley. This book challenges the exclusive focus on anti-racist practice in the caring professions at the expense of understanding different social norms among ethnic communities. It argues for and explores the nature of culturally sensitive practice.

Sue, D.W. (2005) *Multicultural Social Work Practice*. Indianapolis: Wiley. This is one of a number of leading social-work texts in the United States which specifically addresses cultural competence in social-work practice. It makes many observations which are highly relevant to practitioners in the United Kingdom.

4

Communities with Roots in India

Migration and Settlement

India obtained its independence from British colonial rule in 1947 and has since been a democratic and secular state. The population is 80% Hindu with a large Muslim minority of 13% and significant smaller groups of Sikhs and Christians each making up around 2% of the total population. There is also a Buddhist community comprising less than 1% of the population (Office of the Registrar General, 2001). In the United Kingdom, people of Indian descent comprise 1.8% of the population and there are an estimated 1,029,000 people identifying as 'Asian or Asian British – Indian' currently living in England (National Statistics, 2003). The religious breakdown of this ethnic group in Britain is rather different from that in India. Reflecting original migration patterns during the 1950s and 1960s there are, according to the 2001 Census, approximately 559,000 Hindus and 336,000 Sikhs living in the United Kingdom. Of the 1,591,000 Muslims living in Britain, a small number have roots in India, while the vast majority trace their family origins to Pakistan and Bangladesh (National Statistics, 2003).

The migration process began when a number of young men, a large proportion of them Sikh and from the Jat caste (peasant farmers), joined the British Indian Army and during the 1930s settled in Britain. At around the same time males from the Bhatra caste, who traditionally travelled across northern India trading goods, also came to live in England. Most of these single men were from Punjab State which had a long history of migration. When Britain suffered a labour shortage in the wake of the Second World War, commonwealth citizens were encouraged to come and work in the industrial cities of England. Throughout the 1950s and 1960s the process of 'chain migration' meant that Sikhs already living in the United Kingdom assisted fellow villagers from the rural districts of Punjab to join them. Thus close-knit networks of relatives, friends and members of the same caste grew up in many of the industrial centres of England, most particularly in outer London, the Midlands and West Yorkshire. Smaller Sikh communities also established themselves in the seaports of Southampton, Bristol, Cardiff, Newcastle and Glasgow.

Not only did those already settled provide financial assistance for the passage to Britain, they also supplied information on job opportunities and helped new arrivals with accommodation (Ballard, 1994: 94). Since Jats are a landowning caste, many were able to either raise finance from relatives or mortgage their property to obtain sufficient money for the voyage from India to England. For this reason, almost half of those belonging to the Sikh community originate from the first generation of Jats to settle in Britain. By the 1960s immigration controls had curtailed primary migration by single men or couples from India and other commonwealth countries. This prevented large numbers of new arrivals from entering the United Kingdom, but family reunion was permitted. From the mid-1960s onwards many members of immediate families chose to join their relatives already residing in Britain. As these Sikh communities expanded, 'many of the social and cultural styles, conventions and institutions of the Punjab began to be reproduced' (Ballard, 1994: 96).

Hindus from Punjab and Gujarat also migrated to Britain during the post-war years. Smaller numbers came from the southern states of India or its major cities. Like their Sikh counterparts, Hindus also depended upon the material assistance of relatives and members of their own caste already resident in the United Kingdom. Usually, this meant sharing rooms and houses with compatriots. They too formed communities in the industrial centres of England. The first Hindu migrants tended to be young single men who, after the imposition of controls in the early 1960s, then brought their families from India to join them in Britain. Following a similar migration pattern, though smaller in number, were those from India's Muslim minority.

A later wave of South Asian immigrants arrived in the United Kingdom during the 1970s. Unlike the migrant workers of the 1950s and 1960s, they originated not from the Indian sub-continent, but from East Africa. During the late nineteenth and early twentieth centuries Hindus and Sikhs had left Punjab and Gujarat to work in East Africa, which was then under British colonial rule. Many became highly skilled craftsmen and qualified professionals living mainly in the principal cities of East Africa. The countries of Uganda, Kenya, Tanzania, Zambia and Malawi gained independence and a process of Africanisation replaced Indian entrepreneurs and professionals with Africans. This meant that many of those of South Asian ethnicity were either required to leave their jobs or the country in which they were then living. As commonwealth citizens, most East African Asians possessed British passports and during the 1970s there was widespread migration of these families from East Africa to the United Kingdom. Many were successful businessmen or qualified professionals and had savings, and so were normally able to find work in the United Kingdom.

The patterns of migration from India and East Africa mean that there is a diversity of heritage languages among those of Indian descent living in Britain. Those with origins in Punjab and Gujarat will speak a diversity of languages, some of which in their spoken form are mutually intelligible to a greater or lesser extent (see Table 4.1).

The majority of migrants arriving from India took up employment in manufacturing and transport, often because members of the majority white population would not work for the long hours required and for the low rates of pay. Some migrants found self-employment in the service sector, often through the assistance of fellow countrymen already settled in Britain. Of the qualified professionals, emigrating either from India or East Africa, some were able to obtain commensurate employment as teachers, doctors

Table 4.1   Spoken South Asian languages

Language	Punjabi	Gujarati	Hindi
Punjabi		small amount	large amount
Gujarati	small amount		small amount
Hindi	large amount	small amount	
Urdu	large amount	small amount	most of what is said

Source: Adapted from Henley (1979: 163)

and entrepreneurs. Frequently, though, they met with discrimination and experienced downward mobility, at least during the initial years of settlement, as their professional qualifications were not recognised or prejudice prevented their employment (Ballard, 1994: 99–100).

By the 1980s a deep recession had affected the British economy, with the widespread loss of manufacturing jobs. The concentration of males of Indian descent in semi-skilled factory work meant that they were disproportionably affected by the recession and large numbers were made redundant. It is reckoned that during this period up to half of the middle-aged Asian industrial workforce lost their jobs. The Indian community coped with this crisis by turning to self-employment and relying on kin and caste networks to assist them to gain alternative employment or to raise capital for their own small business start-up (Ballard, 1994: 100–1). The 1980s coincided with family reunions and often the wives and children of the first generation of male migrants were drawn into family businesses as either unpaid or low-paid labour. These enterprises tended to be concentrated in the clothes or service sector. Many of these businesses succeeded, so large numbers of the Indian community moved out of the run-down inner-city areas in which they originally settled. Upward mobility has been reinforced by the high academic achievement of many children of Indian descent. As a result, a considerable number have entered the professions, although many graduates are still excluded from employment opportunities corresponding to their qualifications due to racism (Ballard, 1994: 103–4). The search for work, establishing family businesses in new locations and high educational achievement among many families has combined to disperse the Indian community between the suburbs and the inner city in present-day Britain. Despite evidence of social mobility, a lot of people from the Indian community remain in dilapidated housing located in deprived inner-city areas and struggle to make ends meet in the face of employment discrimination.

Families of Indian Heritage in the United Kingdom

Social stratification

Caste, known as *jati* in India, is a form of social stratification which creates a hierarchy between different groups. Hinduism sanctions this system of ranking by reference to ideas of spiritual purity and pollution. The intersection of religious faith with social stratification means that those holding the highest social status are also believed to be the most ritually pure (Shaw, 2000: 113). The teachings of the Sikh Gurus do not sanction caste, but historically it has persisted among many practising Sikhs (Nesbitt, 2005: 117–19). Caste allegiances, though irrelevant among many households in the United Kingdom, remain important to numerous families. These can influence the choice of a partner, which temple to attend and relations between different sections of the same ethnic community (Jackson & Nesbitt, 1992: 34–5; Ballard, 1994: 110).

Strong caste identity may make some parents reluctant to contemplate the marriage of their son or daughter to someone from another caste. Even when religious beliefs around purity are not of concern, social and economic aspects of caste may continue to be important to some Hindu and Sikh families. In Britain, as gradually in India, the traditional occupations of different castes and the complex exchange of goods and services between them has broken down. Consequently, the ranking of castes in terms of their social, educational or income status would be difficult. Upward social mobility has been a common experience for people of Indian heritage regardless of their caste identity. Paralleling this development, notions of pollution through contact with other castes is becoming much rarer (Knott, 1994: 213, 218–28; Hahlo, 1998: 72–5).

Marriage

The marital state is still a social norm within the Indian community with only 2% of Sikhs and Hindu couples reporting that they cohabit in the 2001 Census (National Statistics, 2003). A number of young people of Indian descent, particularly if they are Sikh or Muslim, anticipate an arranged marriage (Hennink et al., 1999; Shain, 2003).

Arranged marriage

Modood et al. (1997: 317), in their national survey of Britain, discovered generational differences between women of Indian heritage whose parents chose their spouse and those who chose their own:

86% of Sikh women over 50 years had arranged marriages
27% of Sikh women under 35 years had arranged marriages
74% of Hindu women over 50 years had arranged marriages
20% of Hindu women under 35 years had arranged marriages

Generally, in India, parents and family elders arrange the marriages of children by identifying suitable partners through negotiation with other parents (Säävälä, 2001: 104–5). Mothers tend to be closely involved in the negotiations regarding the right match, though the final decision will probably rest with the senior males in each family (Säävälä, 2001: 106). Arranged marriages now comprise the minority of unions for people of Indian heritage living in the United Kingdom. Where they do take place, adult children are likely to expect and be given a say over both the timing of the marriage and the choice of partner. As in India, marriage in Britain continues to be a matter between two families as much as it is between the prospective couple (C. Ballard, 1979: 124–5; Barot, 1998: 169).

For a large number of Hindus, caste membership can influence the choice of marital partner. Marrying from within the same caste, or from a closely aligned one, may be important to both the couple and their families. Of course marriages do still take place outside the caste, religious affiliation or ethnic group. While many of these find acceptance among kin, others result in conflict, concerns around damage to *izzat* (family honour) and occasionally social rejection by the *birādarî* (extended kin group). Conversely, among many Sikhs, marriage from within the same sub-caste may not be socially permissible. Nevertheless, people of Indian descent do tend to marry from within their own ethnic group. The *Labour Force Quarterly Survey* for 1997–2002 reveals that 92% of women marry partners of the same ethnicity. Despite the general preference for a partner of the same ethnicity, a small but increasing number of young people are forming sexual relationships outside their ethnic group. The 2001 Census would appear to corroborate this trend by recording 184,000 individuals who identified as 'Mixed – White and Asian' (Office for National Statistics, 2003).

Among the Indian community in the United Kingdom there is considerable variation as regards the payment of dowries. Many parents simply give some jewellery to their daughters on marriage and a few symbolic gifts to her husband's family (Knott, 1994: 222). For other parents the combined cost of the wedding reception, gifts of expensive jewellery to their daughter and the payment of a substantial dowry can reach tens of thousands of pounds (Barot, 1998: 169–70). In Britain a dowry can be anything from a cash payment to jewellery and clothes to buying a car for the groom or his family. Household goods, clothes and/or cash are also given to the bride on her departure from her parents' home. When there are expectations of large dowries and lavish weddings, saving sufficient money to meet the expense of a daughter's marriage can be a source of acute anxiety. A lot of young people express ambivalence regarding dowry, but the prospect for a young couple of gaining considerable material advantage means that many ultimately subscribe to the practice (Jhutti, 1998). Brides, too, often see clear benefits in the dowry system as increasingly they are able to both negotiate their own dowries and retain control over them (Jhutti, 1998: 194–8). Where a young couple gain choice and control over the dowry, it may be a welcome contribution to the expenses of setting up home and having children.

Household structure

In India the ideal household, termed a *ghar*, is a joint family unit comprising three or more generations residing together, pooling their resources, sharing a single budget and holding property in common, participating in ceremonial activities and accepting the authority of the eldest male member. A multigenerational household is formed when married sons follow custom and continue to live in their parents' home. On the death of their father, married and unmarried brothers alike would continue residing together in a joint household (Warrier, 1994: 201). This household arrangement is very much an ideal and is often neither feasible nor desirable for family members. The basis for it is the norm across India of virilocal residence, meaning that women on marriage move to live with their husband's family. This can be a gradual process with the bride steadily spending less time in her parents' home and more in her in-laws' household until after a period of a year or so she makes a permanent move (Wadley, 1995: 97).

The constraints of the housing market in the United Kingdom and the influence of living patterns among the white-majority community mean that few people of Indian descent live in multigenerational households. Although a large proportion of the Indian community in Britain live in nuclear households, many of these change their composition, moving backwards and forwards between nuclear and extended modes. For instance, a household consisting of just parents and children becomes multigenerational when a widowed grandmother migrates from India to reside with her married son. Similarly, a *joint household* emerges when the second of two brothers marries and they both continue residing in the same house with their respective families. Even when, for example, a young couple move out of a parental home, they may well live nearby and the two households share a kitchen and eat daily together. As in India, relatives often come and go from a household, becoming temporary or permanent members of it. This can include family members from overseas making extended visits to relations in Britain. These fluid arrangements are much better described by the term *ghar* than they are by the rather fixed concepts of nuclear and extended families which characterise Western notions of family structure (Warrier, 1994: 201–2).

While virilocal family arrangements in Britain may be less common than in India, it is nevertheless the case that many married couples remain living with the husband's parents for some years before moving into their own home. Often this is a matter of personal choice; often it is dictated by the high cost of buying or renting a house. Where households are joint, they may pool resources or each family unit may keep their finances separate and only share some costs such as utility bills. Conversely, a *ghar* living between several houses may actually comprise a single household with incomes and expenses being shared. Cooking and eating are likely to be regular communal activities with the whole *ghar* coming together at mealtimes.

Gender roles

Traditional gender-role expectations, as among the white-majority population, remain compelling in most families of Indian heritage. Women generally shoulder the bulk of domestic responsibilities while men are expected to be the main earners. The degree to which men participate in domestic tasks and women in paid employment varies considerably from household to household. Large numbers of women attend university and pursue professional careers; many young men are required to curtail their ambitions in order to earn a living wage for their family. Although traditional gender roles are influential, so too are religious orthodoxy, the level of household income, the age and educational achievement of family members and the emphasis on upward social mobility. These factors plainly differ across households and result in different expectations of males and females (Warrier, 1994: 203–6).

A further influence on gendered behaviour is *izzat*, which refers to honour and standing in the community. It is a collectively shared attribute and not an individual one. Therefore a family's social status and dignity can be severely damaged by the misbehaviour of just one of its members. Among many sections of the Hindu and Sikh communities *izzat* is closely associated with women's modesty and chastity. This means that their behaviour is more likely to be scrutinised than that of men, particularly in the context of education, work and leisure activity, when they are likely to come into contact with unrelated males (Ballard & Ballard, 1977: 44–5).

The behaviour of men also has consequences for the prestige and reputation of the *birādarī*, as they can damage their family's *izzat* if they act contrary to accepted social convention (Helweg, 1986: 13). The local Punjabi or Gujarati community may shun a family possessing little *izzat*. Conversely, improving the welfare of the *birādarī* or the local community through service or leadership will increase a man's prestige and therefore the *izzat* of his family. As in India, a man's display of wealth combined with generous gifts to other individuals or community-based organisations will add to *izzat* (Helweg, 1986: 14–17). Generally, where *izzat* is lost it can be regained through commendable acts such as a good marriage, achieving business success or contributing to the community.

Where women's choices around further education or employment outside are constrained by social convention, they may still be working in family-owned businesses. Both women and children among South Asian communities are more likely than are those from the white-majority population to participate in family enterprises. Within this context women may have substantial responsibility for running these small businesses. Children of school age may well be expected to contribute to the family enterprise in their spare time. For both women and children, their labour may be either paid or unpaid (Srinivasan, 1995: 125–8). Wives and daughters not working in family-owned businesses, but whose activity is centred round their home, may instead decide to undertake piece work such as sewing garments or preparing mail shots.

Distinction needs to be made between the public appearance of domination by men and the actual power relations between men and women in the household. Within a British context, many women exercise considerable authority over household decisions as mothers, grandmothers and wage earners. In the United Kingdom, as elsewhere, family decision-making is influenced by the education, employment and marital status of its members alongside the contribution each makes to household income. Family dynamics will also depend on whose kin live nearby. If, for reasons of employment, a man moves to be near his wife's kin, or alternatively if he joins her directly from Punjab or Gujarat, she may have more leverage over decision-making than he. Circumstances modify the degree of authority exercised by men over women and male elders over other members of the *ghar* (Warrier, 1994: 203–6).

Child rearing

In India most children will grow up within the context of an extended family and develop a strong affinity and loyalty to many of their relations aside from parents and grandparents. Sharing the same dwelling or living in one nearby and participating in common domestic and economic activities alongside the joint celebration of religious occasions reinforce kinship bonds (Dwivedi, 2004b: 49). This is in contrast to the family system predominant in Western societies, which promotes the nuclear-family unit and tends to relegate the part played by other relatives in children's lives.

Generally, in India, children are encouraged to spread their affection among a wide range of relations, while the boundaries of the nuclear family are much less emphasised than in Western societies (Dwivedi, 2004b: 50–1).

The combined effects of migration and geographical mobility have reduced the size and influence of the extended family for many households of Indian descent living in the United Kingdom. Nevertheless, uncles, aunts and cousins can continue to play a vital role in the lives of children and to become important sources of support and guidance as they grow into adulthood. Children are likely to be socialised to value the interdependence of kinship relations and to meet their family obligations. In this context the collective good, will usually outweigh that of any single individual. Consequently, children are encouraged to develop emotional self-control, avoid direct confrontation and preserve harmony within the family, even when their own wishes are being frustrated (Dwivedi, 2004b: 55). This approach is plainly in contrast to the endorsement of self-expression and the emphasis on individuality among many families belonging to the white majority in the United Kingdom.

In India it is common for babyhood to be extended and at the same time for children to take on quite adult responsibilities such as looking after younger siblings and assisting with the commercial activities of relatives. Weaning from breast milk may not occur for several years and young children are likely to continue sleeping with their mothers or other relatives for a number of years (Lau, 2004: 96–7). As they grow older girls will generally be expected to care for younger brothers and sisters, while boys are required to help male relatives with their work (Saraswathi & Dutta, 1988; Säävälä, 2001: 185–6). For families of Indian origin living in Britain, these patterns of child rearing have been modified by house design, employment outside the home, the legal requirement for children to attend school and the social pressures exerted by the white majority population. As a result, among many households in the Indian community the weaning and upbringing of children is similar to that within families of the white majority. However, for a proportion of households of Indian descent it may remain the norm for young children to be weaned late and to continue sleeping with siblings, parents or occasionally older relatives until up to four years of age or more (Hackett & Hackett, 1994: 196–7).

Given that co-sleeping arrangements, either in the same bed or in the same room, are adopted by a number of families of Asian background (including those of Pakistani and Bangladeshi heritage), there is considerable scope for misunderstanding between Children's Services and South Asian communities. Mistaken assumptions might be made by social workers that these sleeping arrangements indicate sexual abuse, when in fact nothing could be further from the truth. This is, of course, not to deny the possibility that an adult could sexually exploit a child in such circumstances and then cite custom as a cover for the abuse. Despite the reservations that some social- and health-care professionals from the white-majority community might have around this type of sleeping arrangement, Barn et al. (1997), in their study of referrals to Social Services, found that white children were twice as likely to be referred over allegations of sexual abuse as Asian children. Gibbons et al. (1995) to some extent corroborate this finding by revealing that of all referrals to Social Services for child maltreatment, those for sexual abuse were higher for white children than for those from ethnic minorities combined.

However, Brophy et al. (2003) did discover that of sexual-abuse cases which made it to court, as opposed to just the referral stage, a higher proportion of these involved children of South Asian background rather than white children. These studies do not prove that there is more or less sexual abuse among white families than among those of South Asian or Indian background, but they do challenge any presumption that alternative sleeping arrangements are necessarily harmful to children.

Young people

Girls in Hindu and Sikh families may experience more social restrictions than their peers among the white-majority population. Their social lives will possibly be more centred on their home, family and same-sex friends than is true of young people among the white-majority population. Leisure time with friends is also more likely to be spent at home. By contrast, among teenagers from the white majority, recreation tends to focus around going out with friends to the cinema, clubs and other venues, and often includes the consumption of alcohol. Participation in religious activity has both a social and cultural dimension and can be important to many young people. For Hindu and Sikh girls this is likely to involve going to the temple or *gurdwara* regularly for congregational worship, attending religious instruction or language classes alongside a variety of cultural activities (Hennink et al., 1999). A number of Hindus and Sikhs are non-practising, but even for them activities centring on the temple or *gurdwara* can remain an important source of social identity and community interaction.

The social norms which inhibit girls of Indian heritage from clubbing or socialising with boys differ from household to household. Some girls are permitted to mix freely with the opposite sex while others are not. A lot of parents are likely to feel concern that their daughter's reputation will be damaged if it becomes known in the community that she spends time with boys. Such rumours will diminish *izzat* and therefore the prospects of a good marriage. Peer pressure, which among the white majority often encourages early sexual experiences, among girls of Indian descent usually acts to discourage it (Hennink et al., 1999; Shain, 2003: 69–70). Most young men, like their sisters, spend a great deal of time socialising with relations. However, their movements are likely to be less supervised by their parents. Therefore males tend to spend more time outside the home, often with friends, going to discos, the cinema and sporting activities (Gillespie, 1995: 38).

Conflicts do inevitably arise between parents and their children, which sometimes centre on different cultural outlooks. These have been hyped-up and exploited by media sensationalism which focuses on exceptional incidents of forced marriage or 'honour killings' (Shain, 2003: 8). The relationship between the generations is stereotyped as a clash between over-controlling parents steeped in tradition and rebellious, Westernised youth demanding freedom from restrictive cultural norms (C. Ballard, 1979: 109). On closer examination, most disagreements are concerned with boundary-setting and authority, which are apt to characterise intergenerational relationships in general. Young people may question aspects of their parents or grandparents value system while also possessing a deep sense of identification with those very values. Many young Hindus and Sikhs, whether practising or not, are taken aback by the seeming casualness of family interactions among

the white-majority population. These can appear lacking in commitment or unsupportive
to relatives outside the immediate family. Others perceive the behaviour of teenagers from
the white majority as ill-disciplined and disrespectful to others (C. Ballard 1979: 114–15).
Some young people experience the dominant secular and individualist paradigm in British
society as 'hostile to their family-centred and religious values' (Robinson, 2005: 185).

It is a mistake to suppose that adolescents of Indian heritage are engaged in a process
of inevitable Westernisation. While a number may indeed decide to adopt some of the
norms they encounter in other ethnic communities, they are still likely to embrace
many of their parents' and grandparents' values. These may well include a strong sense
of family loyalty, respecting elders and observing restraint between the sexes. Many
young people of Indian heritage manage the contradictory pressures created by the
dominant norms in British society and those of their parents by switching backwards
and forwards between different conventions of behaviour. Whether they are with their
family, accompanying friends of the same ethnicity or interacting with members of the
white-majority community will affect how people of Indian descent choose to express
their identity (C. Ballard, 1979: 122–3; Jackson & Nesbitt, 1992: 175–6). For those
who synthesise British social styles with those derived from South Asian communities,
racism may prove an obstacle to a positive sense of identity. At the same time, many
young people of Indian descent are choosing to explore, re-adopt and take pride in customary dress codes, religious practices and social norms, which had for a time fallen
out of favour among sections of the Indian community (C. Ballard, 1979: 126–8). In
short, they 'feel that their roots lie in the resources of Asian culture' (C. 1979: 128).

Older people

According to the 2001 Census, those aged over 65 years comprise around 6.6% of the
Indian community in Britain and this figure is steadily increasing (National Statistics,
2003). Many older people with roots in Punjab and Gujarat live in multigenerational
households, but many live with an aging spouse or alone. For instance, a study in
Birmingham found that 25% of older people originally from Gujarat live alone, while
14% of those with roots in Punjab form single-person households. Out of both groups
only half of those aged over 55 years resided in multigenerational households, with one-
third living in two-person family units (Burholt, 2004a: 389). Household size among people of Indian heritage is decreasing, with the result that progressively more older people
are living on their own or with just their spouse. As English is widely used in India, many
older people who grew up in Punjab or Gujarat speak English fluently. For others who
came to Britain relatively late in life and with little formal schooling in India, Punjabi or
Gujarati is likely to remain their primary language of communication (2004a: 392).

There are strong social norms which require younger people to defer to older people,
particularly family elders. Indeed, veneration of elders and repaying filial debt are important religious duties of Hindus (Bhat & Dhruvarajan, 2001: 626). However, older men
and women who are used to exercising authority over their household in Punjab or
Gujarat may find on moving to live with an adult son or daughter in Britain that they have
the status of house guests. Their power as family elders will perhaps be substantially
reduced. This is most likely to happen where adult children are no longer economically

dependent upon parents or reliant on inherited property, as might have been the case in Punjab. Social norms regarding gender and generational relations remain important, but in practice the decisions of males or elders are likely to be constrained by circumstance and the outcome of negotiation with other family members (Warrier, 1994: 203–6).

Transnational families

Kinship networks can be extensive and are often transnational, with frequent communication between family members in Britain and in India. These interactions will probably be a combination of telephone calls, e-mails, exchanges of home videos and extended visits in both directions. These networks are often a source of social identity, financial assistance, advice and general emotional support (Helweg, 1986: 64; Burholt, 2004b). Since relatives in Britain usually earn a great deal more than their counterparts in India, they are more likely to send money than receive it. These remittances are used to regenerate villages and improve the welfare of *birādarī* in India and invest in business ventures or property. Often they are an important source of income to the *ghar* living in Punjab, Gujarat and elsewhere in India (Helweg, 1986: 94–5). Inevitably, such kin networks can also be a source of onerous obligation and scrutiny or censure of an individual's conduct. Close friends may be incorporated into this web of interdependent relationships and often come to be described in kinship terms, such as 'brother' or 'cousin'.

The *birādarī*, despite its transnational nature, remains for many families in Britain a powerful source of emotional and material support. The close-knit nature of such kinship systems means that the decisions of family members may be of concern to apparently quite distant relatives. What seem to be disagreements between parents and children or between spouses may have significance for wider kin. Both the parties in direct dispute and members of the *birādarī* may well acknowledge their common interests in finding a resolution through collective discussion (R. Ballard, 1979: 154). In other instances individuals may regard the interference of *birādarī* members as unwarranted intrusion into a private matter. The importance of and interaction with the *birādarī* differs from household to household. Many families have stronger bonds with friends either from other castes or ethnic groups. For others, the *birādarī* continues to act as a source of social identity, individual affirmation and indispensable assistance.

Social networks

In India, the principle of *vartan bhanji* (meaning 'give and take') obliges members of a *birādarī* to provide assistance to each other. The rendering of material assistance or services to a person or household belonging to the *birādarī* is done in the expectation that this favour will be returned at some stage in the future. The rules of *vartan bhanji*, which are vital to reciprocal exchanges between *birādarī* members, remain important among many families in Britain. Assistance with raising loans, professional advice, property repairs and child care all characterise *birādarī* interactions in the United Kingdom (Ahmad, 1996: 56). When examined more broadly, this system of give and take is not greatly different from the expectations held among the white-majority population of receiving assistance from family members, though *vartan bhanji* is governed by stricter social norms. This includes a hierarchy of obligations between closer and more distant relations. *Vartan bhanji* places a clear moral imperative on *birādarī* to render assistance to each other, whether or not they live in the locality and that this be reciprocated at a later date. Failure to meet the responsibilities created by *vartan bhanji* can damage family *izzat*. As in India, these obligations may create uncomfortable dependencies or indebtedness.

At the same time, the once strong ties of *birādarī* have been weakened through transnational distances, social mobility and the development of alternative loyalties towards friends and colleagues. In these circumstances, help from the wider kinship group may not be forthcoming at all. Moreover, because *birādarī* can operate as close-knit networks, they may exclude other community members on the basis of their family affinity, their caste or religion. Consequently, mutual-support systems often overlook numerous small households and individuals who are not members of established caste or *birādarī* networks and who may not be practising Sikhs, Hindus or Muslims. Alternatively, *vartan bhanji* may be initiated with non-kin who, through the process of mutual give and take, build up bonds of friendship and dependability which are comparable to those between *birādarī* members (Ahmad, 1996: 57–8).

As upwardly mobile adults move from family-oriented businesses into the professions and from areas of ethnic-minority concentration into the suburbs, they may increasingly socialise with members of the white-majority population. Friendships between people of different castes and ethnic groups are common among younger people as they mix with others at school, university, through employment and leisure activities (C. Ballard, 1979). At the same time, racism, combined with a sense of shared values and views with other people of South Asian descent, may well lead to individuals tending to associate with members of their own ethnic community (Ballard & Ballard, 1977: 46–7). Among many of Indian heritage, friendships with members of the white majority and their own ethnic group are both a vital aspect of social identity.

Caste networks may be exploited to increase community solidarity and acquire much needed public resources for a particular locality. Alternatively, they can be a source of factionalism and dispute (Ballard, 1994: 115). A number of people of Indian descent are members of caste associations which help to promote the interests of the *jati* to which they belong. These associations may be local or national in scale. They run cultural and social events for their membership, help to disseminate information, facilitate interaction between caste members, both in Britain and India, and offer material assistance. Often such associations provide services for their local community regardless of caste affiliation, for example establishing evening classes in Gujarati (Warrier, 1994: 209; Hahlo, 1998: 76–8). A large number of organisations deliberately avoid sectarian divisions and aim to serve the whole ethnic community irrespective of caste, religious faith or origin.

Ethnic identification and racism

Some females choose to wear traditional garments such as *shalwar kameez* (trousers and long tunic) with a *dupattah* (long scarf) or sari as against Western clothes. This may simply be because these are the clothes they wore in their country of origin. Such garments also ensure that they are modestly dressed, meaning that their legs, upper arms and breasts are properly covered. For some, wearing a *shalwar kameez* or sari is a matter of pride, ethnic identification and a defiant response to racism (Shain, 2003: 62–3). For others, whether they wear traditional clothes or not is dependent on context. Family gatherings and religious festivals often entail wearing traditional clothes, while the same individual would choose to dress in a Western style at school or work, or when out with friends (Gillespie, 1995: 180; Shain, 2003: 81–2). Likewise, the use of heritage languages alongside English can be both an important aspect of community identity and at times a means of resisting the negative effects of racism by creating private space (Shain, 2003: 63, 119–20).

Racism is frequently concentrated on those who outwardly display their religious faith. Sikh men who do not cut their hair and wear turbans may be particularly vulnerable to racial abuse and employment discrimination. Such racism can have homophobic undertones, for while long hair among Sikh males in Punjab is a sign of manliness, large sections of British society perceive it as effeminate (Helweg, 1986: 5). Sikh men, like members of other ethnic minorities, can be under considerable pressure to conform to the social norms of the majority-white population, for instance, by cutting their hair, abandoning the turban and being clean shaven. This is not to deny that a number of Sikh males simply prefer to have short hair and find wearing a turban inconvenient. Women who choose to wear *shalwar kameez* may similarly find themselves on the receiving end of racial taunts and pressure to abandon traditional styles of dress.

Religious Observance

Hinduism

Hindus believe in one God called Brahman who has different aspects or incarnations. Which incarnation or god a person worships probably depends on family tradition and person choice. Most Hindus in Britain are devotees of Vishnu, known as Vaishnavites, while Shaivites who worship incarnations of Shiva are in the minority. Hindus usually have pictures or sculptures, known as *murti*, of their favourite deities in their home where they are accorded a place of respect. The Hindu religion is not a unified system of beliefs and includes a very wide spectrum of spiritual beliefs and practices.

Principal Beliefs of the Hindu Religion

Samsara – the cycle of reincarnation
Karma – the law of cause and effect
Dharma – doing what is right
Moksa – liberation from *samsara*

Worship, referred to as *puja*, is personal rather than congregational and takes place either in the home or in the local *mandir* (temple). Practising Hindus will set aside a special place in their home, either a room or a shelf, where they will place *murti* as different members of the family are likely to venerate a number of divinities. Domestic *pujas* may be performed by the family on a daily or weekly basis and some individuals may gather in gender-segregated groups, called *satsangs*, in each other's houses for communal devotion. Hinduism places upon women the chief responsibility for their family's spiritual welfare, and female household members tend to take the lead in domestic worship and conduct a number of rituals. In Britain, women continue to exercise an important religious role in many households.

Hindu priests officiate over religious ceremonies, but they do not normally act in a pastoral role towards worshipers. Apart from Brahmin priests, there are holy men known as gurus or *sadhus* who offer religious guidance to devotees. While many Hindus do visit the local temple, known as a *mandir*, for most the home is the main location of religious observance. *Mandirs* provide a communal focus for worship. However, they may be restricted to particular castes or serve wider sections of the community. The *mandir* is not just a place of collective devotion to deities, but also provides a space for social interaction. Few people attend the *mandir* daily; however, most practising Hindus will visit weekly and especially during major festivals. Hindu congregations elect a committee to look after the *mandir* and arrange for a Brahmin priest to officiate.

Major Hindu festivals

Ramnavmi – celebrated in March or April, this is a fast day with abstinence from usual foods although delicacies may be eaten.
Navaratri – also known as *Durga Puja*, it is celebrated around September or October, particularly by those with family roots in Gujarat. It is a nine-day festival devoted to the goddess Durga. People may fast over this period, eating only fruit, and customarily daughters return home to visit their mothers.
Divali – celebrated around October or November, this is the festival of lights which lasts over five days. It is a family event and small lamps or electric lights are lit up in homes and gifts are often exchanged.
Holi – celebrated around March or April in India and February in Britain, it is an occasion for high spirits, the relaxation of social norms and visiting friends and family.

Food for practising Hindus has a psycho-social and spiritual dimension and it has a hierarchy associated with ideas of pollution. Devout Hindus do not consume alcohol and are vegetarian. They will pay particular attention to how food is prepared so as to avoid pollution. As the religious aspect of the caste system has largely disappeared in Britain, anxiety about pollution from other castes is little in evidence. Less devout individuals may consume meat, but are often reluctant to eat beef as the cow is sacred to Hindus. Perceiving food to have a religious dimension is widespread among older and younger Hindus in Britain, whether or not they are practising (Jackson & Nesbitt, 1992: 57–70). However, most young people will also eat from a wide cuisine, including fast food (Gillespie, 1995: 199).

Sikhism

The Sikh religion, founded in India over 500 years ago, draws on both Islam and Hinduism. Sikhs believe in one universal God and are guided by the divinely inspired ten Gurus, who were all born in Punjab. Consequently, there is a strong association between religion and ethnicity. Most Sikhs in India and the diaspora consider their Punjabi heritage an important aspect of social identity. The principal teachings of Sikhism are contained in the Guru Granth Sahib, which is treated with tremendous reverence and is read aloud during congregational worship at the *gurdwara*. Although Sikhs do pray at home or have gatherings at which the whole of the Guru Granth Sahib is read, there is an emphasis on congregational worship at the *gurdwara* which normally takes place on a Sunday. A *granthi* may be appointed to take care of the *gurdwara* and take the lead in collective, worship, but his duties are purely practical and he is not expected to offer pastoral care to members of the congregation. There may be spiritual teachers known as *sant* who attract a following among certain sections of the Sikh community, but again their guidance will be religious rather than pastoral. Like Hindus, Sikhs believe in *samsara*, *dharma*, *karma* and *moksa*.

Sikh religious practice

This requires visible expression by both males and females and commonly referred to as the Five Ks:

Kesh – to keep the hair uncut, closely associated with the turban
Kangha – to wear a small comb
Kirpan – to carry a sword or knife
Kachh – to wear cotton breeches or underpants
Kara – to put a steel bangle on the wrist

Predominant social norms in Britain, legal requirements regarding health and safety and racism have brought changes to religious observance. Many Sikh men now cut their hair and neither wear a turban nor carry a knife. Others may endeavour to observe the Five Ks (Nesbitt, 2005: 95–7). Among both males and females, observing *kachh* and *kara* tends to be quite common, even for non-practising Sikhs (Henley, 1983a: 17). There are differences of opinion among Sikhs as to whether vegetarianism is a religious requirement. Consequently, some Sikhs avoid meat and eggs while others consume most foods, although beef is likely to be regarded as prohibited, as is true among Hindus (Nesbitt, 2005: 63–4). Strictly speaking, alcohol and tobacco are also forbidden to orthodox Sikhs, but some do drink and smoke.

Major Sikh festivals

Vaisakhi – celebrated on the 13 or 14 April, it is a community event with processions through the streets and the public display of the Guru Granth Sahib which is carried by motorcade. Festive foods, presents and cards are exchanged while family come together. There is special attendance at the *gurdwara*.
Divali – this is celebrated by both Sikhs and Hindus in a similar way.
Birthday of Guru Nanak – celebrated in November, alongside festivities there are readings of the Guru Granth Sahib and attendance at the *gurdwara*.

As Sikh communities expanded, the establishment of a local *gurdwara* (temple) for congregational worship became essential. Some *gurdwaras* can be caste-based, which results in members of different castes attending separate temples. The *gurdwara* is a significant centre for welfare support, language instruction, religious education and community interaction (Helweg, 1986: 177; Ballard, 1994: 109). The regular serving of communal vegetarian meals prepared by members of the congregation at the *gurdwara* underlines its contribution to community cohesion and interaction a function emphasised by the occasional provision of lodgings for visitors to the area or those made unexpectedly homeless. Often the facilities of Sikh temples are open to non-Sikhs in the locality. The *gurdwara* committee is appointed to attend to the affairs of the temple. At times, the committee acts as a mediator in disputes and represents the interests of the community it serves.

Health, Illness and Disability

Health beliefs

In India, physical illness or disability is usually attributed to physiological factors or spiritual causes, such as bad *karma*. Health beliefs are also influenced by the principles underpinning *ayurveda* medicine, which is widely respected in India and recognised by the Ministry of Health. Among a large proportion of the Indian population, it plays a major role in conceptualising mental illness. According to the *ayurveda* system, there are three prime qualities intrinsic to every human being, namely *sattwa*, *rajas* and *tamas*. Each individual possesses these in varying proportions which shape their character. Strong emotion, such as grief, fear and anger, can disturb the equilibrium of these qualities and cause mental illness. Different types of food also have *sattwa*, *rajas* and *tamas* and when eaten can affect a person's character as they alter the internal balance of these qualities. A practitioner of *ayurveda*, called a *vaid*, will diagnose the imbalance between *sattwa*, *rajas* and *tamas* and then prescribe herbal or dietary remedies to restore their equilibrium (Healy & Aslam, 1990: 24).

Those of Indian heritage living in the United Kingdom of whatever age tend to hold a variety of beliefs as to the cause of physical illness and disability. These include physiological, psycho-social and supernatural explanations. The range of factors causing ill health is similar to those identified by members of the white-majority population with the exception that more emphasis is sometimes placed on spiritual causes by those of Indian ethnicity (Jobanputra & Furnham, 2005). As among families from the white majority, failure by health- and social-care services to respond with appropriate support exacerbates anxiety, increasing the sense of personal tragedy associated with illness and disability (Jones et al., 2001).

Some people of Indian descent may conceptualise mental health and illness differently from the medical profession in the United Kingdom, which relies on the categorisation of clearly differentiated pathological mental states as defined in the *Diagnostic and Statistical Manual of Mental Disorders* (DSM). Within allopathic medicine, the task of the psychiatrist is to recognise symptoms and identify which mental illness they indicate. Treatment, whether with psychotropic drugs or psychotherapy, is then based on this diagnosis. However, the close linkage between physical and mental states in *ayurveda* medicine means that psychiatric illnesses are not necessarily conceptualised in this way by people who have a South Asian background. Psychological disturbances may be perceived as 'anxiety' or 'sorrow' as opposed to a diagnosable mental illness (Butt & Mirza, 1996: 73). This may permit help-seeking behaviour, which leads to family members and friends providing additional practical and emotional support to the individual without the stigmatisation and distress of (possibly inappropriate) psychiatric intervention. For some individuals, turning to prayer and spiritual healers may be an important aspect of obtaining help and relief (Butt & Mirza, 1996: 80).

There remains among a large number of Hindus in Britain a conviction that food and liquids affect a person's physical and emotional state, especially during a period of illness or distress. For many people the use of 'cold foods' to calm the passions and 'hot foods' to stimulate activity is still essential to achieving mental and physical balance (Henley, 1983b: 46–51). There are compelling parallels between the importance Hindus place on food in relation to their health and growing public concern in Britain over the dietary habits of children. Recent research is revealing strong correlations between food preservatives and children's behaviour, particularly in relation to hyperactivity (Dengate & Ruben, 2002; Schnoll et al., 2003). Evidence is also emerging of links between diet and disability. Autism and epileptic seizures in children treated with prescribed diets appear to reduce the severity of both conditions (Whiteley et al., 1999; Pulsifer et al., 2001).

Health treatment and care

There is likely to be a marked contrast between consultation with a general practitioner and a visit to a *vaid* healer. The doctor will focus on physical symptoms during a short 10–15 minute consultation. A *vaid*, of whom there are a number practising in Britain, will meet with both the patient and his or her family. The *vaid* will spend 20–40 minutes discussing at some length the physical, mental and spiritual health of the patient. By attending to the patient's condition holistically, often *vaids* act as physician, healer and counsellor rolled into one (Healy & Aslam, 1990: 32–6). People consulting *vaids* often do so alongside attendance at a health centre or hospital. In other words, *ayurveda* medicine has become a form of complementary treatment for a number of people of Indian heritage living in Britain (Karseras & Hopkins, 1987: 118–19).

Aside from the help sought from practitioners of allopathic and *ayurveda* medicine the family and wider kin group are an essential source of advice, assistance and direct care for someone who is ill or severely disabled. However, the stereotype of a South Asian *birādarī* consisting of a closely knit extended family bound by mutual obligations hinders effective service provision by health- and social-care professionals. In reality, the extended family unit is usually curtailed by strict immigration control, the growing preference for nuclear households, the fragmentation of social networks due to geographical mobility, the participation of women in the workforce and family breakdown (Katbamna et al., 2004: 399). The amount and quality of informal care may be adversely affected by the stigma attached to mental illness or such diseases as HIV/AIDS. Concern to safeguard family *izzat* may also result in kin isolating both the carer and the person who is disabled. For example, care for older people with dementia is sometimes left to a female relative unsupported by other family members (Bowes & Wilkinson, 2003: 388–9).

It cannot be taken for granted that immediate family members living in the same house will assist with care. Sex roles may mean caring for a disabled relative is regarded as the sole responsibility of a wife, mother or daughter-in-law. Male relatives who appear to cross established gender boundaries to provide hands-on care to a wife or child may find themselves ridiculed by other family members. Prohibitions on females touching males outside their immediate family circle further reduce the options available in terms of informal caring within kin networks (Katbamna et al., 2004). It appears that for a large proportion of households the pattern of informal caring is not greatly different from that among the white-majority population. Often, care is provided by a female relative who is struggling to cope, mostly alone (Butt & Mirza, 1996: 103–4).

Despite some differences between South Asian families and those of the white majority regarding culturally appropriate provision, both generally want the same from health- and social-care services. These revolve around timely and accurate information about the illness or disability, comprehensive domiciliary services to care for the person at home, and service provision which is sensitive to the cultural requirements of different South Asian communities living in Britain (Begum, 1992; Bowes & Wilkinson, 2003). For South Asian communities, domiciliary services can be critical to preserving the health of carers, as for most families residential care is strongly disapproved of given the obligations of kinship (Bowes & Wilkinson, 2003). However, many are willing to consider short- to medium-term residential services for adults and children if these are fully explained and are culturally appropriate (Butt & Mirza, 1996: 94).

Despite the evident need for social-care provision, the up-take of services by people of South Asian ethnicity is generally poor. This is mainly due to a lack of information being disseminated in community languages and the reluctance of many families to avail themselves of services because they do not cater for their religious and cultural needs. For example, meals at day centres often do not meet dietary requirements in terms of religious observance or else provision isolates individuals from others who speak the same language or who have a similar ethnic background. Interaction with social-care staff can be stressful and unpleasant when they do not speak a service-user's language or interpreters are not available. Although people of Indian descent are known to be interested in using services if these were to reflect their specific needs, Social Services departments often cite cost as a reason for only offering mainstream standard provision (Butt & Mirza, 1996: 66–69).

Case Study 4.1

Mr Patel, who is aged 75 years, and his wife, who is 63 years old, live in a two-bedroom ground-floor flat on the outskirts of a city centre. Mr Patel was brought up as a Hindu in a village in Gujarat and obtained work in a construction company in a nearby town, where he quickly obtained promotion. He married a woman who is also Hindu from his own village and then with the financial help of his brothers in India migrated to the United Kingdom during the early 1960s.

Mr and Mrs Patel's youngest son, Karam, is married and lives with his wife and four children aged 9 years, 8 years and twins aged 6 years in a small semi-detached house in a suburb six miles away. Both Karam and his wife work full-time. The couple's eldest son, Naresh, is married with one adult son who is at university and lives two streets away. Naresh damaged family *izzat* by his behaviour five years ago and greatly diminished his father's standing in the local Indian community. Consequently, all contact has ceased between Naresh and his parents. Mr and Mrs Patel's only daughter, Lalita, and her husband live with their two teenage children 70 miles away in another city.

In 1966 Mr Patel obtained work in a local company although lack of formal qualifications and an element of racial discrimination meant that his expertise was not recognised. Employed on low pay in a semi-skilled job he was unable to make adequate contributions to a pension and is currently reliant on a very small retirement income. Mrs Patel undertakes casual work at home sewing garments for a clothes company.

Mr Patel has severe arthritis and asthma. He also has mobility difficulties getting around the flat. His wife had a stroke a month ago and is returning home after a stay in hospital. She is still largely paralysed down her left side. Both Mr and Mrs Patel require assistance to dress in the morning and undress at night. They are both just about able to manage the toilet on their own. Mrs Patel is presently unable to prepare or cook food, which she did prior to her hospitalisation. Mr Patel has never cooked and in any case would no longer be steady enough to do this safely in the kitchen. Mr and Mrs Patel cannot leave their flat without assistance. Karam took his full annual leave from work to help his father during his mother's absence and his wife cooked food which he brought round and heated up for his father. Karam has now returned to full-time work. He and his wife have one car between them.

Mr and Mrs Patel were refused help by a caste association which provides welfare and financial support to other Hindus in the locality on the grounds that they do not belong to the right caste.

Mr Patel speaks Gujarati to his wife and family. He has reasonably good English, but has difficulty understanding complex verbal exchanges in that language. Mrs Patel knows only a limited amount of English and always communicates in Gujarati, although she also understands some Hindi.

OUTLINE OF INTERVENTION

Provide Mr and Mrs Patel with information about adaptations and services.

Ensure that Mr and Mrs Patel are able to claim their full entitlement to benefits.

Arrange personal-care assistance for Mr and Mrs Patel at home.

Arrange meals-on-wheels service.

Negotiate additional help for Mr and Mrs Patel with family members.

Identify voluntary-sector organisations which cater for members of the Indian community and negotiate provision.

Points for Practice

In giving information to the couple you will need to check out which heritage languages they speak and how fluently. Bear in mind that some people (particularly women) who have grown up in developing countries receive limited formal education and are not literate in their heritage languages. You will also need to check out if Mr Patel reads English as well as he speaks it. It has been standard practice for Social Services to produce information leaflets in heritage languages, but depending on their level of literacy the couple may instead need an audio translation in Gujarati. If your agency does not have provision for audio formats, this may be a situation in which you are practising cultural sensitivity, but not cultural competence. In other words, to be culturally competent you would have to challenge at an organisational level a mono-cultural approach which assumes that fluency in a heritage language equates to literacy and therefore makes no alternative provision.

In common with older people from other communities, including the white majority, Mr and Mrs Patel may either not be aware of their benefit entitlements or may feel reluctant to claim them. The couple may perceive claiming as an admission of failure because they think they ought to be able to get by with the help of their family. They may be frightened of having to declare the small amounts of money they receive from extended family or that they still send remittances to Mr Patel's brothers' families in India. Whatever the reasons, culturally competent practice will require more than just referring on to another agency to complete the forms with Mr and Mrs Patel. A proactive approach would most likely involve identifying opinion leaders or ordinary individuals among the local Indian community who would be willing to share their positive experiences of claiming benefits with Mr and Mrs Patel. Bear in mind that institutional racism has damaged the confidence of ethnic minorities in public-sector agencies. So it may be difficult for Mr and Mrs Patel to engage directly with the social-security agency or housing authority without some mediation or reassurance by trusted members of their own ethnic community.

In arranging personal care for the couple you must explore with them any social norms regulating physical contact. You need to treat Mr and Mrs Patel as individuals and explore their particular perspective. Do not assume that they hold the most orthodox or conservative views on this. While it may be preferable to both Mr and Mrs Patel for female care assistants to help her and male workers to help him, this may be negotiable or of less importance than to other couples of Indian descent. You need to check out if either Mr or Mrs Patel have needs related to their cultural background, for example does Mrs Patel regularly wear a sari and have you ensured that the care workers know how to fit one? Are care workers aware of any needs that Mr and Mrs Patel may have in relation to washing, for example having a shower rather than a bath, which many Hindus consider unclean? Are there some aspects of care which Mr and Mrs Patel regard as needs which cannot be met, for example what if Mr and Mrs Patel refused to be touched by a care assistant because he or she was of a lower caste? It is important to realise that there is a difference between cultural competence and cultural relativity. Social workers and care providers cannot collude in oppressive practices by service-users, in this case on the grounds of socio-economic status.

In arranging meals-on-wheels it is important to consider what might be the dietary requirements of Mr and Mrs Patel and also not to assume that they both have the same ones. Are there spiritual or health beliefs linked with food or preferences for traditional Indian dishes? In this case, Mr and Mrs Patel were both brought up as Hindus, but the extent to which they practise their religion needs to be explored and not assumed. Are either of them vegetarian, or do they eat meat, but not beef, or do they no longer observe any food prohibitions while still regarding themselves as Hindus? If Mr and Mrs Patel experience illness, do either of them use 'hot' or 'cold' foods as a means of restoring good health? Do the couple eat from a broad range of cuisines or do they tend to eat predominantly Indian dishes? Are you as a practitioner able to move beyond cultural sensitivity to cultural competence in negotiating with a provider to meet the cultural needs of this couple? If you are unsuccessful in challenging a mono-cultural provider to meet these cultural needs, you may need to support the couple in accessing direct payments. Then they could perhaps employ someone from their own ethnic background who is able to prepare food to meet their requirements.

Many assumptions have been made in relation to the extended kin of families from ethnic minorities. In this case, as in many others, the obligations of adult children towards their own immediate family, geographical distance and family rifts make it difficult to negotiate additional support from kin. Never assume that just because people have extended family members that this means they can easily be on-hand to assist. Like every other aspect of Mr and Mrs Patel's situation, the availability of informal care has to be explored on an individual basis.

There are many voluntary agencies, community-based groups, faith-based and self-help organisations which cater for members of various ethnic minorities. Often these offer services which better meet the cultural and spiritual needs of people than mainstream provision. However, they can sometimes be factional and sectarian, denying assistance to some sections of the local ethnic community while providing it to others. In this instance, Mr and Mrs Patel are refused assistance on the grounds of their socio-economic status and possibly because of the family's loss of *izzat*. In these circumstances, it is necessary to establish what are the couple's needs in terms of socialising, leisure activity and religious practice. You then need to identify organisations which cater for these needs and with which Mr and Mrs Patel would be comfortable. They may wish to attend a luncheon club which caters for people of South Asian descent rather than one for Hindus only or those of a particular caste. They may prefer the multicultural environment of a day centre which caters for people from different ethnic backgrounds, including those of the white majority. Do not assume service-users' preferences for companionship and activity, but check the environments in which they are most comfortable. Finally, it is important to recognise that, like Christians, some Hindus may feel more comfortable attending some temples rather than others, or may prefer private devotion to congregational worship. A culturally competent practitioner will explore with Mr and Mrs Patel their spiritual requirements.

Further Reading

Hennink, M., Diamond, I. & Cooper, P. (1999) 'Young Asian women and relationships: traditional or transitional?', *Ethnic and Racial Studies* 22(5), pp. 867–891. This article examines and compares the relationships of adolescent girls from the majority white population with those from the Hindu, Sikh and Muslim communities in Britain.

Hussain, Y., Atkin, K. & Ahmad, W. (2002) *South Asian Disabled Young People and their Families*. Bristol: Policy Press. This study, based on face-to-face interviews, describes the experiences of young people with disabilities from the Indian and Pakistani communities in the United Kingdom.

Jackson, R. & Nesbitt, E. (1992) *Hindu Children in Britain*. Stoke on Trent: Trentham Books. This book examines the practice of Hinduism in the United Kingdom. In particular, it explores the perceptions of Hindu children about their religion, identity and family life.

Katbamna, S., Ahmad, W., Bhakta, P., Baker, R. & Parker, G. (2004) 'Do they look after their own? Informal support for South Asian Carers', *Health and Social Care in the Community* 12(5), pp. 398–406. This article examines the myths and facts surrounding family care for relatives who have a disability or illness within the Pakistani and Bangladeshi communities.

5

Communities with Roots in Pakistan and Bangladesh

Immigration and Settlement

Presently, according to the 2001 Census, people of Pakistani heritage comprise 1.3% of the United Kingdom's population, while those of Bangladeshi heritage account for 0.5% which equates to 707,000 and 275,000 individuals respectively (National Statistics, 2003). The vast majority of those with family origins in Pakistan or Bangladesh are Muslim, but a few may be Hindu or Christian. In the 2001 Census, 1,591,000 individuals identified as Muslim, which means that there are around 600,000 people residing in the United Kingdom who are either converts to Islam or whose families originate from Muslim countries other than Bangladesh and Pakistan (National Statistics, 2003). There are significant British populations of Muslims with family roots in India, Turkey and a number of Arab and African countries. In fact 12% of Muslims (179,000 people) living in England and Wales are white, many of them from the former Yugoslavia (Peach, 2006: 632).

The initial period of significant immigration from Pakistan and Bangladesh was during the 1950s when mostly single men arrived in Britain to take advantage of labour shortages in manufacturing during the post-war years. Most of these men settled in the industrial heartlands of the Midlands and northern England, taking up low-paid unskilled or semi-skilled jobs in the manufacturing industries of Bradford, Leeds, Sheffield, Preston and to a lesser extent London. Most immigrants from Pakistan and Bangladesh originated from impoverished rural areas with a tradition of economic migration, but a significant proportion were professionals from the major cities. A number of these highly educated individuals experienced downward mobility as discrimination combined with the refusal to recognise their qualifications forced them into menial work (Charsley, 2005: 393). As a result of initial migration patterns, the Pakistani and Bangladeshi communities of Britain have family roots mainly in Punjab,

Mirpur, Kashmir and Sylhet. Even within these regions migration was often confined to a relatively small number of districts. Reinforcing this pattern, on settling in Britain many men sent remittances back to their homeland to sponsor relatives or people of the same village for the passage to Britain.

This 'chain migration' meant that often people from the one family or village were living side-by-side in the same house, street or locality in Britain. Faced with the difficulty of negotiating their way in a foreign country and confronted by poverty and racism, new migrants relied on fellow compatriots to find them accommodation and work. The availability of Pakistani or Bangladeshi-owned rental property, often in poor repair and located in rundown inner-city areas, because they were the only affordable investments, led to the further concentration of these communities in a relatively few urban districts (Phillips, 1998). As a result of chain migration, Pakistani and Bangladeshi communities were commonly as segregated from each other as they were from the majority white population (Peach, 1998: 1664).

The 1960s witnessed a second phase of immigration, heavily influenced by the Commonwealth Immigrants Act 1962, which ended immigration from the Indian sub-continent except for purposes of family reunion. Subsequently, the wives and children of already settled male immigrants arrived in the United Kingdom. These numbers were increased by Pakistanis and Bangladeshis living in Britain who married partners from their own homeland leading to further migration. The expansion and consolidation of Pakistani and Bangladeshi populations in Britain was accompanied by the establishment of mosques and community-based organisations. By the 1970s specialist goods and services, such as *halal* butchers, restaurants and entertainment were also springing up to meet their tastes and requirements. Within a few decades chain migration resulted in the replication of village and kin networks in a number of British cities. Equally, numerous families suffered dislocation as close relatives either remained willingly in Pakistan and Bangladesh or were refused entry to the United Kingdom under increasingly stringent immigration controls.

The 1980s was a decade of accelerated de-industrialisation across the United Kingdom. Many manufacturing industries closed or introduced new technologies which required a smaller, more highly qualified workforce. As casual workers occupying unskilled or semi-skilled positions, often Pakistani and Bangladeshi employees, were the first to be laid-off. Self-employment and employment in Asian-owned businesses concentrated in the service sector had always provided some job opportunities and there was now an expansion in this area of the labour market as men leaving the shrinking manufacturing sector sought re-employment elsewhere (Jones & Ram, 2003: 487). Of the women who had come to the United Kingdom to join their husbands during the 1960s and 1970s many did not speak English and had little formal education. This, in conjunction with traditional gender roles oriented around the domestic sphere, meant that relatively few women entered the formal labour market at this time (Dale, Shaheen et al., 2002: 944). However, substantial numbers of women either worked for little or no money in family-owned businesses or were poorly paid home-workers who sewed garments and toys for the clothing trade (Shaw, 2000: 60).

As a result of these migration patterns, most Muslims living in the United Kingdom who have roots in Pakistan speak Urdu, Punjabi or Mirpuri (a dialect of Punjabi) as their mother tongue. Speakers of these languages will understand quite a lot of what one another say. Pashtun, Sindhi and Baluchi are also spoken by a number of people originating from Pakistan. Those with family roots in Bangladesh will usually speak Sylheti (a dialect of Bengali) as their mother tongue or as a first or second language alongside English. Punjabi or Urdu is incomprehensible to a Bengali speaker and vice versa. Speakers of Hindi from among those families with roots in the north of India will be able to understand a large amount of Punjabi or Urdu, but not Bengali. But, the written forms of Hindi, Punjabi and Urdu which use different alphabets and scripts may not necessarily be mutually comprehensible.

Families of Pakistani and Bangladeshi Heritage in the United Kingdom

Household structure

In Pakistan and Bangladesh the *ghar* or household usually comprises two or three generations who may occupy several dwellings. Living arrangements are normally virilocal or patrilocal, which means that when a woman marries, she either lives in or near her husband's parental home. The ideal household (akin to the British concept of a co-resident married heterosexual couple and their children) is that of a husband, his wife or wives, together with their sons' families and any unmarried daughters or granddaughters. Often referred to as sharing a *common hearth*, members of the *ghar* pool their budgets, jointly own assets and share many of their resources. The relatively low life expectancy of 61 years for both countries means that in reality households tend to be composed of two rather than three generations (UNDP, 2004: 141).

In the United Kingdom the affordability of housing to rent or buy, overshadowed by discrimination, has tended to cluster settlement in inner-city areas. *Birādarī* members arriving in Britain depended upon those already settled to find them accommodation. As would be expected, this often led to individuals from a particular *birādarī* residing in the same locality. Likewise, considerable assistance was often given to recently arrived immigrants from the same village, city or region. To some extent, living arrangements in Pakistan and Bangladesh are reproduced, with several generations coming together in a single household, either in the same house or between several houses. The pooling of budget and resources is usual in these circumstances (Shaw, 2000; Khanum, 2001).

Unrelated families may form 'linked households' which stem from the development of initial contacts with non-kin and are continued through separate households involved in extensive financial and social interactions (Khanum, 2001: 494). Related families may likewise have 'linked household' arrangements. For example, if space became too cramped in a house for parents and the families of both their married sons, one of the son's families might move to a dwelling on the same street. However, the women of the household could continue to cook together in the kitchen of the parental home and the whole family continue to eat there. Similarly, in terms of child care, there may be considerable sharing of responsibilities and interaction between the now separate households. Modified forms of linked or joint households can also exist as between family units living in different cities in Britain or divided between Britain and Pakistan or Bangladesh (Wardak, 2000: 65–6).

Equally, the family may be nuclear due to the migration of only a few kin from Bangladesh or Pakistan. For others, the decision of individuals or couples to relocate away from *birādarī* members may be purely by choice, necessitated by the search for work, or because a higher household income has made it possible to buy up-market property in the suburbs. Generally, in such situations, much contact between *birādarī* members still takes place (C.Ballard, 1979: 112). The need for more space as the household expands is a major factor in the division of *ghars* into different, though often closely situated, houses (Shaw, 2000: 101–2). Family conflict and divorce contributes to the creation of nuclear or single-parent households (Khanum, 2001). In other words, there are many variations of the *ghar* in Britain. The household may be nuclear or extended and residing in one or several houses. It can range from a multi-generational family to a person or couple living alone. It may have strong or weak social and economic ties to other households. Living arrangements may be based around several non-kin households residing together or they may share resources while occupying different houses. Shaw (2000: 101), in a study of the Pakistani community in Oxford, found that out of a sample of 130 families 67% were of a man, his wife and their children while only 15% were joint households comprising several nuclear families residing together.

Marriage

In the United Kingdom among most Pakistani and Bangladeshi households marriage remains an expectation of sons and daughters. Only 3% of those identifying as Muslim in the 2001 Census described themselves as co-habiting (National Statistics, 2003). Preference for partners from the same *birādarī*, particularly first or second cousins, continues to be popular (Shaw, 2001). A number of these marriages are with kin living overseas. These transnational marriages usually require the partner in Bangladesh or Pakistan to migrate to the United Kingdom rather than vice versa. In the past this has usually meant the wife migrating to Britain to join her husband, but increasingly husbands are now leaving their own country to join their British-born wives in the United Kingdom (Charsley, 2005). Suitability and the mutual advantage to be gained by the prospective partners and their families are important considerations. As in Pakistan and Bangladesh, marriages in Britain may also take place between non-kin and indeed are sometimes favoured over those with *birādarī*, depending on circumstances (Shaw, 2000: 148–9). Choices regarding marriage are likely to involve concerns around *izzat* and obligations to kin still living in Pakistan or Bangladesh. Preferring non-kin over kin, if there are eligible partners within the *birādarī*, may cause family frictions (2000: 154). Regardless of whether marriage is with kin or non-kin, it is overwhelmingly likely to be with someone of the same ethnicity. The *Labour Force Quarterly Survey* for the period 1997–2002 reveals that 98% of women of Bangladeshi heritage have a Bangladeshi partner. The comparable figure is 94% for women from the Pakistani community.

Commonly, families adopt a variety of approaches to arranged marriages, which will probably include some marriages to kin as well as non-kin. Many marriage proposals will be initiated by parents, yet there is scope for young people themselves to indicate an interest in a particular partner (Nielsen, 1995: 115; Qureshi & Moores, 1999: 324). If that individual is considered suitable, the two families will begin to discuss the possibility of their children marrying one another. There seems to be a lot of support among young people for the institution of arranged marriage as long as they are allowed some say in the final choice of partner (Wardak, 2000: 140–1; Archer, 2003: 102–3). Dowries continue to figure in negotiations between the families of prospective marital couples, although the practice may be less observed by some households. It is still common for newly married couples to continue living with the husband's family in Britain, although, increasingly, couples are setting up their own households (Qureshi & Moores, 1999: 324). Quite typically, couples move out of their parental homes to live in a separate nuclear household with their own children.

Divorce, which is permitted under Islamic law, and separation are less common in the Pakistani and Bangladeshi communities than among the white-majority population. When marital breakdown does occur it may have severe financial implications for the wider kin group, for example where pooled resources of capital and labour sustain a family business. Relatives may worry about the harm to *izzat* and engage in considerable efforts to reconcile the couple. Where divorce or separation does take place, the reputation (most particularly of the woman and thus her family) may be damaged. Although she may be at risk of rejection by her family or community (and to a much greater extent than her ex-husband) she will have options not available to her counterpart in Bangladesh or Pakistan (Shaw, 2000: 180–1). For example, a single unemployed mother with young children is likely to be found accommodation by the local housing authority and be entitled to benefits. But this is unlikely to compensate for the loss of material and social support from her family and neighbours. Other families, while reluctantly accepting the fact of marital breakdown, remain supportive of the separated couple and their children.

Islam, while sanctioning polygamy with up to four wives, does not advocate it. Polygamy in both Bangladesh and Pakistan requires the consent of an existing wife and the permission of a special court. Islamic teaching requires that a man treat his wives equally, maintaining them and their children (Abd al'Atī, 1977: 117–20). This imposes further duties on any husband embarking on marriage to a second wife. As a result, and contrary to popular Western misconceptions, monogamy and not polygamy is practised by the vast majority of Muslims on the Indian sub-continent.

Polygamous marriages are rare and are recognised in Britain only if they have taken place through a legal process in another country. It is not possible to obtain a polygamous marriage in the United Kingdom and under the Immigration Act 1988 s. 2(2) the right of entry for second wives was removed where a man already has a wife resident in the United Kingdom. In a few instances (although the number is significant), this means that one wife may be living in the United Kingdom with her husband while a second wife remains in Bangladesh or Pakistan (Khanum, 2001).

The fact that the majority of individuals appear to find a reasonably contented life within prevailing social norms in the Pakistani and Bangladeshi communities does not exclude the occurrence of forced marriage, family conflict over what constitutes acceptable behaviour, the mistreatment of children or domestic violence against women (Samad & Eade, 2002; Gill, 2004; Chana, 2005; Gilligan & Akhtar, 2006). The Home Office (2000: 10) draws a clear distinction between arranged marriages, in which parents select a partner but leave the final decision to the prospective couple, and forced ones, which take place without the consent of the young people themselves. No reliable statistics exist, but the Home Office (2000) estimate that around 1,000 forced marriages take place each year in the United Kingdom. These usually involve women in their teens or early twenties marrying a spouse from overseas. This figure needs to be seen against a total population of around 2,500,000 Muslims, Hindus and Sikhs living in the United Kingdom who practise arranged marriage to a greater or lesser extent. In other words, although forced marriage does happen, it affects a small minority of couples. However, this is not to deny that in a number of situations young people may be placed under considerable emotional and financial pressure to accept the spouses picked out for them by their parents (Phillips & Dustin, 2004).

There has tended to be sensationalist media coverage of domestic violence and 'honour killings' within the Pakistani and Bangladeshi communities. Terrible as these are, the estimated 12 honour killings which take place each year need to be considered against a backdrop of approximately 100 murders of women every year by their male partners, most of which are committed by men from the majority-white community (BBC, 2001; *Community Care*, 2006). Prevalence studies across Europe have consistently shown that 25% of all women in European countries will experience domestic violence and almost 13% will be subject to it each year. This is regardless of their race, ethnicity or religion (Council of Europe, 2002). In a report for the Home Office using a breakdown of national British Crime Surveys, Salisbury and Upson (2004: 3) found that individuals among South Asian communities were at half the risk of domestic violence as those from white households. There simply is no evidence to suggest that there are higher levels of domestic violence among families of Pakistani and Bangladeshi heritage than among those from the majority-white community. However, it is important to realise that because many newly wed women go to live with their in-laws, at least for a few years, domestic abuse may be perpetrated by male or female in-laws against them (*Eastern Eye*, 1994). Apart from physical violence, such abuse can include forbidding them to visit relatives or leave the house, preventing them from having access to money or forcing them to undertake extremely onerous household duties.

A number of women's organisations working among Asian minority populations have at times been subject to attack from some sections of their ethnic community for highlighting instances of violence against women. There is concern among some members of the Pakistani and Bangladeshi communities that the exposure of domestic abuse and forced marriage gives ammunition to racist elements within the majority-white population (Gupta, 2003a: 3; Johal, 2003: 40). Others accuse those who draw attention to such matters as upsetting gender relations, undermining social norms, and encouraging women to go against their religion by leaving violent marriages (Johal, 2003: 38–40; Siddiqui, 2003: 71–6). Yet, some organisations representing sections of opinion among the

Muslim population have been willing to lend their support to initiatives which seek to reduce violence against women (Gupta, 2003b: 264–6).

Gender roles

In both Pakistan and Bangladesh, observance of purdah obliges women to avoid contact with men who are not close relations. It also entails an emphasis upon their domestic roles, confining their activity to the house, dressing modestly and abstaining from sexual relations until marriage (Balk, 1994: 23–5, 1997; Amin, 1998; Shaw, 2000: 75). As in all societies, gender roles shape the activities of males and females and their interaction within the home. In Pakistan and Bangladesh, a typical dwelling or compound has separate spaces for different activities as opposed to rooms. For example, the courtyard tends to be the preserve of the females in the household where washing, cooking, the storage and preparation of food all take place. A room may be set aside so that unrelated men can come and go to the house without coming in contact with any of the females of the household (Shaw, 2000: 74–80).

The terraced houses, which characterise the inner cities of Britain's industrial heartlands, have an entirely different layout from the typical housing found in Pakistan or Bangladesh. In comparison, British residential property is often smaller and divided up into more rooms. Plainly there is no demarcated women's or men's area in a terrace house as there is in most Pakistani or Bangladeshi homes. Although layout is different, as Shaw (2000: 82–3) discovered, purdah can still be observed. In numerous homes the front room may be mainly reserved for the male members of the household and their male guests. Equally, it may double as the whole family's sitting room, but when unrelated or distantly related males visit, the women may be expected to retreat elsewhere in the house. As in Pakistan and Bangladesh, households differ as to how they interpret purdah. For some, women sit with the men and join their conversation. On other occasions or in other households this would not be acceptable (Shaw, 2000: 82–3). For instance, long-standing male friends and neighbours may be treated very much like kin, accompanied by a relaxed observance of purdah, but the presence in the home of males who are relative strangers may require reversion to stricter practices. The variation in religious beliefs between one household and another will also determine how purdah is practised in any given home or, indeed, if it is practised at all.

For many households, *izzat* remains important and is realised in terms of family honour and not as the attribute of a single family member. It embraces notions of respect and dignity, combined with possessing wealth yet giving generously to those in need (Wardak, 2000: 83–4). For those belonging to some of the smaller tight-knit Pakistani and Bangladeshi communities in Britain, a family's *izzat* can still be an important social asset. Its loss may have adverse consequences for all family members, even if only one individual is responsible for damaging *izzat*. Since *izzat* is closely associated with women's behaviour, it also has implications for the observance of purdah.

The protectiveness of households towards their female members can take a variety of forms and is likely to reflect different interpretations of purdah. In some homes, education for daughters may be viewed as a stop gap until they marry and so there is an emphasis on their domestic roles. For wives, their activities may revolve around child care, visiting female relations, domestic tasks and contributing to the family business or engaging in home-working for a commercial company. Sons, like their fathers, may enjoy more freedom of movement and more choice in terms of work outside the home or continuing education. They will probably have greater opportunity to mix with their friends and relations outside the home and to engage in a range of activities without being closely supervised. In other households, formal schooling, with the possibility of taking advanced qualifications, is regarded as being as important for daughters as it is for sons (Shaw, 2000).

Even in homes where wives are professionals or daughters are encouraged to go on to take university degrees, distinction may still be made between the permissible behaviour of males and females. Wives and daughters may be chaperoned by a male relative when they go out, and generally their behaviour may come in for more scrutiny than that of men (Basit, 1997; Shaw, 2000). This is evident in the tendency of females to spend more time in there own home and to socialise with friends and relatives there rather than go out to meet friends in the evening or at weekends (Qureshi & Moores, 1999). There is generally an expectation that they undertake some domestic tasks, including the care of younger children. For many Muslims in Britain, as in Pakistan or Bangladesh, there is a code of behaviour between males and females. Outside the family, men and women normally do not shake hands and commonly avert their eyes when in each other's presence. A casual touch of the arm between an unrelated male and female may cause offence or misunderstanding. Even between married partners, public displays of affection can be considered improper. Conversely, touch between members of the same sex is acceptable in most instances.

In some households women are expected to either withdraw or be silent when men or older people are speaking with visitors. Many Muslim girls and women may decide to wear the *hijab* (headscarf) or less commonly the *niqab* (a veil covering the face) when in public. Western feminists generally interpret veiling as a visible sign of oppression, but a large proportion of Muslim women who choose to wear the *hijab* or *niqab* do so to protect their modesty, as religious observance, as an expression of identity or as a political act (Jawad, 2003: 13–14). Others choose to dress modestly by ensuring that their body is fully covered when wearing Western clothes. Social norms regulating behaviour between men and women are central to daily life for many families of Pakistani and Bangladeshi origin. Equally, a number of households do not consider them very important and for others their observance depends greatly on the situation. For example, some women may adopt a more flexible approach at their place of work or as an aspect of their private life and observe stricter social norms around their relatives (*Guardian*, 2006). Similarly, a number of young men may have liaisons with women which they keep secret from their family.

Western feminists have tended to equate traditional gender roles with the oppression of women. This concern is accentuated in relation to Muslim women (Jawad, 2003: 12–13). Yet, paradoxically, it is their uncontested responsibility for domestic activity and child care which can also give women a dominant role within the household. Many women of Bangladeshi heritage emerge as central and influential figures in their families and the lives of their children. It may well be female family members who collect monies from husbands and adult sons in order to budget and decide household expenditures (Dench et al., 2006: 86–7). Furthermore, they may regard the more constrained sexual behaviour of men towards women as respectful and less threatening and predatory than some of the conduct of men from the white-majority population (Dench et al., 2006: 88–9).

Generally, for British Muslims understandings of purdah and *izzat*, as in Pakistan and Bangladesh, are matters of variation, debate and contention rather than of rigid unquestioning observance (Shaw, 2000: 166). For this reason, what is acceptable behaviour for men and women is likely to differ from one household to another. For one family the emphasis may be on daughters not engaging in pre-marital sex along-side a strong commitment to their education, attaining professional qualifications and choosing a career. In another family, male authority may be strictly observed, while purdah requires that the activities of females revolve around the home and that they be chaperoned if walking in the street.

Child rearing

In Bangladesh and Pakistan, where the family functions as a social and economic col-lective, the biological relationships between household members are generally down-played. For example, cousins commonly talk of each other as brothers or sisters. A mother-in-law can influence the lives of her grandchildren much more significantly than their own mother and, indeed, may actually be called 'mother' by her grandchil-dren (Shaw, 2000: 95). Given the deferential relations between younger and older members of the *ghar*, elders may be referred to by the honorary title of 'father' or 'mother'. Non-kin may also be incorporated into the *birādarī* as honorary relations and accorded a title such as 'brother' or 'sister'. Broadly speaking, kinship terminology emphasises social relations rather than biological ones. Even though in Britain house-holds among the Pakistani and Bangladeshi communities tend to comprise nuclear rather than extended families child care responsibilities are often shared among female kin. Titles, which among the majority-white community are used to indicate biologi-cal relationships, may be used within many Bangladeshi and Pakistani households to indicate the nature of a social bond.

The family relationships among the majority-white population, when viewed from the standpoint of those belonging to the Pakistani and Bangladeshi communities, can appear detached, disrespectful, unsupportive and fragmented (Basit, 1997: 48; Archer, 2003: 98). The casual interactions evident between young people of opposite sexes can be perceived as a demonstration of parental indifference within the white-majority community, rather than an expression of trust or tolerance towards teenagers. Likewise the informality with which children of the white majority often address their parents can appear disrespectful to Muslim parents. The relatively high levels of cohabitation and marital breakdown, combined with an apparent lack of moral restraint around sex-ual activity within the majority white community, lead many Muslim parents in the United Kingdom to feel especially protective towards daughters. This is often expressed as a concern that children grow up to respect the authority of adults, are mindful of family honour and practise their faith (Qureshi & Moores, 1999: 315). Negative stereotypes of parents of South Asian descent characterise them as disciplinarians with more punitive approaches to rearing children than is true of the white-majority population. Evidence from research contradicts this stereotype, indicating that South Asian parents actually have similar views to those from the majority community (Maiter et al., 2004).

Young people

Generally, Muslim men in Britain are represented as exceptionally patriarchal and oppressive. Conversely, all Muslim women are lumped together and 'portrayed as passive submissive, inactive and highly dependent on others' (Jawad, 2003: 10). In her wide-ranging study of women of Pakistani descent Shaw (2000: 5) is critical of the way in which they have been stereotyped as 'depressed and isolated in Britain, subordinate to men and confined to the home and childcare within their own communities'. She observes that there is also a pervasive misconception 'that the second generation is torn "between two cultures" – one which offers freedom and one which controls their activities and denies them basic liberties such as a choice of marriage partner and career' (Shaw, 2000: 7). Similar stereotypes abound in relation to the Bangladeshi community in Britain. An increasing number of studies conducted in the United Kingdom challenge these caricatures of culture, gender and social interaction (Basit, 1997; Shaw, 2000; Dale, Shaheen et al., 2002).

The restrictions on, or monitoring of, women's movements and the emphasis on marriage are not inconsistent with either further education or work outside the home. Indeed, many parents are keen for both their sons and daughters to attain a good education before marriage (Basit, 1997; Shaw, 2000; Dale, Shaheen et al., 2002). Many young women, on getting married and having children, may choose to leave their employment or to work from home, as is the case among the majority-white population. Conversely, young men may experience pressure to discontinue with their education in order to enter the labour force and earn sufficient money to fulfil obligations to both their immediate and extended families (Wrench & Qureshi, 1996: 41). Meeting these responsibilities is often closely tied to *izzat* (Dale, Shaheen et al., 2002: 954–5).

The choices of both young men and women are thus influenced, though not necessarily dictated, by gendered expectations. Despite the pressures on both men and women to leave school after the age of 16 years, it is significant that during the 1990s the number of women from the Bangladeshi and Pakistani communities studying for university degrees rose by 71% and 95% respectively. The comparable figures for men were 21% and 44%. This was over a period when the numbers of white males studying for a degree actually fell and only showed a marginal increase for white females (Dale, Shaheen et al., 2002: 960). Contradicting dominant stereotypes that women of Pakistani and Bangladeshi descent are not permitted to work, there exists a wide range of family expectations of women in terms of educational achievement and workforce participation (Dale, Shaheen et al., 2002).

While some young women may resent the restrictions that are frequently applied to them and not their male relatives, many are comfortable with these parameters. Others simply want notice be taken of their views when parents or guardians decide on what they can and cannot do (Shaw, 2000: 181). Some Muslim girls manage the pressures of conformity from their families and the attractions of teenage freedom by adopting different norms of behaviour, depending on whether they are at home or school (Qureshi & Moores, 1999: 320). Boys, too, may manage the demands of religious observance and social expectation by periodically breaking the rules without challenging parental authority or the precepts of their faith (Wardak, 2000: 156–8). To some extent this reflects the inevitable tensions between growing adolescents and parents in any family, including those of the majority white population.

Street protests over the publication of *The Satanic Verses* and the bomb attacks on the London underground during 2005, committed by young men claiming to act in the name of Islam, have resulted in the vilification of Muslim men. They are 'increasingly being constructed as militant and aggressive, intrinsically fundamentalist' (Archer, 2001: 81). These representations are often fuelled by media reporting of incidents involving young Muslim men (Archer, 2001: 81). Stereotypes frequently depict South Asian men generally, and Muslim men in particular, as deeply patriarchal and intent on the 'control' of women. Yet, many Muslim men perceive themselves as taking care on and protecting their wives, daughters and sisters. Furthermore, masculine identity among the majority-white community is often centred on laddishness, such as excessive alcohol consumption, a casual attitude to schoolwork and hedonistic behaviour. Some of these pursuits may or may not be acceptable to a number of young Muslim men (Archer, 2003: 16, 67–72). As a result, racial stereotypes may represent young Asian men as effeminate, in turn creating pressures on many of them to adopt more macho versions of masculinity.

Numerous commentators agree that there can be tensions around religious observance and traditional gender roles within households of Bangladeshi or Pakistani heritage (Basit, 1997; Shaw, 2000). This falls far short of asserting that the majority of young people experience conflict between Western values, which they encounter through schooling and peer interaction, and the norms of the older generation, which are profoundly influenced by their country of origin. This assumption of generational conflict also depends upon essentialised notions of Pakistani and Bangladeshi culture. In fact, most young people appear to negotiate skilfully between the expectations of the white-majority population and its institutions, on the one hand, and those of their own family and community on the other (Basit, 1997; Shaw, 2000). In other words, most young people of Bangladeshi and Pakistani descent seem able to manage a plurality of values and norms without necessarily feeling compelled to choose one over the other.

The emphasis on marriage and heterosexual relationships excludes young gay men and lesbians who can find themselves exposed to homophobia and isolated within their own ethnic communities. The Qur'ān, like the Bible, is often cited to justify the condemnation of same-sex relationships (Yip, 2005: 49–50). Despite some theological challenges to orthodox Qur'anic teaching on homosexuality, it is widely perceived as unnatural and inconsistent with being Muslim (Hélie, 2000). As well as being at risk of rejection by members of their own ethnic communities, gay and lesbian Muslims may be unable to integrate into Britain's gay community because of racial prejudice. The focus of the gay scene around pubs and the consumption of alcohol (as is true among heterosexual young people from the majority-white population) can further alienate Muslims who are homosexual. For some South Asian males, building a positive identity as both a gay man and a Muslim is extremely difficult as both identities are stigmatised within British society (Bhugra, 1997: 555–6). Similar problems confront lesbians.

Homosexuals may be harassed by some individuals from within the Bangladeshi or Pakistani communities who regard their sexual orientation as un-Islamic. As a minority religion in Britain, whose values and practices are under constant attack from Islamophobia, the need to defend Muslim identity can result in the expectation of conformity and a narrowing of what it means to be Muslim (Yip, 2005: 50). For these reasons, Muslim gay men and lesbians adopt a number of coping strategies to deal with hostile reactions to their sexuality. Some choose to conceal their sexual orientation; others retreat into private religious observance and distance themselves from their religious community; a number leave their faith; while others search for an accepting group of individuals within their religious community. These are similar strategies to those employed by many Christians within the Catholic and Protestant churches (Yip, 2005: 48). This needs to be set against the fact that a number of Muslims who are gay or lesbian do come out to family members and find tolerance or support (Yip, 2004: 342).

Older people

Authority structures within the household have been affected by immigration, particularly when members of the *ghar*, commonly its older members, remain behind in Bangladesh or Pakistan. Since relatively few model households of the traditional type have survived migration to Britain, the exercise of authority in families has undergone a degree of change (Basit, 1997: 48). For most families, elders continue to be held in high esteem by younger relations. The pervasive influence, which parents usually exercise over the lives of their children, even into adulthood, is partly due to the fact that most adult children continue to reside in the family home until marriage and often beyond (Shaw, 2000: 95). Where married couples leave the parental home they often move to a house nearby. It is not surprising in these circumstances that the influence of parents or elders may be substantial. Other adult children may decide to leave the area, either through choice or necessity – for them parental opinion may be far less influential.

Though some elderly couples do live on their own, this is relatively uncommon and they are more likely to form part of the household of an adult son or daughter (Khan, 1977: 78; Basit, 1997: 48). Over 90% of older people in the Bangladeshi community have been found to live in multigeneration households (Burholt, 2004a: 389). It is estimated that just 2% of those aged over 60 years in the Pakistani and Bangladeshi communities live alone (Evandrou, 2000). Therefore, a significant, though small, number of older people from these communities do live on their own. Islamic teaching emphasises the duty of adult children towards ageing parents in terms of deference and the provision of material support (Abd al' Atī, 1977: 205). Regardless of the strength of their religious convictions, young people of Pakistani and Bangladeshi descent usually expect to provide for aged parents and think of this as a moral obligation. Their parents, in turn, often anticipate assistance from adult children as part of an intergeneration contract of mutual support (Nesbitt & Neary, 2001: 24–5, 32–3). It is generally still accepted that providing material support for parents is the responsibility of sons rather than daughters (Dale, Shaheen et al., 2002: 953). This does not alter the fact that, in practice, it is the women of the household who provide personal care or domestic assistance to older relatives or close non-kin who are regarded as members of the *birādarī*.

Transnational families

The initial settlement in Britain of male family members, combined with the imposition of ever stricter immigration controls from the early 1960s onwards, has meant the dispersal of *birādarī* between different countries. This fragmentation has been offset by the practice of chain migration. Consequently, segments of the *birādarī* have been replicated in London and many of the older industrial cities of England, while other parts remain in Pakistan or Bangladesh. For instance, several brothers and later their wives may have come to England and may live as a single household or in separate but nearby houses. Their children may have been born in Britain, yet their grandparents and other elders of the *birādarī* remain in Bangladesh. In other instances, the division of the *birādarī* has led to non-kin from the same village or region in the country of origin being incorporated into the family's social network in Britain (Khan, 1977: 77). Inevitably, the dispersal of the *birādarī* in tandem with the movement from a rural to an urban environment, and framed by the culture of a white-majority population, have modified the social organisation of the *birādarī*.

Despite the geographical distance, for most of those settled in the United Kingdom fulfilling obligations towards kin still living in Bangladesh or Pakistan is important. Consequently, many households continue to remit money back to *birādarī* members remaining in their country of origin (Ahmad, 1996: 59). Where members of the *ghar* are dispersed, a father, wife (who may be a second wife) or adult son living in Pakistan or Bangladesh may manage remittances to purchase land and improve the welfare of the *ghar* (Khanum, 2001: 494). For others, as marriage and the birth of children have increased the size of their own households in Britain, it has become more difficult to save and send money overseas (Ahmad, 1996: 64; Shaw, 2000: 99–100; Khanum, 2001: 64–5). In either instance, remitting money to *birādarī* overseas may place a considerable strain on household finances. Extended family members remaining in Bangladesh and Pakistan may, in their turn, act as a source of guidance and support for those living in Britain. For instance, it is estimated that 25,000 telephone calls a day are made from England to Bangladesh (Messent et al., 2005: 332). The preservation of relationships with kin living overseas is an essential aspect of family unity for numerous households (Qureshi & Moores, 1999: 315).

Social networks

The social, domestic and economic relations of the *ghar* and *birādarī* are underpinned by well-established norms regarding reciprocal interactions of exchange and support. Traditionally, these obligations between relatives are governed by age, gender, comparative wealth and position in the family. They are also guided by the custom of *vartan bhanji*. This applies to exchanges between *birādarī* members, ranging from the giving of food and small amounts of money or participation in family ceremonies to large cash sums and performing services involving major commitments of time and effort. In Pakistan or Bangladesh, for example, one *birādarī* member might lend an interest-free loan to another for the purchase of agricultural land. Likewise, relatives might collectively provide free labour to build a brick house for a particular *ghar*. The performance of these services will, in turn, oblige those receiving the benefit of them to act in a like manner towards other *birādarī* members. More modest exchanges take place during life-cycle events such as a birth or a child's first complete reading of the Qur'ān, when small gifts of money or clothing may be given. On a more regular basis, relatives may grant minor favours to each other.

On settling in the United Kingdom, the principles of *vartan bhanji* continue to exert considerable influence on the behaviour of individuals within the *ghar* and *birādarī*. The replication of kinship networks of mutual obligation and support in Britain have been pivotal in securing housing, wage employment and absorbing relatives into established family businesses (Ahmad, 1996: 58). The practice of *vartan bhanji* also facilitates other forms of material support. For example, *birādarī* members may lend each other interest-free loans for property investment, start-up capital for a business venture or the purchase of household items. Likewise, *birādarī* members may support one another's businesses through purchasing goods or services from them (1996: 60–1). These transactions, which take place outside the formal banking system, are reliant on personal connections and trust. Where immigration has brought together people with family roots in the same area of Pakistan or Bangladesh, *vartan bhanji* can also bind non-kin. Such a network of mutual assistance acts as a vital counterforce to the processes of discrimination and marginalisation. However, social mobility may lead some households to rely on assistance from people of a similar professional or educational background rather than their *birādarī* (Ahmad, 1996: 59).

The custom of *lenā-denā*, an aspect of the punjabi gift economy means that a gift, although readily given, establishes a clear expectation that one of equivalent worth will be returned in the future. Indeed, gifts received in this context may actually be thought of in terms of something 'owing' and a mental note kept of the nature of the gifts. Moreover, 'a return gift should be similar in kind and value to the gift received, but worth slightly more, so that while the original debt is "cancelled" another is created' (Shaw, 2000: 228). From a Anglo-centric perspective this might appear rather calculating, but such a viewpoint fails to appreciate the social purpose and effect of these transactions. The system of *lenā-denā* is a means of sustaining and reinforcing relationships between kin. It also redistributes material and non-material resources within the *birādarī*. Since *lenā-denā* is strongly linked to life-cycle events, it provides much needed material support at expensive times for a household, such as the birth of a child or marriage. Gift-exchange is not restricted to kin and can be used to initiate and maintain relations with neighbours and friends (2000: 229). *Lenā-denā* exchanges in Britain (as in Bangladesh and Pakistan) are normally maintained by females, who carry the greater responsibility for preserving kinship contact (Ahmad, 1996: 56; Shaw, 2000). Occasionally, the practice can be manipulated by some individuals seeking advantage of status or power, through giving ever more expensive gifts, which it is then difficult for less wealthy households to reciprocate. The result may be to create an exploitable dependency or cause tensions which finally lead to the disintegration of the relationship (Shaw, 2000: 237).

Despite the transformations and pressures which are brought to bear on households with roots in Pakistan and Bangladesh, the emphasis on the well-being of the kin group as a whole is still a crucial consideration for individual family members. Those who ignore or relegate the concerns and wishes of kin are liable to be seen as pursuing selfish interests to the detriment of the family (Basit, 1997; Shaw, 2000; Archer, 2003: 98–101). If an individual disregards important obligations, such as contributing earnings to support the extended family, or marries without taking account of parental preference, he or she may be viewed as shaming the family. In some instances such actions may result in the breakdown of social relationships, undermine the welfare of relatives or publicly damage the *izzat* of the kin group. For many individuals, the well-being of others is therefore a crucial consideration in making any choice. The repercussions of any decision on the interdependent bonds which exist among numerous households within the Pakistani and Bangladeshi communities are likely to figure in the deliberations of family members.

Ethnic identification and racism

There is a public perception, shared by the Home Office (2001a: 12), that the Bangladeshi and Pakistani communities of Britain are inward-looking and isolationist due to their Islamic beliefs, frequent use of heritage languages and socialising within their own ethnic community. These are deemed to inhibit integration into mainstream British society (Alexander, 2004). Studies show that although communicating predominantly in their heritage language may be a source of disadvantage for older women (who may speak little or no English), the younger generation is usually bilingual and able to converse effectively in several languages (Basit, 1997: 37; Home Office, 2001a: 12). The choice of language is in fact most likely to depend on the social setting, for instance whether the person is at home or at work, or spending leisure time with friends (Lawson & Sachdev, 2004: 54–5). Using heritage languages is an important aspect of individual and group identity, particularly in the face of racism. It is therefore not surprising that a number of community schools have been set up by Pakistani and Bangladeshi parents to ensure that their children have the opportunity to learn to speak, read and write in their heritage language (Blackledge, 1999: 183–5).

Far from being a static prescriptive culture, the understanding of what it means to be Asian and Muslim differs from household to household. Conceptions of being a good Muslim or what it means to belong to the Pakistani or Bangladeshi community are disputed and vary across groupings (al-'Azmed, 1993). Individual and community identity comprise layers of identification which contribute to a complex and rich sense of selfhood and social affiliation. For some individuals, their region of origin, such as Punjab or Sylhet, alongside their mother tongue of Punjabi or Bengali, may be an essential aspect of identity. Others, particularly those born in Britain, may feel that regardless of their family origin they share a strong common identity with the Pakistani and Bangladeshi communities of Bradford or London.

For yet others, religious faith provides a crucial aspect of individual and community identification. It can be with pride that women veil to protect their modesty or men decide to grow beards and wear prayer caps, making these also public statements of their religious convictions and shared identification (Werbner, 2004: 906). A number of studies reveal that for the majority of those brought up in the Islamic faith, their religion constitutes a more important aspect of personal identity than is the case among the majority white population. This remains true even for those who no longer consider themselves practising Muslims (Saeed et al., 1999). All of these dimensions of identity are likely to contribute in some degree to a person's sense of themselves and are often deployed selectively, depending on social context. Many members of the Pakistani and Bangladeshi communities report feeling more or less British, more or less Asian and more or less Muslim, depending on the social circumstances in which they find themselves. Accordingly, they may express some aspects of their identity in certain situations while being reserved about others (Rosenthal, 1987; Knott & Khokher, 1993; Modood, et al., 1994; Basit, 1997).

These debates are mediated by assertions of what it means to be British and the apparent rejection by the majority-white population of 'a new generation of British Asians claiming in full the right to belong to Oldham or Burnley and the *nation*, but whose Britishness includes Islam, *halal* meat, family honour and cultural resources located in diaspora networks' (Amin, 2002: 10). The failure of the white-majority community to appreciate the different priorities and preoccupations of these minorities has reinforced community identification. Poverty, racism and rising Islamophobia expose members of the Pakistani and Bangladeshi communities to exclusion, intolerance and inequality. Many have reacted by drawing back into their own communities in order to protect themselves from harassment, racial attack and prejudice. For others, the sense of shared experience and outlook provides the context for socialising among kin or friends from their own ethnic community (Basit, 1997: 99–101).

Religious Observance

Within the Islamic faith social relations are governed by Sharī'ah, which is a system of rules based on the Qur'ān and the deeds and sayings of the Prophet Muhammad. These govern not just the social conduct of individuals, but their behaviour in relation to economic and political activity. Sharī'ah, comprises a comprehensive guide to the proper conduct of Muslims and may to a greater or lesser extent form the basis of the legal system of an Islamic country. The Qur'ān and Sharī'ah, law have a profound influence on the relationships between family members. These regulate sexual relations, marital roles and the obligations of parents and children towards each other (Abd al Atī, 1977), but the extent to which Sharī'ah governs family relationships and activities will differ from household to household. This is particularly true in the United Kingdom where the process of migration and settlement has brought to bear many new influences.

The devotional practices of Islam mean that while most males attend the local mosque for prayers, particularly on Fridays, females usually pray at home. A number of mosques in the United Kingdom now have a women's section so that they can also attend services. Women may occasionally congregate in a relative's or friend's home to perform *khatmī-Qur'ān*. This involves reading the whole Qur'ān at a single sitting and is believed to bring Allah's blessing or protection to the household. As places of worship, education and welfare provision, mosques comprise more than just a place for congregational prayer. Buildings are planned to offer facilities for a variety of functions, ranging across weekly Qur'ān school for children, advice centres, youth centres, day-care for older people and starting points for self-help and community-based associations (McLoughlin, 2005: 1048, 1060).

Different mosques are often associated with distinctive versions of Islam. In Britain, each mosque is an independent institution with its own religious leaders and Islamic scholars. The *imam* (preacher) does not normally have a pastoral role, but undertakes all religious functions and teaches the Qur'ān to young people at mosque school. The pastoral role, which is customarily performed by a minister in the Christian faith, is carried out by respected Muslim men and women within the local community. While the *imam* wields a degree of influence over his congregation, the mosque is actually run by an organising committee, usually made up of prominent community members who decide which *imam* to employ and for how long.

The Five Pillars of the Islamic faith

- Belief in Allah as the one and only God and to recognise Muhammad as his last prophet.
- To pray five times a day at appointed times.
- To observe *zakāt*, which requires giving a portion of one's income to the poor.
- To fast during the month of Ramadan.
- To undertake the *Haj* (pilgrimage to Mecca) at least once in a lifetime.

Alcohol, pork and eating meat which has not been slaughtered in a prescribed manner are referred to as *haram* (unlawful) and are forbidden to practising Muslims. These dietary restrictions include foods containing lard, gelatine, glycerol or rennet, and therefore can apply to products as diverse as jelly and biscuits. The meat from animals which have been ritually slaughtered is known as *halāl* (lawful) and is acceptable to practising Muslims. A number of specialist butchers in the United Kingdom now sell *halāl* meat. Food which is *halāl*, such as vegetables and fruit, can be contaminated and become *haram* if it comes into contact with prohibited foods such as pork. This in part explains why many households of Bangladeshi and Pakistani heritage continue to eat traditional dishes originating from the Indian sub-continent (Kassam-Khamis et al., 2000).

Muslim religious festivals

Ramadan – during this period Muslims are required not to eat or drink from sunrise to sunset.

Eid-ul-Fitr (Festival of Almsgiving) – held at the end of Ramadan and includes praying, feasting, visits from relatives, and buying new clothes and giving presents or money to young family members.

Eid-ul-Adha (Festival of Sacrifice) – this marks the end of each year's pilgrimage to Mecca.

First of Muharram – this marks the commencement of the Islamic year.

Tenth of Muharram – some Muslims may fast over this period.

The interpretation of Islam and the degree to which it is practised differs from person to person, as is true for Christianity and other religions. Some will consider themselves Muslim because they were brought up in that faith and believe in Allah. Others strictly observe purdah, the prohibition on alcohol and eating pork or meat which is not *halāl*, abstinence from pre-marital sex and the Five Pillars of Islam. A large number of Muslims fall somewhere between these two positions (Basit, 1997: 37–43). Regardless of the extent to which individuals practise their religion, it is likely to play an important part in their lives, either because of personal belief or the religious observance of their kin or due to the Islamophobia which they encounter.

Health, Illness and Disability

Health beliefs

Some individuals among the Pakistani and Bangladeshi communities may hold beliefs which view illness or disability as a punishment from God. But, contrary to the widespread Western perception of fatalism among Muslims, this does not normally prevent them from actively seeking medical attention or advice. Indeed, lack of information and the language barrier are perceived by those of Pakistani and Bangladeshi descent as much more prohibitive in accessing health-service provision (Ismail et al., 2005: 501). Some people do interpret illness within a spiritual framework, believing that it is Allah's will or caused by malevolent spirits known as *Jinns*. Many others within the Bangladeshi and Pakistani communities clearly associate mental distress with their experiences of social and economic disadvantage aggravated by regular racist abuse (Kai & Hedges, 1999). Regardless of the perceived cause of the illness or disability, as among the majority-white community, attempts may be made to hide it out of shame or to prevent stigmatisation of the whole family (Gatrad & Sheikh, 2000: 67).

In difficult circumstances Islamic teachings may be a vital source of comfort and guidance, as may consultation with an *imam* or holy man (Begum, 1992: 62; Dein &

Sembhi, 2001). For many, the Qur'ān offers an explanation of illness and disability, interpreting them as a test or opportunity sent by Allah to improve oneself through patience, commitment and effort in the face of difficulty (Ahmed, 2000: 31–2; Yamey & Greenwood, 2004: 457–8). The Qur'ān associates disease with failings in faith or a preoccupation with the material world. It is notable that religious faith and prayer for some individuals of Pakistani heritage actually reduce depression (Loewenthal, 1993; Cinnirella & Loewenthal, 1999: 515). Illness and disability, whether affecting oneself or others, is sometimes regarded as a chance to refocus on the spiritual aspect of living. Qur'ānic teaching also expects individuals to take care of their health and seek treatment to that end (Ahmed, 2000: 31–2). Equally, a section of the Bangladeshi and Pakistani communities perceive little connection between illness and disability, on the one hand, and spirituality on the other. Their views tend to be similar to those of the majority white population and, for them, cure is a matter of seeking out the right medical treatment. Ultimately, there is little difference between the reactions and concerns of people within the Pakistani and Bangladeshi communities towards disability and those of the majority-white population (Ismail et al., 2005).

Stereotypically, parents of a Bangladeshi or Pakistani background are thought to either believe that their child's disability is a punishment from God or to adopt a fatalistic attitude which frustrates any action to improve their child's circumstances (Ali et al., 2001: 962–3). Contrary to this prejudiced view, while some people do draw on religious accounts of illness or disability, more often than not these are combined with physiological explanations. They very rarely inhibit individuals from seeking medical assistance (Bywaters et al., 2003: 508). There is evidence to suggest that disability is negatively regarded in the Bangladeshi and Pakistani communities (Bywaters et al., 2003: 506). This is not greatly different from the prejudice and stigma which attaches to disability within the white-majority population. In large part, the failure of doctors and other service providers to give sufficient information, guidance and support is a key reason why Asian parents and carers experience extreme feeling of confusion, guilt and immobilisation (Begum, 1992; Ahmad et al., 2000; Mir & Tovey, 2003).

Aside from religious faith, *Unani* medicine, which is derived from approaches to healing first developed in ancient Greece, can also influence health beliefs. Within this system, everything is believed to be formed out of the four elements, namely fire, air, earth and water. Consuming food and liquids transforms these elements into the four humours within the body – yellow or black bile, blood and phlegm. Since each individual is deemed to have a natural balance between the four humours, illness is attributed to an imbalance in these humours. Under the *Unani* system, foods are defined as hot or cold, not in relation to temperature, but depending on how they affect the humours. Such an approach focuses holistically on a person's mental and physical well-being. Conversely, Western medicine generally works on the presumption that illness is the consequence of a definable physiological dysfunction. Consequently, allopathic medicine tends to compartmentalise physical and mental illness and normally treats them separately (Shaw, 2000: 196–9). Since most Eastern medical traditions do not treat the mind and body as separate entities, sometimes people of Asian background may express mental distress through physical symptoms. This is also true for some members of the white-majority community (Holland & Hogg, 2001: 88–9).

Health treatment and care

The reluctance of Asian parents and carers to engage with social and health services has sometimes been interpreted as hiding away those with disabilities out of shame (GLAD, 1987). In fact, for many Asian families the cultural insensitivity of service provision, such as male staff mixing with female service-users or meals-on-wheels ignoring dietary restrictions, is the principal reason for their decision not to use the service (Karseras & Hopkins, 1987: 123; Ali et al., 2001: 964; Merrell et al., 2005: 554). For other families the problems of racism were ignored by the service provider, for instance attendance at a day facility for people with learning difficulties located on an estate notorious for racial violence (Ali et al., 2001: 959). The greatest obstacle to accessing social-care services was simply not being told about them in the first instance, or else not being informed of their scope. The language barrier appears to be a major contributor to this state of affairs, particularly where information is not translated into community languages or interpreters are not readily available (Butt & Mirza, 1996: 109–11).

For a number of service-users and their carers the problem was not the impairment but the nature of social-care provision. Deaf service-users, in particular, often find themselves marginalised by deaf culture, which is mainly shaped by people from the white-majority community. As a result, it tends to lack a spiritual aspect or to be affected by racism. Indeed, deaf people from the white majority may express a range of Islamophobic attitudes and behaviours. At the same time, deaf individuals of Pakistani and Bangladeshi descent can find themselves cut off from their own heritage because very few people from their ethnic groups use British Sign Language and there is little provision for lip-reading any language except English. Inevitably, many parents, together with other family members, worry that their deaf relatives are being exposed to experiences and activities which remove them ever further from the values and religious observances which would be easily shared with hearing children. The consequence for some deaf people was that a positive deaf identity was accompanied by confusion over ethnic identity. This was due both to the lack of deaf role models from within their own minority community and communication difficulties even with close family members (Ahmad et al., 1998).

There is a widespread assumption among service providers that the Pakistani and Bangladeshi communities 'look after their own'. This is powerfully reinforced by the perceived concentration of these communities in relatively few cities and the mutual assistance and interdependence of the *birādarī*. Many households do comprise extended families, live in the same locality as other relatives and enjoy a close and mutually supportive affiliation with other kin. Many other households do not. Immigration to Britain may separate close kin: older people may live alone as their adult children move elsewhere; family disputes may result in a young mother being cut off from the *birādarī*; conflict and disagreement may have dissolved the once strong bonds between kin and non-kin alike; economic necessity may force a newly wed couple to live at a distance from their extended families. Racism and substandard housing in deprived localities, which disproportionately affect the Pakistani and Bangladeshi communities, may further isolate individuals and households from wider social networks and amenities. Low income, lack of knowledge regarding benefit entitlement and the language barrier are likely to increase the difficulties carers face above and beyond those confronting members of the white-majority population. These factors can leave many individuals and households among Pakistani and Bangladesh communities in need of assistance from service providers (Butt & Mirza, 1996: 104–9; Hatton et al., 2004; Merrell et al., 2005: 552).

Case Study 5.1

Jameela is 20 years old and has learning difficulties. She is unable to read or write and can find it hard to follow or remember verbal instructions. She is able to understand and communicate in short, simple sentences. Jameela is well liked by her family and is generally affectionate. She can become distressed by unfamiliar people or surroundings and then she starts to shout loudly and occasionally hits out.

Jameela's grandfather, Khaliq Arif, and grandmother, Fatma Begum, migrated from Punjab in Pakistan with their young family and settled in Britain during the early 1960s. The couple now live in a four-bedroom terraced house in an inner-city area together with their adult son Mohammed Mansur, who is Jameela's father, and Jameela's mother, Sabera. Jameela's married brother Yusif and sister-in-law, along with their 3-year-old son and 2-year-old daughter, also live in the same house. Jameela's elder sister Zeenat lives with her husband Tariq and his parents in a terraced house on the next street. They also have two young children. Jameela's recently married younger sister Aziza lives two miles away with her husband, whom she met through a mutual friend and obtained her parents' approval to marry. There is regular telephone contact and occasional visits to *birādari* still living in Punjab. Jameela's home is in a locality where there is a large concentration of people who have family roots in Pakistan.

All family members speak Punjabi. Jameela's grandparents speak very little English, while her parents are fluent in it, as are her siblings and their partners. Jameela communicates in a mixture of Punjabi and English and is completely comprehendible to anyone who speaks both Punjabi and English.

Jameela's grandparents are in their 70s and receive a state pension. Her father, Mohammed Mansur, works as a cab driver and mother Sabera is a housewife. Yusif works for a computer company while his wife is a part-time nurse. Zeenat and her husband Tariq are both teachers. Aziza has gone back to university as a mature student and her husband owns and manages a small local supermarket. Aziza also works part-time in the shop.

A new day centre was opened in the area for people with learning difficulties. Jameela attended for three days a week over a two-month period and then abruptly stopped coming. During Jameela's short time at the centre, she told several members of staff about her upcoming arranged marriage to a cousin in Pakistan. Care staff reported this to the manager of the day centre and also observed that Jameela seemed quite agitated and started to speak loudly when discussing the prospective marriage. The day-centre manager is concerned that Jameela is being married without consideration of her ability to give consent or even her well-being and protection. The day-centre manager also suspects that the family feel shamed by Jameela's disability and have stopped her coming to the day centre. The manager contacts Adult Services and requests social-work intervention.

OUTLINE OF INTERVENTION

Protect Jameela as a vulnerable adult.

Identify and address reasons for Jameela's withdrawal from day centre.

Arrange any additional care provision required for Jameela.

Arrange support for Jameela's carers.

Points for Practice

An arranged marriage is not a forced marriage and should not be treated as such. You need to explore with Jameela's family the circumstances surrounding the proposed marriage. You need to establish who holds the most influence over the decisions made in the family. In this case, although women in the family are publicly deferential to the men and often observe a respectful silence in front of strangers, in fact Fatma Begum is the principal decision-maker regarding the upcoming marriage. Both she and Sabera have been actively looking for a suitable partner for Jameela. It will always be a temptation (particularly where interpreters are difficult to organise) to converse mainly with those family members who are fluent in English. This fails to meet the requirements for a holistic assessment and may well exclude crucial decision-makers and carers from care planning.

On exploring the background to this arranged marriage, you discover that Jameela herself is excited by the prospect of marriage and very much wants to be like her elder sister Zeenat and her sister-in-law. Jameela adores playing with their children and wants her own. Fatma Begum and Sabera have settled on a young man in Pakistan called Iqbal, who is also Jameela's cousin. There has always been a lot of contact between the two families and Jameela has met Iqbal on two previous occasions when they appeared to get along quite well. It is the fact that the two families know one another that enables Fatma Begum and Sabera to conclude that Iqbal is a quiet, unassuming and gentle-natured young man who is likely to be a suitable match for Jameela. The parents of the two families have agreed that Jameela's dowry will pay for Iqbal's flight to the United Kingdom and the deposit on a house for the couple. There are plans to purchase a house near Jameela's family home. Although Jameela cannot cook on her own, and indeed is not safe in the kitchen, this does not matter greatly as the extended family usually eats together in Mohammed Mansur's and Fatma Begum's house, where there is a large dinning kitchen. The intention is to employ Iqbal in the local supermarket run by Aziza's husband, where Jameela may also work part-time. When Jameela has children, it is anticipated that she will join the other young mothers In the family who often congregate in Mohammed Mansur's and Fatma Begum's house and generally spend a great deal of time together. In other words, this arranged marriage has been agreed between the families with considerable attention to Jameela's interests and needs. In this situation, cultural knowledge of arranged marriage and open-minded cultural encounter, combined with the skill to collect cultural information, prevent negative stereotyping and resort to cultural imposition through the initiation of adult protection procedures.

Most family members downplay Jameela's learning disability as they do not perceive it to interfere with her ability to engage in social relationships, family obligations or religious observance. Jameela's parents actually withdrew her from the day centre because, first, although it served halal meat, staff continued to give Jameela meals during Ramadan. Secondly, a service-user at the day centre of Vietnamese heritage made fun of Jameela's hijab and several times tried to remove it. Despite complaints about this from Mohammed Mansur, staff did not act and it continued.

Cultural knowledge cannot just consist of a few isolated facts about other religions. It requires practitioners to take time to read up on other faiths. In this case, the day centre needs to be challenged to explore the place of food within a range of faiths and to cater for different service-users' spiritual needs. Cultural competence also includes the ability to identify and address racism, whether it comes from members of other minorities or the majority-white community. As the involved social worker, you must take responsibility for confronting racism and oppression at both an individual and an institutional level. Discussion with staff is important to establish why they failed to prevent racial abuse of Jameela. Were staff members actually complicit because they perceived the grabbing of Jameela's headscarf as harmless fun? Were they reluctant to intervene because both those involved were service-users and from ethnic minorities? You need to explore with staff how they propose to tackle Islamophobia at the day centre.

In arranging other services for Jameela and her carers you need to explore what their aspirations are for the future. A community centre nearby offers training courses in independent living and basic employment skills. Jameela's parents and grandparents object to this on the grounds that Jameela will be encouraged to mix with young men, which might harm her reputation and thus derail her marriage. Secondly, they do not see the point in supported independent living as Jameela, on marriage, will continue to interact with her family much as before. Jameela's domestic life, rather than her employment, is perceived to be the priority by both her parents and grandparents. Jameela, for her part, wants to be like the other married women in the family, does not like unfamiliar places away from close kin, and is happy to go along with the decision of her parents. The ability to act as a cultural broker requires that you openly acknowledge the clashes between the values and goals of social work and those of service-users or carers. You also need to consider the extent to which ideas around independent living are based on Anglo-centric values. In this instance the service-user and her carers value the interdependency of kin and not independence from kin. They also foresee Jameela's life as being essentially domestic.

Acting as a cultural broker in these circumstances, you could explore some of the skills which Jameela and her family do value, for example being less open and friendly towards unrelated men and caring for a baby. You are aware of a portage scheme which is offered to parents of adults with learning difficulties. This service involves a home teacher training parents to teach their adult children tasks and skills which are practical rather than cognitive. You reach agreement with the family that if the home teacher is female and either speaks Punjabi or is accompanied by a female interpreter, so as to closely involve Fatma Begum, this service would be very welcome.

Further Reading

Ahmad, W.I.U. & Atkin, K. (eds) (1996) *'Race' and Community Care.* Buckingham: Open University Press. This text comprises chapters by different contributors which examine the experiences of Pakistani and Bangladeshi communities regarding kinship relations, community care and the benefits system in the United Kingdom.

Basit, T.N. (1997) *Eastern Values, Western Milieu: Identities and Aspirations of Adolescent British Muslim Girls.* Aldershot: Ashgate. This book, based on interviews with adolescent girls from Britain's Bangladeshi and Pakistani communities, explodes some of the myths around arranged marriage, *purdah* and family honour.

Hatton, C., Akram, Y., Shah, R., Robertson, J. & Emerson, E. (2004) *Supporting South Asian Families with a Child with Severe Disabilities.* London: Jessica Kingsley. This book explores the experiences of families from the Pakistani, Bangladeshi and Indian communities who are caring for a child with severe disabilities. It also examines their experience of service provision.

Shaw, A. (2000) *Kinship and Continuity: Pakistani Families in Britain.* Amsterdam: Hardwood. Based on empirical research, this book documents the continuities and discontinuities for families living in Britain who have roots in Pakistan. It explores social organisation, gender relations, religion and issues around arranged marriage and forms of mutual support.

6

Communities with Roots in the Caribbean

Migration and Settlement

From the seventeenth century until the early nineteenth century, Africans were transported to the Caribbean islands as slaves to work on the sugar and cocoa plantations established by Europeans and later Americans. Most Africans transported to the Caribbean during this period were from West Africa. Migration from Africa during the middle of the nineteenth century consisted of indentured agricultural workers who replaced the slave labour, which was gradually being abolished. Africans who survived the voyage across the Atlantic Ocean found themselves living alongside people of different tribes, languages, regions and customs. Dislocation from their own families and communities meant that many Africans could not reproduce either their kinship structures or the social institutions of their homeland. As a result, the growing African populations of the Caribbean islands developed their own communal languages, traditions and kinship systems, which drew on the heritage of their homeland. These adaptations also acted as a form of resistance to the harsh conditions of slavery (Alleyne, 1989: 69, 83).

Most of the Caribbean islands were originally colonised by Britain, France or Spain and there is a great deal of diversity in language and culture between modern-day island nations. As different European colonial powers occupied different islands with Africans transported there from a variety of regions, each Caribbean island has developed its own patois. In Jamaica, for example, the languages of the Akan peoples of West Africa were predominant and Creole, which is widely spoken in Jamaica, comprises elements of West African and English languages. Present-day Jamaicans speak in a number of different registers along a continuum from Creole to Standard English. It is Jamaican Creole, originally brought to Britain by migrants from the Caribbean, which has been highly influential in the development of Black English in the United Kingdom.

The labour shortages of the post-war years in Britain and elsewhere in Europe witnessed large-scale migration from the Caribbean in search of employment during the 1950s and 1960s. In 1951 there were only around 15,000 people from the Caribbean living in Britain, but by 1971 this had risen to approximately 225,000 (Foner, 1977: 125). Mass migration to the United Kingdom has tended to be from former British colonies in the Caribbean, where English is the official language. Currently, around 64% of those with Caribbean roots living in the United Kingdom trace these to Jamaica, 10% to Barbados, 8% to Trinidad and Tobago and 10% to Guyana (Plaza, 2000: 86). By the time of the 2001 Census, 561,000 people living in England -identified themselves as 'Black or Black British – Caribbean' (National Statistics, 2003).

Many immigrants were from poverty-stricken communities so they sought employment opportunities abroad; others had vocational skills and qualifications which they hoped to use in their adopted country. Chain migration meant that the voyage from the Caribbean was often sponsored by friends or kin already living in the United Kingdom. As a result, the settlement patterns of Caribbean populations often reflect island origins. For instance, in London, those of Jamaican heritage are concentrated in Lambeth, Southwark and Lewisham, while people with roots in the Dominicans are clustered around the Paddington area (Peach, 1998: 1667). Seasonal and permanent migration from the Caribbean, predominantly by single men, has resulted in one-third of households in the islands being headed by women. Absentee fathers due to emigration, is linked to extremely high female-labour participation rates. In many Caribbean nations women account for around 40% of the workforce (Lloyds-Evans & Potter, 2002: 42). To some extent this situation has resulted in single women themselves migrating to the United States and Europe in search of employment. Many are already mothers and engage in 'shift migration', whereby they emigrate alone, but once established in another country send for their children one by one to join them (Plaza, 2000: 83).

The greatest concentration of the newly arrived immigrants during the 1950s and 1960s was in Greater London and the industrial centres of the West Midlands. To a lesser extent African-Caribbean men also settled in Greater Manchester, Leeds and Bradford. It was in these areas that mainly young single males took up employment in the manufacturing and transport sectors or filled unskilled menial jobs in the service industry. This was true even for those with qualifications, as widespread discrimination kept them out of more highly skilled occupations (Plaza, 2000: 88). During the post-war years women's employment was mainly in nursing or semi-skilled jobs. Currently, the majority of women of African-Caribbean descent work in public administration, usually in junior positions although increasingly they are entering the professions (Reynolds, 2001: 1060). The necessity of accepting low-paid jobs, combined with discrimination, meant that many first-generation immigrants and their families were forced to live in overcrowded rented accommodation (Plaza, 2000: 90). People of African-Caribbean heritage continue to be concentrated in these urban centres, reflecting the settlement patterns of the first migrants (Peach, 1998: 1662). Although there is still clustering in inner-city areas due to poverty and unemployment, many people of African-Caribbean descent now live in the city suburbs and in the new towns of the south east of England. Exposure to racial harassment also means that a substantial proportion of people choose to locate in districts where there are large numbers of people of African-Caribbean heritage (Peach, 1998: 1674).

Families of African-Caribbean Heritage in the United Kingdom

Household structure

In a critical overview of previous ethnographic research, Miller (1994: 139) notes that the African family in the Caribbean is often portrayed as dysfunctional. African-Caribbean fathers are represented as absent or marginal figures in family life. Family organisation is described in matriarchal terms and mothers are typified as sending children to be brought up by their grandmothers and aunts. The bond between fathers and mothers and between them and their offspring is commonly depicted as casual and lacking in commitment. Many of these racial stereotypes are now being challenged by more recent research in the Caribbean which demonstrates that a variety of family forms actually exist. These include *friending* or *visiting* relationships, in which men, although they do not live with their female partners or children, are frequent visitors and provide material support. Many men value their roles as fathers and some are willing to share domestic tasks (Brown et al., 1997: 93). Alongside these arrangements, nuclear and extended family living is common, as is the formalisation of unions (Miller, 1994: 193–40; Wyss, 2001: 406). However, for many couples their relationship with each other and the contact they have with their children is influenced by social norms which stress the importance of filial rather than conjugal bonds. In other words, affection and material and social support are more closely associated with a parent's own parents rather than with his or her sexual partner (Foner, 1977: 139; Plaza, 2000: 78–9). That is why, overall, there is a tendency for households to be matrifocal, with children living either with their mothers or grandmothers and fathers being non-resident but frequent visitors (Leo-Rhynie, 1997: 38; Peach, 1998: 1675).

In the United Kingdom, contradicting matrifocal preconceptions of the archetypal African-Caribbean family, there are in fact fairly equal numbers of male- and female-headed households among the African-Caribbean community (Peach, 1998: 1677). Reflecting social norms in many Caribbean countries, women of African-Caribbean descent have the highest participation rate in the formal economy among all ethnic groups. It is estimated that 77% of women from the African-Caribbean community in Britain are in full-time employment (CRE, 1997). Despite this relatively high female-employment rate, the fact that around half of families consist of lone mothers results in many continuing to live in social housing and deprived neighbourhoods (Peach, 1998: 1675). Even in circumstances where both parents live together, their employment, which is often semi-skilled, poorly paid and requires shift work, can make it difficult to meet household bills and provide round-the-clock childcare. At the same time, these parents may be saving money to send as remittances back to kin still living in the Caribbean (Plaza, 2000: 89–90). In these circumstances, grandparents, if living nearby, may provide short-term or (less commonly) long-term care for the children (2000: 94). Working mothers on higher incomes have the option of paying for a nursery place or childminder, but those who have neither relatives living nearby, nor the qualifications to earn a good income, will of necessity be dependent on the state to some extent (Reynolds, 2001: 1057–8).

Women of African-Caribbean heritage are often positioned differently within their families and communities from those of the white-majority population. Patriarchy shapes their lives, as it does that of women in most societies. However, black feminists argue that this needs to be understood in the context of race. Feminists, who are overwhelmingly white, have interpreted the family as oppressive of women. But feminists of the African diaspora contend that the black family is a site of resistance to the racism of white North American and European women as well as men. African-Caribbean family structures are treated as problematic when compared with the white middle-class ideal of a co-residential nuclear family founded on the romantic love between heterosexual marital partners and a mother who leaves employment during her children's formative years. The economic independence of most women of African-Caribbean descent, 'visiting' relationships outside marriage and the 'shifting' of children to relatives is viewed as detrimental to both women and children by dominant discourses controlled by the white majority (Cardy, 1997: 46–8; Reynolds, 2001: 1054). In other words, these family forms are perceived not merely as different, but as inferior. Seldom are the family arrangements of those with an African-Caribbean heritage recognised as simply the expression of a preferred living arrangement.

Just as among couples of the white-majority population, for some women of African-Caribbean descent, their relationship with a partner from the same ethnic background becomes physically abusive. This can create similar dilemmas as for women of the majority-white community, but it can also generate additional considerations. Those from minority groups may be pressured by community members to put their ethnic loyalties before themselves. This can be particularly acute where minority communities are subject to vicious racism and know that instances of abuse will be used to reinforce stereotypes of violent African-Caribbean men (Mama, 1989: 84). On the other hand, this kind of predicament is not particular to people from the African-Caribbean community or other ethnic minorities. Frequently, women from the white-majority population are compelled by relatives and friends to endure domestic abuse for the sake of their children and wider family (Burman et al., 2004: 337). In other words, women generally are often required to put 'appearances' before their own interests.

Gender roles

Stereotypes abound of the African-Caribbean superwoman who combines single parenthood with a successful career while an unreliable male partner makes little material or emotional commitment to family life (Reynolds, 1997: 97). The over-emphasis of the media on the absence of men from the black family portrays single motherhood as particular to the African-Caribbean community. In fact, the 2001 Census revealed that nationally 23% of children live in one-parent families, the vast majority of them with single mothers (National Statistics, 2003). Furthermore, the concentration on the absence of African-Caribbean men from the family home neglects their contribution as fathers, grandfathers, uncles and brothers (Reynolds, 1997: 105). It also ignores the support of men involved in long-term *visiting* relationships as partners and parents. In fact, almost four-fifths of women of African-Caribbean heritage defined as lone mothers are reckoned to be in long-term unions, often with men who pay maintenance and contribute to domestic responsibilities (Mirza, 1992; Reynolds, 2001: 1052–3). This is particularly vital in circumstances where migration or moving to a different town have separated female kin.

The positioning of men outside the black family is compounded by what Alexander (2001: 103) argues are racist portrayals of them as 'an aggressive, anti-authoritarian and anti-social collectivity, whose life revolves around endless parties, alcohol, drugs, and unspecified debauchery'. The leisure activities of African-Caribbean males are commonly associated in the media with violence, substance misuse and criminal activity (2001: 103). Yet, research indicates that drug use is actually much lower among African-Caribbean young people than among their peers from the white-majority population. In fact, under 18s from the white-majority population are more likely to have tried alcohol or tobacco than young people of either Asian or African descent. It is therefore unsurprising that alcohol-related problems are estimated to be 50% lower among African-Caribbean communities than in the majority-white population (Wanigaratne et al., 2003: 40, 42). While the incidence of arrest and incarceration of African-Caribbean men is higher than among the majority-white population, there appear to be racist stereotypes in play which account for this (see Chapter 1).

Child rearing

The child-rearing practices of African-Caribbean families have come in for particular scrutiny from statutory agencies. African-Caribbean parents are often caricatured as working mothers and absent fathers who parcel out their children to different relatives. Chand (2000) criticises racist portrayals which characterise them as disciplinarians who frequently resort to physical chastisement to manage their children's behaviour. For their part, many parents of African-Caribbean heritage perceive themselves as trying to bring up children in a permissive British society which is eroding the authority of parents over children. Passing down a value system which draws on some aspects of Caribbean life and inculcating a positive black self-image can also be important aspects of parenting (Exploring Parenthood, 1997). Actually, there is no evidence to suggest that parents of African-Caribbean ethnicity chastise their children any more than those from the majority-white community (Cawson et al., 2000).

Research does reveal that parents of Asian, African or African-Caribbean backgrounds are more likely to be referred to Social Services for using an implement to physically punish their children than are those from the white-majority community. Yet, in these instances, injury was no greater than if inflicted directly by a hand (Gibbons et al., 1995). It appears that the use of something to hit a child with, such as a belt or shoe, results in Social Services reacting more quickly to intervene than would be the case if no implement were used (Chand, 2000: 68). A representative survey found that 10% of mothers and 15% of fathers who are white use an implement to hit their children (Nobes et al., 1999). Possibly, the racial stereotyping of African-Caribbean parents as more aggressive contributes to twice as many children of African-Caribbean descent being referred to Social Services because of physical injury caused by an implement as compared with children from the white-majority population.

There are pervasive negative stereotypes held by many members of the general public and a number of professionals which view Asian and African-Caribbean parents as over-controlling disciplinarians who readily resort to corporal punishment of their children. Contrary to expectation, survey samples reveal that white children are more likely to be referred to Social Services because of concerns around physical abuse or neglect (if instances of 'home alone' are excluded) than are children from visible ethnic minorities. On the other hand, children from ethnic minorities are more likely than white children to be referred for complex reasons which are not always clear. Many of these tend to revolve around maternal deprivation and mental health overlaid with communication difficulties caused by the language barrier. It appears probable that a significant, though small, number of these cases, together with 'home alone' referrals for ethnic-minority children, are not, strictly speaking, about child abuse. They seem to relate to parental distress caused by unsuitable accommodation, lack of child-care facilities and failure to claim benefits. While many of these families are subsequently removed from the child-protection system, this is not before parents are subjected to even further distress through allegations of child abuse (Thoburn et al., 2000). Of child-protection cases resulting in legal proceedings, physical abuse is more common among white families, while ethnic-minority parents are disproportionately involved in cases based chiefly on risk assessment (Hunt & Macleod, 1999; Brophy et al., 2003). These findings do not conclusively establish that there is more physical abuse of children in white families than in those of ethnic minorities, but they do indicate that, outside racial stereotyping, there is no evidence to suggest that parents of African-Caribbean (or indeed Asian) heritage are any more likely to physically abuse their children than those belonging to the white-majority community.

Research indicates that ethnic-minority families are over-represented among referrals to Social Services because children are left unsupervised. In one survey, these account for 16% of referrals of ethnic-minority children compared with just 11% of those from the white-majority community (Thoburn et al., 2000). Another study found that the majority of children from ethnic minorities who come to the attention of Social Services because of inadequate supervision are typically from homes where a parent was in employment and 'whose child care arrangements had broken down or who had not arranged alternative care' (Gibbons & Wilding, 1995: 17). Given that people from African-Caribbean and dual-heritage backgrounds experience some of the most deprived conditions, it is inevitable that arranging substitute child care will be more problematic for many of them than for those in higher-income groups. It is also probable that those who have recently immigrated from the Caribbean or elsewhere may not be aware of childcare practices or legal requirements in the United Kingdom. Consequently, based on notions of childhood and adulthood in their home country, they may expect older children to take on more adult responsibilities at a younger age than is normally accepted in Britain (Thoburn et al., 2005: 82).

It appears likely that the over-representation of children from an African-Caribbean or dual heritage background in the care system is because social workers fail to engage with families at a sufficiently early stage, are overly influenced by their socio-economic difficulties, and are reluctant to return children to African-Caribbean families which they perceive as less adequate than families from the white-majority community (Barn, 1993).

The lack of available support from kin due to migration and the additional family stresses caused by poverty and racism are also contributing factors to over-representation (Lees, 2002). Finally, the failure to take into account the diversity of child-rearing practices in a multicultural society results in idealised versions of child care among the white-majority population being defined as 'normal'. Differences in approaches to discipline, supervision or substitute care arrangements adopted by a number of parents of African-Caribbean descent are not inferior to those of the white-majority population (Chand, 2000: 72). What is more, there are as many different approaches to child rearing among the African-Caribbean community as among families of the white-majority population. It simply is not possible to identify a culturally distinct African-Caribbean form of child rearing. Individual parents and carers bring up children, not cultures.

People of African-Caribbean heritage are more likely than those of other visible ethnic minorities to have a partner who is from the white-majority population. Half of British-born African-Caribbean men and one-third of women will have chosen a white partner, while two out of five children who had a parent identifying as African-Caribbean also had a white one (Modood et al., 1997: 27). In the 2001 Census, 231,000 people in England identified as 'mixed – White and Black Caribbean' (National Statistics, 2003). Professionals and researchers frequently assume that children of mixed heritages experience problems in their social development. They are portrayed as having identity conflicts and feelings self-hate. Most children of mixed heritages actually develop sophisticated and multidimensional self-concepts (Goldstein, 1999: 288–9). Many of the problems that do arise for these children are a consequence of essentialising their identity.

For those children who have a white parent as well as a parent of African-Caribbean descent there has been a tendency to treat the child as having only a black racial identity. This has often resulted in both rendering invisible the white parent and ignoring the child's European heritage (Goldstein, 1999: 291). On the other hand, mixed heritage children brought up exclusively in the company of people from the majority-white community may find that they are constantly measured against Anglo-centric norms which undermine their African legacy (Ifekwunigwe, 1997: 140–2). The concept of dual heritage rather than multiethnic identity can, of itself, devalue personal histories which draw upon numerous cultural traditions (Ifekwunigwe, 2002). For example, a white parent may be the son of Georgian and Russian *émigrés* who settled in Britain when he was a child. His partner could be born in Britain of an African-Caribbean mother and an Indian-Caribbean father. Children who are the product of several different heritages are often forced to make choices between them to the detriment of their self-esteem and personal sense of identity. It is this forced choice, rather than their multiple ethnic identifications, which precipitates an identity crisis for children and young people of mixed parentage (Owusu-Bempah, 2005).

Young people

As among boys of the majority-white population, manliness may be defined in terms of physical strength and a hyper-masculine heterosexuality which is typically homophobic (Sewell, 1997: 87). This is exacerbated by stereotypes of black men which emphasise their physicality, assume they have greater sexual potency and ignore their mental abilities. The 'black macho' image is to some extent a reaction to white male power which creates societal inequalities that economically and politically disempower men of African-Caribbean descent (Alexander, 2001: 136). For a number of men, adopting machismo is an attempt to exercise authority and recover self-esteem in the face of racism. For others, it is but one expression of masculinity, largely confined to nights out with male friends. Their relationships with female partners are often a place of compromise and negotiation, resulting in alternative versions of masculinity (Alexander, 2001).

The sexuality of women of African descent has also been constructed differently from that of white British females. It is determined as much by racism as it is by patriarchy. Black women were and are negatively stereotyped as oversexed, immoral and promiscuous, a perception which is employed to rationalise their sexual exploitation. These ideas of black women are perpetuated by media images and commentary (Marshall, 1996: 28). Multiple pregnancies and single motherhood leading to scrounging off the state are misconceptions about those of African-Caribbean heritage commonly held by people from the white-majority community. By contrast, dominant representations of white women portray them as sexually restrained and generally intent on having children within marriage or a long-term relationship. Prevailing Anglo-Saxon conceptions of what counts as beauty, such as having blond hair, blue eyes and fair skin, denigrate the physical features of those with black African roots. Consequently, some people of African-Caribbean heritage develop a negative self-image based round notions of white femininity. Conversely, many have relied on each other and the wider African diaspora to achieve positive self-definitions as black women, mothers and sexual partners (Marshall, 1996).

The majority of parents of African-Caribbean heritage place a high value on education. Despite this, children from the African-Caribbean community attain fewer academic qualifications than pupils from the white majority. This is partly attributed to the absence of material concerning the African diaspora from the curriculum. The place of people of African descent in history and their contribution to science, the humanities and politics is normally not covered in schools. Many pupils of African-Caribbean heritage cannot identify with what is being taught and feel bored by, or indifferent to, their schooling (Lyle et al., 1996). Paradoxically, girls attain higher educational qualifications compared with boys (see Table 1.1). Possibly this is because boys from an African-Caribbean background are subject to more negative stereotyping than girls within the educational system, which frequently escalates into pupil–teacher confrontation and school exclusion (Cross et al., 1990: 9; Wrench & Hassan, 1996: 60). Expressions of African-Caribbean ethnicity in dress style or wearing dreadlocks are frequently labelled as deviant by teachers. The use of patois or Black English is often perceived by teachers to be a corruption of Standard English rather than a heritage language. Consequently, in school African-Caribbean pupils are likely to face constant correction of their use of English. The effect is to provoke conflict, resulting in the characterisation of such pupils as disruptive (Gillborn, 1990: 29; Sewell, 1997: 7). As most teachers are from the majority-white community, a large proportion of them have no contact with people of African-Caribbean descent. They may perceive black pupils as aggressive or intimidating, feel fearful and over-react with a punitive response (Sewell, 1997: 3).

In response, some pupils of African-Caribbean heritage develop a form of 'raceless-ness'. They tend to minimise their contact with people of African descent and African-Caribbean culture. Ultimately, they may even negatively stereotype members of the African-Caribbean community (Sewell, 1997: 13–15). Others form gangs based on black pride and an anti-school culture. Some pupils, particularly girls, may choose a qualified form of deviance, which is essentially pro-education but anti-school. This often results in being punished for 'bad behaviour' without incurring serious punishment such as school exclusion (Gillborn, 1990: 64–7). Difficulties at school can be exacerbated for boys by the pervasiveness of machismo, which values physical prowess while characterising mental activity and academic success as effeminate (Sewell, 1997: 103–4). This is an issue for male pupils from the white-majority population, which partly explains their lower grades compared to girls (see Table 1.1). Nevertheless, a greater proportion of pupils from African-Caribbean backgrounds participate in post-16 education than from the majority-white community. What is more, African-Caribbean males leave school with better vocational qualifications than any other ethnic group, including youths from the majority-white population (Wrench & Hassan, 1996).

Many of African-Caribbean descent, who are academically or professionally success-ful, continue to be confronted with the same dilemmas that were posed during their school years. A large number discover that their essentially middle-class status is still shaped by their ethnic origins. A section of the majority-white population regards prosperous African Caribbeans as an unsettling contradiction of negative stereotypes. Their racism undermines the achievements of people of African-Caribbean descent, relegating them to a place virtually outside the class system and below that of the white population. There is also ambivalence among a number of young people of African-Caribbean heritage towards success as defined by a society dominated by white people. These difficulties have been resolved in various ways. Some individuals may strongly identify with the British class system regardless of the racial prejudice they encounter. Others, acutely aware of their struggle against discrimination, may retain strong links with the African-Caribbean community in the area. Yet others choose a thoroughly individualist perspective and neither identify with the African-Caribbean community nor the white middle classes (Daye, 1994: 282).

Older people

There is a pervasive ideal among Caribbean societies that older people are respected and cared for within their extended families. The matrifocal character of most Caribbean families in such countries as Jamaica, Trinidad and Barbados means that grandmothers are looked to as a 'social safety net' for parents, often providing mater-ial support and childcare services (Plaza, 2000: 81). In reality, the migration of younger people has dispersed the extended family. Many elders actually live alone and some attract derision due to their physical incapacity (Kelley, 2005a). For a propor-tion of older people, their ability to offer services and benefits to kin or non-kin, such as earning an income, caring for grandchildren, providing access to land or property or looking after small livestock in rural areas, secures them a place in a social network of mutual exchange (Kelley, 2005b). For some elders, particularly women, church membership complements, and occasionally acts as an alternative to, the provision of material, emotional and spiritual support from families (Kelley, 2005a).

The dispersal of African-Caribbean families due to migration from their country of origin, restricted housing choices in Britain and the necessity to move away from kin in search of employment, has resulted in small household size. More often than not families are nuclear rather than extended, and are sometimes single-parent or single-person households. It is estimated that almost one-third of African-Caribbean elders live alone (Luthra, 1997: 278). As a result of state provision and the dispersal pattern of members of the African-Caribbean community, many grandparents find themselves more peripheral and less-respected members of their extended families than is generally true in the Caribbean (Plaza, 2000: 92–3). For many, a lifetime of low pay and casual jobs will mean poor pension provision (Thomas, 1990: 46). Those from low-income backgrounds may find there is little scope for material support from relatives, even when they live nearby. Consequently, for a significant proportion of African-Caribbean elders, isolation, deprivation and racism combine to create a hostile environment and exposure to increased physical and mental ill-health (Thomas, 1990). This needs to be set against the fact that a large number of older people among the African-Caribbean community live in multigenerational households, often with an adult daughter and her children. Usually they are integral to mutually supportive relationships, for example providing childcare while a parent goes out to work. In many families there remain valued social norms which obligate kin to care for older relatives (Thomas, 1990: 19).

Social networks

Despite all the pressures to which African-Caribbean families are subject in the United Kingdom, many continue to draw on the strengths of African social organisation which, according to Graham (2002: 107–9), are underpinned by African-centred values.

African-centred values

Graham (2002: 107–9), in her comprehensive overview of African centeredness, identifies a number of important values:

Survival of black families – they have endured the processes of enslavement, colonisation and racism and yet remain foundational to communities of African descent.
Strong religious and spiritual orientation – spirituality, whether within the context of established churches or not, contributes to the resilience of the family.
Strong achievement orientation – black families place emphasis on the importance of education and reject the limitations placed on their children by the education system.

Strong kinship bonds – historically in African societies all family members, including older siblings, took part in parenting. The notion of family embraces those who are not biologically related and is open to community involvement.
Tradition of communal self-help – based on the principle of reciprocity, community-based groups facilitate mutual assistance among their membership.
Adaptability of family roles to new environments – flexibility in family roles and the sharing of responsibility to meet the needs of the family as a whole.

For a large proportion of families, their kin network is not confined to the United Kingdom. It includes relatives still living in the Caribbean and those who have migrated elsewhere, such as to the United States or Canada. Moreover, because parents frequently migrated on their own and then requested children to join them one by one, some siblings are geographically separated. Some first-generation migrants living in Britain may choose to return to the Caribbean, usually after retirement, further dispersing the family. For others, changes in the fortunes of family living overseas may result in prolonged stays abroad to provide much needed support. These transnational families keep in contact through telephone, e-mail and visits. Such kinship bonds are a source of identity, affection and sometimes material assistance (Goulborne, 2004; Sutton, 2004).

Strong kinship bonds and communal self-help are central to communities of the African diaspora (Graham, 2002: 108). But the realities of migration and settlement combined with geographical and social mobility mean that these are under extreme pressure. The growing dispersal of second- and third-generation members of the African-Caribbean community across Britain has increased the emphasis on fictive kin. Not all those of African descent feel a sense of collective identity with one another. However, a feeling of shared experience and culture is common to many in the African diaspora. This is often expressed through the close friendships between people of African-Caribbean heritage, who come to be regarded as relatives. This implies a degree of loyalty and mutual support that more usually defines kinship relations rather than friendships among members of the majority white community.

Ethnic identification and racism

Patois from different Caribbean islands was originally used by first-generation migrants when island identity tended to be more significant than it is in present-day Britain. By contrast, second- and third-generation African-Caribbeans have tended to adopt a form of Jamaican Creole to affirm both camaraderie and a broad-based common identity. Many individuals switch between patois or a Black English inner-city dialect and Standard English depending on the setting and to whom they are speaking (Sewell, 1997: 81). Code-switching can be between patois, Black English, cockney and Standard English. For example, patois may be used between African-Caribbean youths going out clubbing together, while they revert to Standard English to communicate with teachers in school the following day (Toulis, 1997: 184–5). For many African Caribbeans, their identity is actively developed over time, often in the face of negative stereotypes. These identities may draw on African, Caribbean and African-American sources, alongside the Black Power movement and Rastafarianism. They can also be expressed through choices over music, lifestyle and diet (Bhui et al., 2005: 262–3).

The Rastafarian worldview, reggae, hip-hop and rap, the use of patois and the adoption of African-America styles of dress have also shaped the sub-cultures of youths from the white majority community. Young white males often pick-and-mix from these cultural forms in order to develop their own individual or group identity (Jones, 1988: xxiii–xxv). Although rap and versions of Creole have entered the mainstream of youth culture, for many people they remain important markers of African-Caribbean identity in Britain. Often these musical forms, together with community radio, carry social commentary and express political viewpoints. In doing so, they help to affirm a positive collective identity. This is not to deny that sometimes 'slack' music promotes violence, sexism and homophobia (Hylton, 1999: 8–9). House parties, blues dances and black clubs are also social venues which reinforce a sense of common identity. These are also essential alternatives to clubs frequented largely by people from the majority-white community, where sometimes individuals of African-Caribbean descent can feel unsafe (Alexander, 2001: 106–19).

For many people, the church is not only a place of worship and guidance, but provides an important social space in which to meet other members of the African-Caribbean community. For a significant proportion of older women it is an integral part of their spiritual and social lives (Toulis, 1997). Many churches are engaged in welfare and self-help initiatives. Some of these are confined to their own congregations, while others serve the wider community (Toulis, 1997). Aside from organisations connected to religious institutions, various voluntary groups have been set up by people of African-Caribbean descent. These support a very wide range of activities from general welfare to leisure to African heritage and spiritual exploration. Political activism is also a prominent aspect of many community groups. What they tend to have in common is a strong African-centred approach (Hylton, 1999: 34).

Religious Observance

Christianity

African-Caribbean immigrants of the 1950s and 1960s expected to be welcomed into the Christian congregations of England and many brought letters of introduction from the clergy or elders of their own churches. While some churches did welcome newly arrived migrants, many of the historic churches were indifferent and even hostile to their presence in the congregation (Toulis, 1997: 111). Many African Caribbeans were taken aback by the lack of solidarity and support which had been an integral aspect of the congregations they had known in their homeland (Howard, 1987: 9–10; Kalilombe, 1998: 177–9). As a direct result, large numbers of immigrants started to set up and attend their own black-led churches. Currently, almost two-thirds of church-going Christians among the African-Caribbean community in Britain are estimated to be attending black-led churches as opposed to historic Catholic and Protestant denominations (Kalilombe, 1998: 192). This contrasts with church attendance in the Caribbean where two-thirds of Christians are members of the historic churches.

In Britain, black-led churches are predominantly Pentecostal or Seventh Day Adventist, some with strong links to sister churches in the United States. There is a strong doctrinal tendency among the majority of these churches towards a conservative evangel- ical interpretation of biblical scripture (Howard, 1987: 13). Black-led churches have a black leadership and a majority black congregation, but draw their membership from the African, African-Caribbean and, to a much lesser extent, the Asian and majority- white populations (Howard, 1987: 11). The affirmation of cultural identity and the re-establishment of mutually supportive relationships through a common spiritual com- mitment are further reasons for the successful founding and growth of black-led churches (Toulis, 1997: 59). For a substantial number of people, their church became a refuge from racism and discrimination, an affirmation of identity and a source of self-empowerment (Kalilombe, 1998: 189).

Increasingly, African and African-Caribbean pastors perceived their role as catering to the whole of their local ethnic community and not just those who were members of the congregation. Numerous black-led churches are involved in youth work, assistance for the unemployed and providing for African-Caribbean elders. Often such churches are a source of material support and an increasing number of their pastors are speak- ing out on issues of social injustice and other matters affecting their local community (Howard, 1987: 12, 23). Ministry is normally open to both men and women. Although outnumbered by males, a relatively high proportion of leadership roles within black- led churches (compared with the historic churches) fall to women (1987: 19). Women also make up the majority of the congregation in most black-led churches, in which there is usually a more even demographic spread than is true of the aging congrega- tions of the historic churches (Toulis, 1997: 50). Despite the obvious importance of black-led churches in the lives of their members and the wider community, only one- fifth of the African-Caribbean population is estimated to attend church regularly. This plainly limits the significance of black-led churches for the greater proportion of people of African-Caribbean heritage (Howard, 1987: 20).

Rastafarianism

Rastafarianism evolved in Jamaica during the early twentieth century and is influential on a number of Caribbean islands. It does not have a single unified structure and is made up of individuals and groups who hold the Rastafarian faith. Indeed, a fundamen- tal value of Rastafarianism is the rejection of doctrine. Followers differ in their precise beliefs, but these have a common foundation in Christianity and the oppression expe- rienced by members of the African diaspora since the transatlantic slave trade. Rastafarianism developed out of the contradictions between a black African heritage and the white archetypes of a Euro-centric Christian religion. It has been described as 'grounded in the very essence of what it is to be black in a society charged with White bias and discrimination. The beliefs of Rastafarianism replace European values with val- ues which celebrate Africanness and Blackness: belief is congruent with ethnic identity'

(Toulis, 1997: 169). The norms of white societies are considered detrimental to the well-being and advancement of black populations.

Christian interpretations of the Bible, which are necessarily based around Euro-centric conceptualisations, are rejected. A different understanding of the Bible is sub-stituted. For many Rastafari, this re-interpretation includes the revelation that Haile Selassie, the Emperor of Ethiopia who died in 1974, is the Messiah. Since he is black, it is possible for those of African descent to fully identify with him. The world of spirits is rejected and the nearness of God is stressed. As God is believed to commu-nicate through visions, the use of ganja (cannabis) is important to many Rastafarians. Africa, and particularly Ethiopia, is regarded by Rastafarians as their spiritual home-land. For many believers, America and Europe are regarded in terms of ancient Babylon where black people are held in exile from their true homeland of Africa, often referred to as Zion. Even for those who are not Rastafarians, the ideas around dispossession, suffering and estrangement have proved influential among black peo-ple given their experiences of prejudice and discrimination in a predominantly white society (Jones, 1988: 48).

There is much emphasis on God as the loving and omnipotent Father, reflecting the ideal role for Rastafari men in their domestic lives. This reinforces the strong patriar-chal aspect of Rastafarianism, which is numerically dominated by men. In contrast to the matrifocal bias in many African-Caribbean societies, males in the Rastafarian faith are placed firmly at the head of the family, both spiritually and socially. Women and children are therefore required to accept a subordinate position, but at the same time fatherhood is regarded as an extremely important role (Toulis, 1997: 216–17). However, in Britain, African-Caribbean women have been influential in adapting the ideas of Rastafarianism to resist racist stereotypes as sexualised erotic objects of white male desire. Instead, they have forged a notion of Rasta-womanhood centred round communalism, kinship and children (Jones, 1988: 49). This has in turn tempered the patriarchal bias of Rastafarianism. For practising Rastafarians, dreadlocks, vegetarian-ism and respect for nature are important aspects of religious observance. Some believe that life is a temporary state ended by death, while others hold the conviction that the true Rastafari does not die. For this reason, a number of Rastafari do not attend funer-als or engage in mourning the dead.

Disability, Health and Illness

Health beliefs

In the Caribbean, a range of folk medical traditions, which draw on the knowledge passed down by the first African slaves, have developed and been elaborated upon through experimentation. It is a dynamic system of knowledge which attributes illness to natural or spiritual causes and is constantly changing in its application as new cures are discovered and disseminated. The ongoing process of trial and error means that those treatments which appear ineffective are abandoned (Laguerre, 1987: 2, 5). In most Caribbean countries, aside from allopathic medical facilities, there are a number of folk healers who use medicinal plants, prescribed diets and spiritual guidance to treat illness. Nowadays, most folk healers use patented drugs alongside herbal remedies and are likely to refer more serious cases to clinics or hospitals (Laguerre, 1987: 4). Some people turn to folk healers because they cannot access medical care due to poverty or as a last resort when allopathic treatments have failed. Others rely on home remedies based on folk traditions for minor aliments, but attend a medical doctor for more serious illnesses. Often these home remedies are passed down from generation to generation within the family (Laguerre, 1987: 5).

Unlike allopathic practice, which is based on methodical written accounts of diseases and treatments, folk medical traditions are largely dependent on oral transmission from one generation of practitioners to the next. As a result, folk medicine in the form of home remedies can consist of fragments of knowledge confined to a relatively small number of people, for instance a village community or kinship group (Laguerre, 1987: 6). Like *Unani* and *Ayurvedic* medicine, folk medical traditions have been discredited and marginalised by the supremacy of Western medical practice (Laguerre, 1987: 9–11). Founded on scientific premises, allopathic medicine has historically attributed illness to purely physiological causes. Within the British health-care establishment, other medical traditions, which make close connections between diet, daily routine, spirituality, and mental and physical health, continue to be viewed with suspicion.

The combination of a dominating allopathic medical tradition, access to free treatment on the National Health Service and the loss of oral knowledge due to the passage of time and migration means that folk medicine is unknown to large sections of the African-Caribbean community in Britain. For others, it persists as home remedies passed down from generation to generation within a particular family. For those with strong religious conviction, faith healing may remain an important complement, or occasionally an alternative to allopathic treatment. Faith healing is a common practice in the historical Protestant and Catholic churches as well as in the Pentecostal ones. It is usually performed through anointment or the laying on of hands and is founded on the belief that a person is restored to health through the grace of God (Laguerre, 1987: 74–5). For some Christians, whether of African-Caribbean descent or not, illness and disability are interpreted as a punishment for sin or a test from God, and emphasis is placed on spiritual reconciliation with God (Laguerre, 1987: 76).

Health treatment and care

The engagement of people from the African-Caribbean community with health and social services is problematic. Compared with members of the white-majority population, they are up to twelve times more likely to be diagnosed with schizophrenia, experience higher rates of compulsory placement in secure psychiatric units, are less likely to receive psychotherapy or counselling, and are more liable to police involvement in detainment under the Mental Health Act 1983 (see Chapter One). It is therefore unsurprising that people of African-Caribbean heritage under-utilize mental-health support services and repeated contact with them actually tends to decrease service use (Mclean et al., 2003: 658). African-Caribbean mental-health service-users also report lower satisfaction scores than white British users (Mclean et al., 2003: 658). Additional reasons for avoiding mental-health services include fear of stigmatisation by people inside or outside the African-Caribbean community and anxiety about ill-treatment in a psychiatric ward (Keating & Robertson, 2004).

The over-representation of people of African-Caribbean descent at the compulsory end of the mental-health system is attributed to several factors. First, there are cultural misunderstandings by white professionals who also employ Anglo-centric constructs in their interpretation of a patient's behaviour. Secondly, stereotypes of people of African-Caribbean ethnicity as dangerous and violent result in higher drug dosages being administered to them and the greater use of physical restraint. Thirdly, the standard-ised services offered by staff, who are overwhelmingly from the majority-white popu-lation, leaves little room for specialised provision which addresses the needs of a particular minority group (Mclean et al., 2003: 659). These experiences have led many people of African-Caribbean heritage to advocate specialist and voluntary-sector ser-vices which are dedicated to the needs of their community (Secker & Harding, 2002; Campbell et al., 2004).

For those with physical impairments, African-Caribbean culture may be treated by social care professionals and service care providers as indistinct from mainstream British culture, which is constructed through the values and perspectives of the white majority community. Usually no special arrangements are made for those of African-Caribbean heritage, who are just expected to fit into existing service provision. This can create difficulties for people of African-Caribbean descent who experience them-selves as different both in terms of outlook and experience from those of the white majority (Ahmad et al., 1998). Those with learning difficulties in residential care have been particularly disadvantaged by a lack of opportunity to mix with other people of African-Caribbean descent. Their low self-esteem appears related to limited interaction with people of their own ethnicity. Even aspects of their physical needs, such as special attention to the skin and hair care of black people, are sometimes ignored (Lewis, 1996; Morris, 1998).

Older people of African-Caribbean heritage tend to have less knowledge and make less use of social-care provision than those of the white-majority community. For many who do receive services, what matters most is to be treated equally and with respect as opposed to being treated in a special way related to their cultural background (Butt & Mirza, 1996: 65–7). Others, however, want the opportunity to reminisce and partici-pate in activities with people who, like themselves, trace their origins to the Caribbean, and consider this an important aspect of social care (Dadzie, 1993: 31–3). Given that African-Caribbean households are more geographically dispersed than those of many other ethnic minorities, the chance to meet older people of a similar background may be particularly valuable.

Despite racial stereotypes which assume that people from ethnic minorities live in multigenerational extended family units, the reality is that for people of African-Caribbean heritage, most are caring in much the same way as are those from the white-majority community. In other words, informal care is chiefly provided by female kin, often with little aid from other family members. However, the greater likelihood of inadequate pension provision, unemployment or employment in low-paid work and poor housing among the African-Caribbean community is likely to compound the problems of caring for a disabled relative in many households. Racial harassment could become a further factor restricting carers' options in terms of activity or literally confining them to their homes for long periods (Butt & Mirza, 1996: 103–7).

Case Study 6.1

Alice, a teacher in adult education, is 39 years old and is the third daughter of Jamaican parents who migrated to the United Kingdom during the 1960s. She is married to Kwame, aged 44 years, who originally came from Ghana during the 1980s to take a degree in computer science and then decided to settle in England after receiving a job offer from a large company, for which he still works. Alice and Kwame have two children, Kofi aged 15 years and Grace aged 13 years. They all live together in a modest detached house in the suburbs of a large city. Alice's mother, Josephine, resides with her eldest daughter, Rachel, and Rachel's two teenage sons, a few miles away from Alice and Kwame. Alice's other sister, Shirley, lives with her partner near the city centre. They have no children. One of Kwame's four brothers, George, also migrated to the United Kingdom and now lives on his own a few miles away from Kwame's house. Alice was brought up as a Protestant in the Anglican tradition and attends church each week with her mother and elder sister. Kwame grew up in the Catholic faith, but is no longer practising and neither of his children have strong religious convictions.

Kofi and Grace attend the same local school and up until a year ago were both considered by their parents and teachers to be hardworking pupils who were expected to do well at GCSE level. Grace's academic work continues to be commended by her teachers, but there has been a substantial deterioration in the standard of Kofi's school work. Over the last year he has been excluded from school on a number of occasions for fighting with other boys on school premises. He is also alleged to have been rude and physically threatening to a female teacher. Several months ago Kofi began stealing merchandise at a local shopping mall with a number of white youths. Having already been caught twice before and issued with a final warning by the police, Kofi has now been brought before the Youth Court and given a four-month Referral Order, which requires him to attend community reparation sessions at the weekend and weekly meetings with a Youth Offending Social Worker. He is also banned from the local shopping mall. Kwame and Alice are appalled by their son's behaviour and have confiscated his bicycle and skateboard and grounded him during weekdays.

Kofi recently told his parents that he is gay. Kwame was disgusted and told Kofi he had better change his mind quickly otherwise he will have to go and live elsewhere. Alice thinks he is just going through a phase and will grow out of it when he meets the right girl. Since his initial disclosure, which met with such a hostile reaction from his parents, Kofi has not mentioned his sexuality at home.

OUTLINE OF INTERVENTION

Explore why there was a change in Kofi's behaviour.

Obtain detailed information about the incidents at school and shopping mall.

Assist Kofi to reduce offending behaviour.

Work in partnership with Kofi's parents to reduce his offending behaviour.

Points for Practice

You find out that up until about a year ago Kofi hung out with four other boys in his class at school. Three of them are of African-Caribbean heritage and the other one has Pakistani parents. The five boys frequently spent time together – playing football, going to the cinema or playing computer games in each other's homes. When Kofi told his friends that he was gay they refused to associate with him anymore, claiming everyone would think that they too were gay. All four boys have been heard, both by pupils and teachers, to shout loud homophobic abuse at Kofi in the playground. As a result, many other pupils keep their distance from him and several have shoved him in the school's corridors. It is because of these instances of physical and verbal abuse that Kofi has had several fights at school with male pupils who are mainly from the white majority. As a result of these, he has been excluded on several occasions, despite the fact that the white pupils involved were only given reprimands. A female teacher who broke up one of the fights claimed that Kofi behaved towards her in a threatening manner, although no specific details of this were ever presented.

You also discover that after school over the last year, Kofi has been hanging out with a small gang of older white youths from a local college. All the white youths are heterosexual and treat Kofi's sexuality as one of his eccentricities, but they do not make a fuss about it. A lot of the time the gang spends together is centred round dares relating to petty theft, excessive alcohol consumption and recreational drug use.

There appears to be a close correlation between Kofi's disclosure of his sexuality to friends and family, their negative reactions and the changes in his behaviour. There is also evidence of racial discrimination at the school and a failure to tackle homophobic bullying. In the midst of this Kofi appears to have no positive role models for being black and gay.

Racial discrimination requires challenging and eradication wherever it takes place and in this instance you could liaise with the education officer on your Youth Offending Team. This would ensure that teaching staff examine their approach to exclusions, particularly in relation to Kofi, but also more broadly within the school. Oppression is multidimensional and in this instance Kofi is subject not only to racial discrimination, but to homophobic abuse which the school appears to condone through inaction. This is a further issue which needs to be explored. Does the school have an anti-bullying policy and how are pupils protected? Is sexuality addressed in any aspect of the school curriculum and if so does this include homosexuality? If not, how does the school propose to deal with homophobia and abusive behaviour among its pupils? It is important to remember that cultural competence is not an alternative to anti-oppressive practice – each is equally integral to good practice and you must work within both frameworks simultaneously.

It is crucial to involve Kofi's parents in your work with him. They need to be made aware of the linkages between his emerging sexuality and the changes in his behaviour and choice of friends. You could explore whether there are other members of Kofi's family who identify as gay or lesbian or who have an anti-oppressive perspective. Otherwise you could consider the possibility of involving a gay African-Caribbean mentor who would provide a positive role model for Kofi while at the same time helping him to examine the triggers for his offending behaviour. You could also try to identify gay-friendly youth clubs or facilities in the local area. Another option would be to search the internet to find safe and supportive virtual networks of African and African-Caribbean gay and lesbian youth. All these courses of action are likely to yield important resources if Kofi is to develop a positive self-image as a gay African-Caribbean man.

Further Reading

Alexander, C. (2001) *The Art of Being Black: The Creation of Black British Youth Identities*. Oxford: Oxford University Press. This book describes leisure activities among youth of African-Caribbean heritage and the different expressions of black youth culture in Britain. It also explores masculinity and the relationships of young men and women.

Graham, M. (2002) *Social Work and African-centred Worldviews*. London: Venture Press. This book describes an African-centred worldview and uses it to critique the philosophy and Enlightenment ideas which underpin social-work practice in the United Kingdom. Alternative models of practice are suggested which mobilise the strengths and values of African societies and communities of the diaspora.

Okitikpi, T. (ed.) (2005) *Working with Children of Mixed Parentage*. Lyme Regis: Russell House Publishing. This book considers the challenges for duel-heritage families. It particularly focuses on issues of identity, racism and the implications for social-work practice.

Plaza, D. (2000) 'Transnational grannies: the changing family responsibilities of elderly African Caribbean born women resident in Britain', *Social Indicators Research* 51, pp. 75–105. This article examines the roles of grandparents in the families of people of African-Caribbean heritage. It also considers the transnational character of many families in the African-Caribbean community.

7

Communities with Roots in China

Migration and Settlement

In the 2001 Census, 221,000 people identified as ethnically Chinese, forming one of the largest ethnic minorities in the United Kingdom (National Statistics, 2003). Of these, it is estimated that 80% originated from Hong Kong, whose population is almost entirely ethnic Chinese. The rest have family roots mainly in China, Taiwan and Vietnam, with smaller numbers tracing their origins to Singapore, which is three-quarters ethnic Chinese, and Malaysia where the population is around one-third ethnic Chinese (Shang, 1988: 20). The vast majority of ethnic Chinese who practise a religion are influenced by Confucianism, Taoism, Buddhism and ancestor worship. There are, however, significant minorities of Christians and Muslims living in mainland China, Hong Kong, Taiwan and Singapore or who have come to Britain as refugees from Vietnam.

Hong Kong is made up of Hong Kong Island, the Kowloon peninsula and the New Territories. Due to its strategic location as a major trading centre, Hong Kong became a prosperous British colony. Its population rose from half a million to 2 million between 1945 and 1951 as large numbers of refugees displaced by war and civil turmoil flooded into Hong Kong from mainland China (Pearson, 1997: 96). Poverty among the Hakka people of the New Territories, who were mostly small-hold farmers, led many of the younger generation to migrate to the urban centres of Hong Kong and abroad. As citizens of Hong Kong, rather than refugees from mainland China, most had an automatic right to a British passport, which up until 1962 granted unrestricted entry to the United Kingdom. As a result, it was mainly Hakka people who left for the United Kingdom in response to the British government's call during the 1950s for migrant labour. But as the numbers of refugees from the Chinese mainland swelled in the New Territories during the 1950s and 1960s, many obtained identity papers from the Hong Kong authorities and later migrated to Britain (Taylor, 1987: 23). Both single and married men migrated to Britain, often sending remittances back to relatives in Hong Kong. Their wives and children normally joined them a few years later after they had found work and accommodation.

Prior to the 1950s there was a very small number of ethnic Chinese living in Britain, many having previously served in the navy or on merchant vessels. Though relatively few in number, they often assisted their fellow countrymen from Hong Kong to find work and accommodation in England. This initiated a system of chain migration among the Hakka people who, on settling, helped others from their village to make the voyage to Britain. As villages in the New Territories were established and maintained through lineages, this meant that settled migrants were, in effect, assisting members of their own extended family. The voucher system introduced under the Commonwealth Immigrants Act 1962 to limit immigration meant that in order to obtain entry to the United Kingdom migrants needed to prove that they had arranged a specific job with a named employer. Furthermore, work permit holders could not transfer to another employer without the express permission of the Department of Employment. Thus would-be immigrants from Hong Kong relied on being offered employment in the growing Chinese catering industry. Consequently, many of those recently arrived from the New Territories joined kin or fellow villagers in family-run restaurants, takeaways and related businesses (Cheng, 1994: 16). By the 1980s it was estimated that around 90% of the ethnic Chinese workforce in Britain were employed in some aspect of catering (Taylor, 1987: 59–60). In subsequent decades this enclave economy was to provide a route for upward social mobility and a fallback in times of recession (Cheng, 1994: 146).

Chinese immigrants were not only from rural areas in the New Territories, who often had limited formal education and found themselves working in unskilled and semi-skilled occupations. A substantial number of professionals and highly educated graduates also migrated to the United Kingdom from Hong Kong city and the urbanised Kowloon peninsula. Usually these individuals had been educated through the Anglo-Chinese education system in Hong Kong, which meant that they spoke fluent English. Despite racial prejudice, many of these immigrants obtained employment in the professions and skilled jobs in the service sector (Cheng, 1994: 15–19). In the run up to 1997, when the handover of Hong Kong to China was to occur, around 50,000 families were given British citizenship. The vast majority of these were from the professional classes and a number left Hong Kong to settle in the United Kingdom during the 1990s. The smaller populations of ethnic Chinese Singaporeans and Malaysians first came to England as students or skilled professionals and later decided to remain and have since been joined by their dependants (Parker, 1998: 74–5). This is a similar pattern of migration as that from Taiwan to the United Kingdom.

The majority of those originating from Vietnam made their way to Britain during the 1980s via Hong Kong and were refugees from the political and social turmoil of their homeland. In 1979 China invaded North Vietnam, with the result that Vietnamese people who were ethnically Chinese were widely suspected of being collaborators and were subject to harassment. Consequently, large numbers of ethnic Chinese began to flee to Hong Kong. During this international emergency the British government agreed to accept an initial 10,000 refugees from camps in Hong Kong. This number was increased in subsequent years and the United Kingdom continued to receive refugees throughout the period 1975–1992, though later arrivals were mostly family reunions (Duke & Marshall, 1995: 1). Out of the total number of adult refugees from Vietnam, approximately half were either semi-skilled or unskilled, with very few having professional qualifications. Many were not literate in their own language and this inevitably compounded the difficulty of learning to read and write in English (Dalglish, 1989: 52–3, 59).

On arriving in the United Kingdom new Chinese immigrants (excepting Vietnamese refugees) were generally reliant on those already settled to find them accommodation. As a result, multiple occupation of inner-city housing was common-place. This settlement pattern was reinforced by the clustering of Chinese businesses, forming 'Chinatowns' in large industrial cities, such as London, Manchester, Birmingham, Liverpool and Glasgow. As competition increased and new opportunities opened up, many individuals established their own restaurant or takeaway elsewhere in the city or moved to another town altogether. Often dependent on the financial assistance provided by immediate family or lineage members, individuals often purchased dual-purpose premises, comprising a shop on the ground floor and living accommodation above. As these family-owned businesses expanded to draw in more labour, free accommodation became an important incentive for recently arrived immigrants. The growing prosperity of people of Chinese descent and the increasing diversity of their career choices has changed the initial concentrations of the Chinese community in Britain. Nowadays a substantial proportion of people of Chinese heritage have entered the professions, commerce and other areas of the service industry apart from catering. These individuals and their families are located in the suburbs of cities or small towns across the United Kingdom and not in the original inner-city areas where their predecessors first settled. Indeed, among ethnic minorities, those of Chinese descent now have one of the most geographically dispersed settlement patterns (Taylor, 1987: 49–51).

The experience of Vietnamese refugees was different from that of economic migrants from Hong Kong. This was because the British government pursued a dispersal policy and placed the first accepted quota of 10,000 people in small clusters around the United Kingdom. The dispersal programme was heavily reliant on voluntary organisations, and housing authorities were not placed under any obligation provide public housing to the refugees in their area. Consequently, Vietnamese families were often located in far-flung parts of the country and isolated from other members of their ethnic community. The result of this policy was, first, unemployment rates of up to 85% because there was no attempt to match skills to local labour markets. Secondly, 51% of Vietnamese relocated within five years of their initial settlement by the government in order to be close to kin and compatriots. Overwhelmingly, secondary migration has been to London (and to a lesser extent Birmingham, Leeds and Manchester) where there were already established communities of Vietnamese refugees (Dalglish, 1989: 77; Sims, 2007: 6–8).

The dominance of economic migration from the New Territories and urban Hong Kong has meant that the principal dialects spoken among the Chinese community in Britain are Cantonese and to a lesser extent Hakkanese. Mandarin is spoken by approximately 70% of people on mainland China as it is the official language. Similarly, in Taiwan, Mandarin was promoted as the national language. But as people from these regions form a minority in Britain's Chinese community, it is used only by a small percentage. Likewise, there will be relatively few speakers in the United

Kingdom of Vietnamese. Cantonese, Hokkien or Mandarin may be spoken by members of the Chinese community whose families originally came from Malaysia or Singapore. Multilingualism is not uncommon, but often those born in Britain will only have a good command of one Chinese dialect. This is significant because speakers of Cantonese and Mandarin will not be able to understand each other. Similarly, Hokkien and Vietnamese are unlikely to be understood by those using another Chinese language. Conversely, written Chinese is the same regardless of its spoken dialects and is equally understood by those originating from Hong Kong, mainland China or Taiwan.

Families of Chinese Heritage in the United Kingdom

Household structure

In the New Territories of Hong Kong, up until the mid-twentieth century, it was customary for sons to remain in the village of their birth and to marry and raise their families there. This meant that when women married they normally had to move to live with or near their in-laws. Usually, households consisted of multigenerational families, as large extended kin groups were perceived as prestigious and more effectively supported complex livelihood systems in rural areas. The customary practice of patrilocal and virilocal residence meant that commonly villages were dominated by a single patrilineage. In other words, the majority of male villagers were related to one another and could trace their ancestry, sometimes up through 30 generations, to a common male forbearer. This was of central importance in agricultural communities because farming land belonged to the lineage and could only be inherited by males (Watson, 1977: 185–7).

In agricultural communities, such as those of the New Territories, the family was crucial to people's social network, their livelihoods and survival. This was underpinned by the notion of the ideal family promoted by Confucianism (Taylor, 1987: 14–15).

The Confucian concept of the family

There are five fundamental relationships identified in Confucian philosophy, generally reflecting dominant–subordinate associations. These are arranged below in descending order from the most to the least significant:

- Ruler–minister
- Father–son
- Older brother–younger brother
- Husband–wife
- Friend–friend

The greatest emphasis in Confucianism is on the father–son relationship, which is the model for a person's behaviour towards the leader of their community or country and within the context of the family. The relationship between father and son revolves around the concept of 'filial piety'. This obliges sons to treat their fathers with respect and obey them. Since this relationship is primary and forms the basis for all others, every elder is owed respect. Within this social arrangement women are required to submit to the 'three obediences', which are deference to fathers, husbands and sons. Confucian ideas make the family the focus of loyalty rather than the nation and individual goals subordinate to those of the family as a whole.

Migration from Hong Kong and other countries of origin caused the initial fragmentation of the family. Social and geographical mobility within the United Kingdom have further dispersed many extended families. Undoubtedly, norms among the white-majority community regarding smaller household size have also exerted some influence on those of Chinese descent. The culmination of these factors has resulted in a multitude of social arrangements which include multigenerational households and single-parent families, although nuclear families are the most common. For some, these changes have resulted in a degree of social isolation, with single families of Chinese heritage living in vicinities which are predominantly composed of people from the white-majority community. Some elders can find themselves virtually without social support (particularly if not fluent in English) as adult children move out of the locality in search of work or to join their partners. For others, leaving a place where there is a distinctively Chinese community presents the welcome challenge of developing a greater diversity of social networks.

Gender roles

The primary importance of the father–son relationship, which once characterised the family in China, has mostly given way to an emphasis on the bond between husband and wife, although for many families special importance still attaches to the eldest son, who by custom becomes head of the family on his father's death. For a number of households, a circle of close friends has come to replace the centrality of kinship which was foundational to a Confucian worldview (Taylor, 1987: 76–7, 82; Wah et al., 1996: 50). As in mainland China and Hong Kong, male dominance over women has generally become less autocratic and more amenable to negotiation, especially where wives and daughters work (Song, 1995). The once central position of senior males in household decision-making is often replaced by tactful acquiescence in norms established by adult children. Where older parents come to live with their son or daughter, the confusion between being a host or guest can result in them adopting a low profile in family decision-making (Chiu & Yu, 2001: 695).

The first generation of female Chinese immigrants who came to the United Kingdom from Hong Kong during the 1950s and 1960s are now retired. The vast majority either travelled with their husbands to Britain or migrated within a few years to join them. Many of these women were either housewives or contributed substantially to family businesses, which were at that time predominantly concentrated in the catering industry. This is in contrast to the present generation of young women of Chinese heritage, who are among the highest achieving educationally, even when compared to peers of the white-majority population (see Table 1.1). They also have unemployment rates only slightly higher than those of their white British counterparts (see Table 1.2). While women of Chinese ethnicity continue to shoulder much more domestic responsibility than their male partners (as is true among heterosexual couples of the majority-white population), they are entering many of the professions in ever greater numbers.

Child rearing

Confucius emphasised the importance of scholarship and learning. Partly, this is reflected in the high value placed on schooling by parents in both Hong Kong and Taiwan. Likewise in mainland China, after the upheavals of the Cultural Revolution under Mao Zedong during the 1960s (when professionals were viewed as class enemies), formal education returned to its former pre-eminent status. This Confucian concern with education remains influential among a substantial number of families. It is also true that many parents are simply keen for their children to branch out into other occupations in order to avoid the harsh demands of the catering trade. Doing well at school and obtaining academic or professional qualifications is regarded as the main route out of family-run restaurants and takeaways (Taylor, 1987: 271–7). For many parents, their own experience of hardship as first-generation migrants or the long hours they had to put into a family business has shaped their attitudes to education. Others perceive an emphasis on learning as an integral aspect of their own Chinese culture. Thus, for some, it acts as a cultural marker distinguishing them from other ethnic groups, including the white-majority community (Archer & Francis, 2005). There is no reason to suppose that parents of Chinese descent are much different from most others in wanting their children to gain sufficient qualifications for a well-paid job and a decent standard of living.

The widespread involvement of members of the Chinese community in the catering trade based on small family-run businesses means that the labour of women and children is sometimes absorbed into unpaid or poorly paid employment. Working hours in the catering business are usually long and unsociable. This type of work can place substantial strains on family life, particularly for mothers who are usually expected to work in the family business while undertaking the majority of domestic responsibilities (Parker, 1998: 84). Despite the inevitable pressures, individuals, by and large, manage a balance between contributing to the family business, their education and leisure activity. While many parents do expect children to devote some of their time to assisting with a family business, this is generally weighed against the importance of school and the need to study. Among some families this may be part of a wider expectation that children ought to actively contribute towards the material welfare of the household (Taylor, 1987: 69–71, 94).

In multigenerational households or where grandparents live nearby, child care may be provided by elders while parents work for long hours (Taylor, 1987: 95). In other words, the majority of grandparents are more likely to be contributing to family welfare than to be dependants. At the same time, elders can find themselves relatively isolated where family-owned businesses, dual-career households or full-time education result in kin having less time to spend with older family members. This may be equally true, whether or not older relatives are residing with their adult children, live nearby or are in another town (Chiu & Yu, 2001: 694–6). Progressively, more second-generation ethnic Chinese are moving out of the catering business into other service industries or the professions. Consequently, there is less likelihood of third-generation children working in a family takeaway or restaurant as the Chinese community is now diversifying out of this enclave economy.

A substantial number of families are transnational and bilingual, with frequent and extended visits of relatives back to Hong Kong and vice versa (Taylor, 1987: 125; Wah et al., 1996: 38). These visits often coincide with major festivals such as the Chinese New Year. Visits to the Chinese mainland and Hong Kong for children born in Britain can be a significant contribution to gaining competence in their parents' or grandparents' mother tongue and to developing a sense cultural identity. Since the structure of written English is so different from that of Chinese, children of Chinese descent can be confronted with considerable challenges in trying to develop literacy in both their heritage language and English. For many who have been born or spent their formative lives in Britain, their grasp of English may be better than that of Chinese. Indeed, while the older generation may continue to read Chinese-language papers, the younger generation often prefer English-language medium. Children may also tend to use English with their peers and Chinese when conversing with parents or grandparents. Even within the family, alternative languages may be used for communication, according to who is interacting with whom (Taylor, 1987: 143, 151; Wei, 1994: 96). This differs from household to household depending on country of origin, socio-economic background, the timing and the circumstances under which family members came to live in Britain.

Occasionally, there can be language difficulties between the generations. If parents or grandparents speak a Chinese dialect to the exclusion of English, while children never learn fluency in their heritage language, sometimes viewing it as irrelevant to their daily lives, there can be a breakdown in communication (Taylor, 1987: 248–9). A large proportion of children can no longer write effectively in their heritage language (Wei, 1994: 138–9). Nevertheless, speaking a Chinese dialect is likely to be considered an important aspect of a child's identity. For this reason, some parents send their children to Chinese Sunday schools which offer supplementary teaching in written Chinese (Taylor, 1987: 156–8; Wei, 1994: 57). In circumstances where small family units are dispersed and interaction with people of Chinese descent is limited, the mother-tongue language may be a vital point of contact with cultural heritage. This should not disguise the fact that some young people see little point in learning a heritage language and have virtually lost the ability to read, write or speak in Chinese. Additionally, their friends and social contacts are mostly outside their own ethnic community (Wei, 1994: 183).

Young people

Families differ in the degree to which they conform to a Confucian ideal of kinship. Aspects of this approach to family life may continue to influence people's interactions, for example deference to elders or loyalty to the extended family. Some elements of Confucianism may be retained in a modified form. For instance, the complete obedience owed to parents by their children may be substituted by the expectation that young people are amenable to parental guidance and are reasonably courteous (Taylor, 1987: 240). This is evident in relation to arranged marriages which do still take place within the Chinese community. Nowadays these tend to be based on 'introductions' by parents, with adult children then deciding whether they are interested in a prospective spouse. In fact, among young people of Chinese descent born in the United Kingdom, a combination of social and geographical mobility has often meant that many seek out their own sexual partners (Wah et al., 1996: 50–1).

The interaction of young people of Chinese heritage with members of the white-majority population has resulted in an increasing number of inter-ethnic marriages. Based on national samples, it is estimated that 15% of children of Chinese heritage have one white parent. This compares to 39% of children of African-Caribbean descent, 3% of children of Indian heritage and just 1% of those with a Pakistani or Bangladeshi parent (Modood et al., 1997: 31). Intermarriage between people of Chinese heritage and those from the white-majority population appears to be gradually more accepted among both communities. This does not lessen the possibility of children of mixed Chinese and European heritage being subject to racism at school or elsewhere. Given the wide dispersal pattern of Chinese families, such children may in fact be more exposed to prejudice than those living in more ethnically concentrated housing in large cities.

Whether of mixed or Chinese ethnicity, individuals are also influenced by the social norms adopted by people from other ethnic communities in Britain and inevitably pick-and-mix from a variety of attitudes, behaviours and lifestyle options (Taylor, 1987: 76–7, 82). Indeed, even these may be tailored, depending on the social situation. For example, the Confucian concept of deference which is owed by a son to his father is, strictly speaking, the starting point for all junior–senior relationships. Yet a young person may choose to act deferentially towards a grandparent while not doing so towards a teacher. Ultimately, their choice of attitude and behaviour is as likely to be influenced by their family background as by their peer group at school or the television. Where the values or behaviours of older and younger generations do differ, these may lead to tensions. For example, parents may conclude that by adopting some of the casual habits of communication used by a lot of young people among the majority-white population, their children are actually being disrespectful (Wei, 1994: 50). Tensions between the generations are unlikely to be greatly dissimilar from those among families of the majority-white community, although they may be over different issues.

While schooling can be instrumental in achieving social mobility for young people of Chinese ethnicity, it is also a site of racism. Pupils of Chinese heritage are frequently harassed by their white peers. Racial stereotyping by pupils and teachers from the white-majority population characterises them as 'geeks', 'naturally clever' and 'high achievers'. These labels can be used by some white pupils as a pretext for racial abuse. Similar labelling by teachers can place unwelcome expectations on pupils of Chinese descent, who then feel pressured to outperform their white peers.

Girls (and to a lesser extent boys) may be typified as 'passive' or 'repressed'. Often this is attributed by teachers to Chinese or Asian culture, which is conceived in terms of authoritarian fathers and restrictive home lives. Labelling of this kind can make those of Chinese heritage the target of bullying by white pupils who assume they will not fight back. Teachers may also use these stereotypes to pathologise the behaviour of pupils of Chinese heritage, characterising them as non-participative. Conversely, boys of Chinese descent are sometimes associated with violence and the martial arts. This racial attribution can create ambivalence among a number of ethnically Chinese male pupils, who resent assumptions that they are passive or have a soft masculinity. Consequently, some may play into this combative stereotype with the assertion of a calculatedly aggressive persona. For others, regardless of their actual behaviour, the assumption that they are versed in the martial arts leads to constant goading from white male students who want to square-up to other males (Archer & Francis, 2005).

Older people

Historically, familism and filiality have been central to social organisation in China. Kinship ties, and the obligations they imply, are thus generally more important than those owed to the state or its officials. Broadly, this means that social organisation was based on leadership by older men both within the family and within the community. Economic factors also underpinned the superior position of elders and men within the family in mainland China and Hong Kong. Older men often held specialist knowledge regarding cultivation, particularly vital in an agriculturally based community. They also controlled property and other assets as women could not inherit. Consequently, senior males were usually the primary decision-makers in households (Chiu & Yu, 2001: 685). The institutional form of Confucianism no longer survives in mainland China or elsewhere. But, the essential moral principles of Confucius' teachings do infuse the ethical and social perspective of many people of Chinese origin. Deference to seniority, prioritising kinship, preserving harmony within the family and courtesy usually influence social dynamics (Chan & Lee, 1995: 86).

Despite the persistence of Confucian values among many households of Chinese heritage, older people can find themselves disempowered within British society as a result of migration. A small proportion of first-generation immigrants may be literate in neither Chinese nor English as the introduction of free compulsory education in Hong Kong did not occur until the 1970s. For ethnic Chinese from other countries, poverty and political upheaval in their homeland may have disrupted early formal schooling. This means that among the older generation there remain those who missed out on an education both in their country of origin and their country of adoption. For those affected, their lack of English-language skills or literacy in their mother tongue can act to isolate them within the broader community. This is particularly the case if there are few people living in the vicinity who share the same Chinese dialect. It is equally true that for older people who grew up in urban Hong Kong and who came to Britain as skilled professionals, their combined command of English and Cantonese may well be superior to that of their children or grandchildren.

The situation of those brought up in the United Kingdom, who acquire a knowledge of English through formal education, contrasts with a significant number of older people, mainly women, who are not able to communicate in English (Taylor, 1987: 137–8; Parker, 1998: 85). Older women in particular may have a social network restricted to members of the Chinese community who speak their dialect. This is in contrast to their children and grandchildren, who are often fluent in English and have expanded their social contacts to include people belonging to other ethnic communities and the majority-white population (Wei, 1994: 124). Obviously, formal employment and schooling offer adults and young people opportunities for interaction with people from other ethnic backgrounds whereas Chinese elders are more likely to be retired and working within the household, either assisting with domestic responsibilities or the family business (1994: 125).

Social networks

Despite the transition from agriculture to commerce and the effects of migration, most people in Hong Kong, and among the Chinese diaspora, rely on the obligations of kin towards each other before relying on the state or civil society (Taylor, 1987: 14–15; Huque et al., 1997: 17). Characterised as 'utilitarian familism' in Hong Kong, this approach results in an extremely strong emphasis on mutual assistance among family members, a weak involvement in groups beyond the family and the de-politicisation of social issues as their resolution is sought within the family. This makes the household the focus of welfare provision and financial assistance in times of need (Siu, 1993: 182; Wilding, 1997: 256–7). It also means that economic interdependence is a significant aspect of family dynamics alongside the recruitment of apparently quite peripheral family members into a strong reciprocal network of relations (Chan & Lee, 1995: 88).

In China, extensive social and economic support networks known as *guanxi* are built up through complex, long-standing social contacts with kin, friends and colleagues. Derived originally from the rural gift economy, *guanxi* has for centuries been an aspect of social life in China. Families and individuals may devote considerable effort to developing, maintaining and extending these networks. It is particularly important to integrate people who have influence or power into the network. *Guanxi* can be called upon for material and non-material assistance. They are more formalised than those between friends because they impose very real obligations in terms of an ongoing exchange of favours. Binding social norms within the network make it difficult for members to refuse a favour when requested. As these networks are usually quite enduring, many favours are not repaid immediately. They can be outstanding for a long time before an approach is made for a reciprocal favour. Although many transactions can be mutually beneficial, unequal relationships can be created between the more powerful and less powerful members of the network. This can result in exploitive and abusive patron–client relations (Michailova & Worm, 2003: 510–12; Thelle, 2004: 248–9).

Although *guanxi* networks may remain vital to recent immigrants, particularly those from the Chinese mainland, they are likely to be much less important to those of Chinese ethnicity born in the United Kingdom or who have spent many years living in the country. This is because those settled in Britain will normally have resort to more formal sources of economic and social support, including the banking system, Social Services and welfare benefits. Furthermore, the catering trade, which once accounted for 90% of total employment among people of Chinese descent, has exercised a profound influence on settlement patterns, family size and community dynamics. Most particularly, the enclave economy has meant direct competition between families in the same locality or the necessity of moving to another one to set up a new business. The reality of competition and geographical dispersal has often made community ties secondary to economic necessity. While there are a number of cohesive Chinese communities in some areas, for many people interaction with members of their own ethnic community is mostly restricted to immediate family and public Chinese festivals (Chau & Yu, 2001).

Ethnic identification and racism

The dispersal of families of Chinese heritage throughout the United Kingdom has acted as a constraint on collective action or public representation (Parker & Song, 2006: 183). Dispersal can also make it difficult for voluntary organisations serving ethnically Chinese people to reach all sections of the community. For this reason, the internet can be a key channel of communication between members of Britain's Chinese community. The website www.britishbornchinese.org.uk was established in 1999 and sets out to 'provide a forum in which British born Chinese can share experiences ideas and thoughts'. Besides posting current new items likely to be of interest to people of Chinese descent and e-mailing out a regular newsletter, it hosts around 25 thematic forums and offers near real-time discussion boards. By 2005 the site had 7,000 registered users, 38% of whom were aged between 16 and 34 years. A number of users have increased the interactivity of the discussion forums by adding hyperlinks to their own personal websites and blogs at the end of their posted messages. The British-born Chinese website also hosts Chinatown Online, which provides updated information on events going on within the Chinese community across the United Kingdom. It publicises everything from traditional Chinese recipes, to lifestyle matters, to business activities (Parker & Song, 2006).

Another website, www.dimsum.co.uk, offers online commentary on issues of concern to people of Chinese heritage in Britain. It seeks 'to be able to give voice to the views of ethnic minorities that have, until now, been silent or ignored'. Chinatown Online is a portal for people interested in Chinese culture in Britain and is widely used by members of different ethnic communities, including the white-majority population (Parker & Song, 2006: 184–6). These sites not only provide forums for discussion and access to information, but also facilitate meetings between members of the Chinese community, who are liable to be quite geographically dispersed (Parker & Song, 2006: 187). Print media, such as *Chinatown, the Magazine*, a bi-monthly English-language paper which has a circulation of around 10,000, has also gone online at www.chinatownthemagazine.com. The web has also presented opportunities for often subordinated identities within ethnic communities to develop a public profile. For example, lesbians among the British Chinese community have set up their own website www.bbclesbian.co.uk as a space for discussion (Parker & Song, 2006: 193–4).

There is a widespread public perception that the Chinese community as a whole is educationally and economically very successful, achieving high upward social mobility. This has created a number of difficulties for a proportion of those with Chinese origins. Often referred to as the 'invisible minority' because of presumptions that they experience no problems, people of Chinese descent are frequently ignored in terms of policy-making and service delivery. The relatively high educational attainment of a large proportion of ethnic Chinese pupils, alongside the business success of their parents, has been interpreted as evidence that few, if any, people of Chinese descent are subject to discrimination or require special attention (Chau & Yu, 2001: 107–8; Archer & Francis, 2005: 388–9). This can result in the voluntary and statutory sectors ignoring the specialist needs of people who are ethnically Chinese. Those with disabilities, particularly older people living alone, or those excluded from welfare benefits and service provision by the language barrier, are most likely to be disadvantaged by this widely held positive stereotype of the Chinese community.

Religious Observance

In Hong Kong, Protestant and Catholic missionaries came to work in the colony from the mid-nineteenth century onwards and presently 8% of its population are Christians. There are also small communities of Muslims and Hindus, but the vast majority of Hong Kong's population practise Buddhism or Taoism. For this reason, a small number of people who are ethnically Chinese and living in Britain, practise Islam, Christianity or Hinduism. Chinese religion is, in essence, a blending of different belief systems rather than devotion to a single, organised faith. Confucianism, Taoism, Buddhism and ancestor worship influence the religious observances of most Chinese people.

Confucianism

Confucius is believed to have lived in the sixth century BC and developed a system of thought and behaviour based on the conception of people as social and moral beings. His sayings are set down in the *Analects*.

The principal concepts of Confucianism

Humanity (*ren*) – this refers to humaneness or kindness towards others and is centred round notions of developing oneself and then assisting others to develop.
Ritual propriety (*li*) – this is the correct form of behaviour in every situation which expresses the moral character of the humane person.
The superior person (*junzi*) – the *junzi* is someone who is committed to becoming a humane or *ren* person. Self-examination and devotion to learning are the prime characteristics of the *junzi*.

Taoism

Taoism is associated with a number of sages rather than one particular man and developed later than Confucianism. The main teachings of Taoism are contained in the *Laozi* and the *Zhuangzi*. In Taoism, human beings are understood to be natural beings and must strive to harmonise their thinking and behaviour with the *Way* or *Tao*, meaning the patterns and rhythms of nature. Taoism emphasises a person's relationship with nature rather than (as in Confucianism) a person's relationship with other people. It places considerable emphasis on private meditation. The focus of Taoism on harmony between mind, body and spirit has made it central to the development of Traditional Chinese medicine.

Buddhism

The founder of Buddhism was a contemporary of Confucius. A number of texts or *sutras* where written in later centuries codifying the teachings of Buddha.

The principal concepts of Buddhism

Karma – this is a doctrine of 'moral causality' in which every intentional action has an effect which will be encountered by the person at some later point in time.

Samsara – this refers to the cycle of birth, death and rebirth. When a person dies their immortal soul is reborn into a new body. This rebirth is conditioned by unresolved *karma*, because the effects of intentional actions are not necessarily experienced during a single lifespan.

Nirvana – literally this means 'extinguishing' and is the final goal of Buddhists. The intention is to prevent rebirth into a life of suffering and difficulty.

Popular religion

This refers to popular religious practice comprising divination, ancestor worship, and devotion to a pantheon of different gods. The temples used for the worship of gods are independent of each other and are maintained by the local community. They may have a resident priest or be visited by religious functionaries, including diviners, who perform rituals and offer services at the request of those who come to the temple. There is no central authority or administrative structure presiding over these temples, as is the case for the Catholic and Anglican churches in Britain. In popular Chinese religion the world is believed to comprise gods, ghosts, ancestors and humans, who all inhabit the same realm. This contrasts with Christianity, which defines heaven as a place distinct from and beyond the world of human beings. Much of the devotional activity associated with popular Chinese religions takes place within the confines of the home and among kin.

Devotional practices

In the United Kingdom many people of Chinese heritage continue to observe religious practices. In areas where there are communities of ethnic Chinese, Buddhist temples have often been constructed or created out of refurbished buildings. These form a centre for devotion and, as in other Chinese societies, usually enable worshippers to consult with diviners as well (Wah et al., 1996: 68). Diviners, who can be either male or female, may be consulted in temples, offices or homes. For those who believe in divination, it is often used to identify the source of a problem and to suggest the means of resolving it. For example, a spirit-medium may be employed to help settle a dispute between two families rather than legal professionals. Essentially, diviners endeavour to restore harmony between the spiritual and human worlds. Some people of Chinese descent may no longer possess a deep spiritual faith, but nevertheless occasionally seek the advice of a diviner when confronted by personal problems or illness.

A large proportion of people of Chinese descent continue to revere their ancestors and often have a shrine devoted to them in the home where daily or weekly offerings of burnt incense and fresh food are made by relatives. The ancestors revered in this way usually only go back a few generations, but some shrines are to ancestors over many generations. While most people in the United Kingdom now venerate rather than worship their ancestors, others still believe it is important to avoid giving offence to the ancestors in case they punish family members. A number of people of Chinese heritage attend local Christian denominations or churches, some of them specifically established to cater for the local Chinese community (Taylor, 1987: 100). For many others, traditional Chinese religions continue to exert an influence on their moral and social lives, whether or not they regularly attend a temple or engage in family devotional practices.

Due to the geographical dispersal of the Chinese community in the United Kingdom many people of Chinese heritage may find that there simply is no public focus for their faith. In these circumstances, observance may be largely confined to the household or attending religious festivals. Ancestor worship may still be practised or modified as reverence for deceased grandparents and great-grandparents. Close ancestors may be given a small shrine in the household, adorned with their portrait, and continue to be called upon by family members for guidance and protection (Wah et al., 1996: 48–50). Buddha or popular gods may be regularly worshipped and their statues given a special place within the house or workplace (Wah et al., 1996: 67–8). A considerable number of people of Chinese descent continue to be concerned for the spiritual harmony of their environment and will consult a *Fung Shui* expert on how to arrange the interior of an office or home. Even among those with little religious belief in the forces of nature, the choice of décor or the arrangement of furniture in a room may remain an important consideration (Wah et al., 1996: 68–9). As in mainland China, Hong Kong and Taiwan, many people are eclectic in their worship. They may combine religious beliefs and practices from Buddhism, Taoism and popular forms of Chinese religion.

Principal festivals of Chinese religions

Chinese New Year – this is the largest Chinese festival and emphasises renewal. It is a time of family reunion, celebration and the exchange of gifts. Festivities are usually over two weeks, culminating in public lantern processions and dragon dances. Many people will also attend a local temple during this period.

Ching Ming – known also as 'The Pure Brightness Festival' this is likely to involve going to the cemetery or visiting the family's country of origin in order to pay respects to ancestors.

Dragon Boat Festival – this is usually observed through the serving of a special meal consisting of rice wrapped in a lotus leaf called *Zong Zi*.

Mid-Autumn Festival – gifts are exchanged and special delicacies cooked, especially moon cakes in the shape of animals.

Health, Illness and Disability

Health beliefs

Traditional Chinese medicine encompasses a wide range of different health treatments which were established and developed over many centuries in China. These include herbal remedies, acupuncture, cupping, massage and regimes of physical exercise (e.g. Qi Gong and Tai Chi). In mainland China and Hong Kong, these approaches may be used in combination or to complement allopathic treatment. The treatments which comprise traditional Chinese medicine share several underlying concepts regarding the human body and the nature of physical and mental health. *Yin* and *Yang* are terms for the original cosmic forces out of which the universe evolved. They express the fundamental dualism which underpins relationships in the world. *Yin* is associated with heaven, heat, dryness and light, while *Yang* is identified with the earth, night, water, cold and the dark. Tao or 'the way' is a means of maintaining or restoring harmony between the two opposing elements of *Yin* and *Yang*. As harmony is so fundamental to good health, traditional Chinese medicine has always focused on prevention as well as cure. Diagnosis, for the traditional practitioner, focuses on the physical state of the patient, including their facial expression and quality of voice. It is likely to involve finding out about basic human functions, such as sexual activity, sleep patterns and dietary habits. Both the nature of a patient's symptoms and their pulse are also important aspects of diagnosis (Jewell, 1983).

Even when people of Chinese descent in the United Kingdom no longer subscribe to Buddhism (requiring vegetarianism) or Taoist ideas about human physiology, which underpin the belief that certain types of food affect bodily equilibrium, they often still influence dietary habits (Taylor, 1987: 241). Choices of food are often influenced by concerns to maintain a healthy diet based on the concepts of *yin* and *yang* foods which make up familiar Chinese dishes (Taylor, 1987: 241). Most fruit and many vegetables produce *yin* energies and are referred to as 'cold foods' and have cooling properties. Meat, fats and oils are 'hot foods' and produce *yang* energies which possess heating properties. A person requires a proper balance between *yin* and *yang* foods in order to maintain physical and mental health. For others (e.g. practising Buddhists), food preparation and consumption are a matter of religious observance and vegetarianism is strictly followed. Although many families of Chinese heritage have adopted diets similar to those of the white-majority community, and with the same degree of diversity, a large proportion have retained traditional Chinese methods of food preparation and serving. This has been made more possible by the growing number of outlets in large cities which specifically cater to Chinese cuisine, making available traditional ingredients often imported directly from Hong Kong or the Chinese mainland (Taylor, 1987: 96–7).

Health treatment and care

In the United Kingdom up to one-third of the population use complementary and alternative medicine to take care of health problems ranging from minor aliments to major diseases (Harris & Rees, 2000). A substantial number of these treatments are based on Chinese traditional medicine. Besides being utilised by a large section of the Chinese community, these alternative treatments are now widely used by people from other ethnic minorities and the white-majority population in Britain. In major cities, practitioners of Chinese traditional medicine, the herbalist shops which supply their prescriptions, and acupuncture clinics are often readily accessible to people of Chinese descent (Wah et al., 1996: 109). Generally, traditional Chinese doctors tend to be consulted for more minor illnesses and practitioners of Western medicine for more major ones. Usually, Chinese and Western approaches to treatment are perceived by people of Chinese descent as complementary to rather than in conflict or competition with each other (Gervais & Jovchelovitch, 1998).

People of Chinese heritage, like members of other communities, will probably not have a systematic knowledge of traditional Chinese medicine or the way in which 'hot' and 'cold' foods affect the body. It is more probable that they will pick-and-mix from a range of health beliefs and treatments drawn from both allopathic and traditional approaches. For example, some people may believe that Western treatments work more quickly than those offered by Chinese traditional medicine. Others may regard allopathic approaches as only addressing symptoms while a practitioner of Chinese medicine is more likely to treat the deep-seated causes of an illness. There is a common perception that GPs are only interested in symptoms whereas a practitioner of Chinese medicine will take a more holistic view of the person in arriving at a diagnosis. Inevitably, a wide range of opinions are held regarding Chinese traditional medicine. These may be influenced as much by gender, age and country of birth as by health beliefs handed down through the family (Prior et al., 2000).

Older Chinese people, particularly if they have spent their formative years in China, may prefer to consult with a practitioner of Chinese traditional medicine rather than a general practitioner (Wah et al., 1996: 109; Prior et al., 2000: 825). It is not purely coincidental that Chinese elders also face substantial difficulties accessing health services due to the language barrier and the lack of interpreters available in

GP surgeries or hospitals. This is exacerbated by the absence of voluntary or statutory services geared for people of Chinese descent in those districts where there are very few people from that ethnic community. As a result, many older people tend to rely on their families for assistance to the exclusion of other services (Chau & Yu, 2001: 115; Chinese Community Network, 2006: 4). This does not mean that their families are necessarily able to meet all their care needs. Often there are gaps in the assistance provided, particularly in relation to personal care. The working lives of relatives mean that while they can carry out many domestic tasks for older family members, they are sometimes unable to meet personal needs. This is because activities such as ironing or repairs to the home can be undertaken at a time reasonably convenient to the family member, for instance after work. By contrast, the personal care needs of elders, such as assistance to the toilet, has to be performed immediately when the need arises (Chiu & Yu, 2001: 693–4).

As among the majority-white population, mental illness remains largely stigmatised by people of Chinese descent, although there may be a greater range of viewpoints than exists within the majority-white community. Psychiatry, which evolved from the positivist scientific worldview which underlies allopathic medicine, interprets behavioural symptoms in terms of physiological or intra-psychic processes, whereas a number of people of Chinese heritage perceive unusual behaviour as indicating a social problem of some kind. Consequently, a range of behaviours will be interpreted as non-medical and matters to be addressed by the family rather than referred to a psychiatrist or therapist (Prior et al., 2000: 831–2). In this connection it is significant that people of Chinese descent have the lowest rates of out-patient appointments or consultations with GPs (Smaje & Le Grand, 1997). While this has typically been attributed to fears of 'loss of face', in fact it may be due to different interpretations of what constitutes illness (Prior et al., 2000: 832).

Domiciliary, day-care and residential services frequently fail to meet the needs of members of the Chinese community in terms of heritage languages, food preferences and the need for contact with others of a similar ethnic background. This has resulted in many turning towards the voluntary services provided from within the Chinese community. This may be the only realistic option in metropolitan areas with a concentration of ethnic Chinese people. Often those of Chinese descent are confronted either by poorly resourced voluntary-sector services, which better meet their cultural and social needs, or statutory services which fail to address their most basic requirements (Taylor, 1987: 92). A large section of older people among the Chinese community are unaware of the services available to them, while others reject them because they fail to meet their requirements – typically meals-on-wheels fails to attend to the dietary preferences of many ethnically Chinese people (Chiu, 1989).

The language barrier, lack of information about specific services, facilities or benefits and at times a lack of trust result in a large section of people within the Chinese population turning to family, friends and Chinese community organisations as a source of assistance rather than public provision (MOOA & CIBF, 2004). Chinese voluntary organisations have been to the forefront of creating places for people of Chinese descent to meet and engage in recreational activities. These tend to take better account of people's needs in terms of language and lifestyle preferences (MOOA & CIBF, 2004: 50). Many older people still feel that there is little which caters specifically for their desire for social and leisure activities. A number cannot speak English fluently or else they feel a strong identification with life in Hong Kong. Consequently, they tend to experience mainstream provision as isolating rather than integrating (Yu, 2000).

Case Study 7.1

Mr Tan and his wife came to live in the United Kingdom during the 1960s when they migrated from Hong Kong. Mr Tan was an accountant and worked for a large company. His wife was a qualified primary-school teacher. Mr Tan is now 78 years old and was widowed five years ago. His two sons, Seng and Hock, emigrated to the United States 30 years ago – one now lives in New York City with his wife and the other with his partner in Detroit. Their adult children also live in the United States. Throughout the years Mr Tan and his sons' families have regularly spoken by telephone and occasionally exchanged letters. Mr Tan also kept in contact with extended family in Hong Kong, particularly his nephews and nieces and their families. Up until ten years ago Mr Tan and his wife used to make extended visits to the United States and Hong Kong to stay with relatives. Before his stroke Mr Tan still regularly telephoned them.

Mr Tan has severe arthritis. He was already experiencing mobility difficulties in his second-floor city-centre apartment when a stroke resulted in his admission to hospital. Over the last two months in hospital Mr Tan has recovered only very limited movement and his ability to speak has been seriously affected, although there has been no deterioration in his cognitive abilities. Mr Tan now requires two people for most personal-care tasks and it is generally extremely difficult for people to make out what he is saying, even though he is a fluent English and Cantonese speaker. He continues to have regular appointments with a speech therapist. His right hand is partially paralysed and he cannot write anymore. While the hospital consultant expects Mr Tan to recover some more movement and gain a little improvement in his speech, he will never be able to meet his own personal-care needs.

Mr Tan reluctantly agreed to be moved to residential care after acknowledging that he would be unable to manage at home on his own again. The residential unit is located ten miles away from where Mr Tan originally lived, as it was the only one in the local-authority area with a single room available. This makes it very difficult for Mr Tan to keep in contact with his longstanding neighbours and friends in the locality.

The manager at the residential home was informed by the hospital social worker of Mr Tan's ethnic background. He thought that meeting Mr Tan's cultural needs would not be a problem as Mrs Wong aged 68 years, who emigrated from China as a young woman, is already having all her care needs met. At the first review meeting after Mr Tan's move into residential care, the manager expresses his frustration at Mr Tan's refusal of a medical examination, while Mr Tan insists on being moved elsewhere.

OUTLINE OF INTERVENTION

Explore the reasons why Mr Tan wants to leave the residential home.

Discover why Mr Tan is reluctant to see a doctor.

Identify Mr Tan's cultural and religious needs and negotiate with the service provider to meet these.

Identity Mr Tan's social and leisure needs and negotiate with the service provider to meet these.

Points for Practice

The hospital social worker only had two meetings with Mr Tan in hospital. Due to other priorities and the additional time required to understand Mr Tan's impaired speech, the social worker did not explore Mr Tan's background in much detail. The focus of the two interviews was on the paperwork necessary for setting up the care package. As a result, the care home received little information about Mr Tan. Instead, staff at the home relied on their experience of working with Mrs Wong and made the same arrangements for Mr Tan. He is served only vegetarian meals which, according to him, lack any real variety. According to Mr Tan, he has tried to ask several care assistants why other residents are given meat dishes, but he cannot get a satisfactory answer. He is also transported weekly, along with Mrs Wong, to attend a small Buddhist temple in a converted terraced house in the locality.

Through discussion with Mr Tan you discover that he is not a Buddhist. In fact, his parents were part of the Christian community in Hong Kong. Mr Tan does not have a strong religious faith and has not attended church for many years. From previous cultural encounters you appreciate that many people pick-and-mix from different value systems and beliefs. So it does not surprise you to learn that while Mr Tan is nominally Christian, he enjoys attending the Chinese New Year and usually celebrates the Mid-Autumn Festival with friends from the Chinese community. Although Mr Tan believes that a balance between *yin* and *yang* foods is important to maintain his mental and physical health, he is not a vegetarian. The manager of the residential home assumed that because Mrs Wong was Buddhist, all people of Chinese ethnicity are normally practising Buddhists and therefore vegetarian. While Mr Tan thinks that allopathic medicine is effective for many illnesses, he believes that practitioners of Western medicine have done all they can to treat his condition. However, Mr Tan is still experiencing considerable discomfort and wants to receive further treatment from an acupuncturist. As a culturally competent practitioner, you need to be able to both impart your cultural knowledge to others (in this case staff at the residential home) and advocate on behalf of service-users to bring about multicultural provision in predominantly mono-cultural organisations.

You discuss with Mr Tan his preferences for contact with family, friends and members of his own ethnic community. Mr Tan thinks of himself as cosmopolitan and has no interest in attending facilities exclusively for people of Chinese ethnicity, although he does miss reading Chinese-language newspapers. At the same time he does want to maintain contact with his many friends, who are from diverse ethnic backgrounds. Furthermore, contact with his extended family in American and Hong Kong has been severely curtailed since his stroke, despite its centrality in his life. Past cultural encounters alert you to the fact that people identify with their ethnic group to a greater or lesser extent, and that this may change over time. Your ability to draw on cultural knowledge means that you appreciate how diverse any single ethnic group can be in terms of the spiritual beliefs, social norms and lifestyles of its members. But like the vast majority of people, regardless of their ethnic background, Mr Tan wants frequent contact with family members and no less so because they live overseas.

You discover that many of Mr Tan's friends and family members have internet access. Mr Tan used a word processor for a short period as an accountant, although he has never used a computer. As Mr Tan has sufficient movement in both hands and wrists to use a keyboard and mouse he agrees that the World Wide Web might be a workable alternative to communicating by telephone. However, Mr Tan thinks a computer would be too difficult to understand and is worried about making a lot of mistakes and appearing foolish. He agrees to have a try on condition that you can get someone to instruct him on a one-to-one basis for the first few sessions.

You ask the manager why residents do not have any internet access. The manager tells you that to his knowledge none of them has ever used a computer and would not be able to understand how it works. Cultural competence does not mean setting aside anti-oppressive practice and you need to challenge disablist and ageist assumptions about service-users which restrict their lives. In this case, it is feasible to arrange for someone from the local Volunteer Bureau to offer basic instructions to residents interested in using the World Wide Web, if the manager authorised provision of several internet-ready computers. This would enable Mr Tan to communicate directly with his relatives and friends and to access Chinese-language media.

📖 Further Reading

Archer, L. & Francis, B. (2005) 'Constructions of racism by British Chinese pupils and parents', *Race Ethnicity and Education* 8(4), pp. 387–407. This article explores the racist assumptions and attitudes of pupils and teachers from the majority-white community towards students of Chinese descent. It uses semi-structured interviews to investigate the impact of racism on pupils of Chinese heritage.

Chiu, S. & Yu, S. (2001) 'An excess of culture: the myth of shared care in the Chinese community in Britain', *Ageing and Society* 21, pp. 681–699. This article questions the assumption that Confucian norms play a major role in the families of people of

Chinese descent. It particularly challenges the notion that they are in a position to care for older people in the absence of assistance from adult social services.

Prior, L., Chun, P.L. & Huat, S.B. (2000) 'Beliefs and accounts of illness: views from two Canonese-speaking communities in England', *Sociology of Health and Illness* 22(6), pp. 815–839. This article examines the health beliefs of people of Chinese descent living in Britain. It also describes the range of opinion which exists in relation to Chinese traditional medicine and Western medicine.

Wah, Y.Y., Avari, B. & Buckley, S. (1996) *British Soil Chinese Roots*. Liverpool: Countrywise. This book, illustrated with photographs and diagrams, gives a brief overview of the beliefs, experiences and lifestyles of families in Britain with roots in Hong Kong.

8

Economic Migrants and Refugees

Recent Trends in Immigration

Historically, immigration has been synonymous with visible ethnic minorities originating from the Caribbean, Asian and Africa. In fact, as the 2001 Census revealed, there are 1,308,000 people residing in England who identify themselves as 'White – Other' as opposed to 'White – British' or 'White – Irish' (National Statistics, 2003). Some of these respondents are members of post-war refugee communities of Poles and Ukrainians who settled in England in the aftermath of the Second World War. In addition, the twentieth century witnessed a continuous stream of people arriving from North America and Western Europe to live in Britain. In contrast to the wave of post-war immigration from the New Commonwealth and the family reunions of the 1960s and 1970s which followed, recent migrants to the United Kingdom are generally from other developed countries.

During the 1990s around 85% of immigrants arriving in the United Kingdom were from countries of the Old Commonwealth (Australia, New Zealand, Canada), the United States and the European Union. Of all those coming to Britain during this period, approximately 54% intended to stay for less than four years (Hatton, 2005: 721, 724). It is significant in this connection that in any one year there are likely to be up to 300,000 overseas students studying at higher education institutions in the United Kingdom (BBC, 2005b). During 2003 this translated into 10.5% of full-time undergraduates and 38% of full-time postgraduates in Britain coming from other countries. Of these, 32,000 came from mainland China and a further 10,000 from Hong Kong; 11,000 were from India; 10,000 came from Malaysia; and well over 70,000 foreign students were from other EU countries (Böhm et al., 2004).

The socio-economic profile of migrants to the United Kingdom has also changed dramatically over the last 40 years. Of those who came to Britain in 1971, just 40% had managerial or professional skills, while of those arriving in 2000, around 72% had professional qualifications or experience (Hatton, 2005: 725). The difference in the skills levels is in part explained by Britain joining the European Community in 1973, which meant the free movement of people between member states. It is also attributable to changes to government policy which act to discourage unskilled migrants while attracting skilled workers from abroad through the issue of work permits with the possibility of permanent settlement in the United Kingdom (Home Office, 2001b). During the years 2004–2005 work permits were granted to approximately 261,000 people from outside the European Union who were accompanied by 87,000 dependants (BBC, 2006).

Economic Migrants from the New Accession States of the European Union

The Treaty of Rome 1957 provided the legal framework for the European Union and granted the free movement of goods, services, people and finance between the countries of all the Treaty's signatories. Yet, until, recently, there had been limited migration to the United Kingdom from other countries of the European Union, mostly due to the existence of similar economic conditions elsewhere. The small numbers of people originating from other EU nations came mainly from France, Portugal and Greece. They tended to congregate in Greater London and the south east of England (White, 1998: 1729). This changed significantly when, in 2004, ten new countries, eight of them from the former Eastern Bloc, joined the European Union. Three years later Romania and Bulgaria became the newest member states, making a total of 27 countries belonging to the European Union. Ten out of the 12 nations which joined the EU from 2004 onwards were originally under communist rule. Most of these countries still have low-wage economies and continue to experience the social and economic disruption caused by transition from a centrally planned economy to a free-market one.

Across Eastern Europe the standard of living deteriorated as state revenues fell sharply during the 1990s and the majority of post-communist countries were left with grossly under-funded health, education and welfare systems which retained their infrastructure without effectively delivering provision (Milanovic, 1998; Micklewright, 1999; Sandu, 2005). A number of post-communist states have experienced a degree of economic recovery since the 1990s, particularly those joining the European Union, which have benefited from its funding. These improvements have not been substantial enough to offset the day-to-day realities of low wages and relatively high unemployment. As a result, many citizens in former Eastern Bloc countries joining the European Union have taken advantage of the free movement of labour to migrate to Western European nations.

When ten new countries joined the European Union in 2004 the United Kingdom was one of only three existing member states to grant full rights of employment to their citizens. Consequently, Britain has been a popular destination for economic migrants from former communist countries. During the period May 2004 to June 2006 the government approved approximately 427,000 applications from people living in a former Eastern Bloc country and wishing to work in the United Kingdom. Of these applications, around 62% were from Poland alone, the rest being from the Czech Republic, Slovakia, Hungary, Slovenia and the three Baltic states. Out of the total of 427,000 successful applicants, 350,000 were aged 18–34 years and 36,000 brought dependents with them to live in Britain. It is reckoned by the Association of Labour Providers that at least a further 100,000 workers arrived in the United Kingdom without officially registering (BBC, 2006).

Refugees from former Eastern Bloc Countries

The refugees from Ukraine, Russia, Poland and other East European states who settled in Britain during the 1940s and 1950s are now aged. Some find themselves living alone as their adult children or grandchildren have moved elsewhere in the country to raise families of their own. Others decided not to marry, had no children or lost close relatives during the Second World War. For a number of older people, a limited grasp of English and little contact with other native speakers may result in isolation (Bowling, 1993: 5–6). The fact that they are white can result in their difficulties being overlooked and thus compounded by service provision which fails to cater for differences of language, religion and custom (Bowling, 1993: 5–6). These historical refugee communities have more recently been joined by people fleeing conflict in Eastern Europe in the wake of the collapse of communism.

For a significant proportion of those fleeing war or harassment in post-communist countries there has been no established diaspora of fellow nationals in the United Kingdom. Ethnic Albanians escaping persecution in Serbia during the 1980s found few people from their homeland living anywhere in Britain. When circumstances worsened, culminating in the mass flight of Albanians from Kosovo as Serbian troops advanced across the province during 1998, only then were there sufficient numbers concentrated in London to form the nucleus of a community. For some refugees there may be very few people to whom they can directly relate, in terms of personal experience, language or culture. Where this is the case, the government's dispersal policy can compound their plight. Provisions introduced under the Immigration and Asylum Act 1999 mean that asylum seekers are located to regional centres such as Barnsley in South Yorkshire, Glasgow in Scotland, Birmingham in the Midlands or Cardiff in Wales. Should they later be granted refugee status, they will be allocated social housing in the local-authority area to which they were originally dispersed. Inevitably, this can result in further fragmentation of already small ethnic communities (Kostovicova & Prestreshi, 2003: 1079–80).

The Traumatic Experiences of Refugees

Many refugees experience feelings of loss, sadness, distress, trauma and isolation, which can be exacerbated by their reception in the country where they seek asylum if they are then subject to ostracism or racial harassment (Drumm et al., 2001: 468). Those who have been tortured or witnessed violence may also feel profound anger and hostility, sometimes expressed through aggressive behaviour (Ekblad et al., 2002). Some women fleeing from persecution and war may have suffered ill-treatment or (as in Bosnia and Kosovo) been systematically raped as a weapon of war. Families may be split up as men take up arms to fight and women are required to find a place of safety with their children (Drumm et al., 2001: 468). In other cases, men are imprisoned for their political opinions or activities and female partners are left with the sole responsibility for child care. In these circumstances, the women who seek asylum with their children are effectively single parents who have become heads of households (Drumm et al., 2001: 468–9). In other cases, women may have been involved in political activity themselves or pursued successful careers in their country of origin. The effect of seeking asylum often means depriving them of these roles. A British context may not be favourable to continuing with their political activities, while the language barrier or the non-recognition of professional qualifications and expertise may prevent women from taking up work similar to that in their country of origin. If they are single parents wrenched from the kin they had to leave behind and unable to make contact with new networks of fellow expatriates, their difficulties are likely to be magnified (Al-Ali, 2002: 254).

Those women and children subjected to the violent events of war in Bosnia and Kosovo may experience post-traumatic stress disorder resulting in sleep disturbance, flashback and poor concentration. Where they are supported by other family members or are enabled to develop new social networks, these will act to facilitate adjustment and reduce mental-health problems (Drumm et al., 2001: 470). The enforced passivity caused by the asylum process in Britain and often followed by unemployment or difficulty in accessing educational or leisure activities can induce boredom and intensify feelings of loss and isolation. This is particularly the case where refugees do not have ready access to media in their own language. Likewise, uncertainty about the whereabouts of other family members or even whether they are alive or dead can increase the day-to-day anxiety experienced by refugees (Drumm et al., 2001: 478, 480).

For many men, the processes of seeking asylum and then settling in the United Kingdom, where they may not be able to fulfil their previous role as breadwinners, can lead to re-negotiation of gender roles within the family. For a substantial number of men these experiences may also cause considerable stress and some loss of personal identity. This is particularly so if families are dependent on income support or men can only obtain low-paid, unskilled work despite their actual expertise and abilities. Where families have left societies with strong patriarchal structures, these changes can demand great effort to adjust. Equally, a number of men, particularly if they have made the journey into exile with partners and children, invest in other aspects of their social identity, for instance as husbands and fathers (Al-Ali, 2002: 255).

Ethnic Identity in the United Kingdom

The experiences of refugees in their countries of origin can generate enormous sensitivity when attempting to re-establish their lives in the United Kingdom. Aspects of employment, education and social engagement may be strongly associated with traumatic events in their country of origin. For instance, many Albanians from Serbia who came to Britain during the 1980s and early 1990s were leaving a country in which their language schools were being closed and they were facing widespread discrimination in education and employment. The Albanian language is perceived by the majority of Kosovar Albanians as a fundamental aspect of their identity (Kostovicova & Prestreshi, 2003: 1082). For many Albanian parents, sending their children to schools in Britain, where they are necessarily taught in English, can generate ambivalence, particularly as for some children this results in the loss of fluency in their own heritage language.

Culture shock, which creates confusion and disorientation, is also likely to be an aspect of settling in Britain. For Bosnian teenagers, like many young refugees, the preservation of their heritage in another cultural context can assist adjustment. This can be facilitated through opportunities to use their own language, fulfil family commitments, meet people of the same ethnicity, practise their religion, partake in their own cultural traditions, participate in local youth culture and build a future through education and information (Weine et al., 2004: 925–6). At the same time, people from the same ethnic group are likely to have different understandings of their identity and may seek to assert this in different ways. For example, some Bosnian Muslims who have settled in England find religious practices more important than previously. This can include both greater observance of rituals and a greater sense of affiliation with the *ummah* (world community of Muslims). For others, their religious faith is an aspect of ethnic identity which may coexist with consuming alcohol or eating meat which is not *halāl*.

By contrast, a number of Bosnian Muslims living in the United Kingdom think that religious sectarianism contributed to the civil war in their country and consequently tend to be more secular in outlook (Al-Ali, 2002: 250, 257–8). Similarly, Kosovo Albanians living in Britain practise Islam in different ways. For some, it is one aspect of an otherwise secular lifestyle. For others, religious observance helps to restore a sense of identity after the dislocation of war and exile. For this reason, there can be differences in religious observance and in the interpretation of Islam between Muslims from the former Yugoslavia and those whose family roots are in Pakistan or Bangladesh (Kostovicova & Prestreshi, 2003: 1090–1). In other words, there is no one way to be Muslim any more than there is one way to be a Christian.

Refugees from Bosnia may also differ in their identification with fellow nationals. Where people are fleeing civil war or persecution in their homeland inevitably there will be community divisions which are likely to persist in the receiving country. In many parts of Bosnia, Orthodox Serbs and Catholic Croats were in violent confrontation with Bosnian Muslims. Many refugees from the former Yugoslavia have witnessed the brutal deaths of family members or been forced from their home during campaigns of ethnic cleansing. It is understandable that the anger and resentment which these actions caused will persist in a new country and may detrimentally affect community relations between ethnic groups. For this reason, the creation and sustaining of mutual support networks among recent refugees in Britain can be complex and fraught with tensions. Divisions between those who came from rural areas and urban areas, between those who were professionals and those who were unskilled labourers in their home country are also likely to affect the cohesion of refugee communities in the United Kingdom (Al-Ali, 2002: 250).

Development of transnational families

Those granted refugee status may never return to their homeland. Instead, they settle and raise their families in the United Kingdom, but they are likely to remain connected to their country of origin. Their exile may greatly affect their engagement with the relatives, friends and, indeed, the community they left behind. These new transnational relationships may involve endeavours to support those who remain behind, for example through remittances. It may consist of frequent exchanges through telephone calls and the internet or even visits. For other refugees, communication may be difficult in circumstances of continuing community tensions in their homeland. The displacement of family and friends within the country of origin or to other countries in Europe may reduce the scope for ongoing contact. Even in a situation of relative peace and ease of communication, resentment may be felt by those who stayed behind to fight or who could not escape and those who managed to get out of the country (Al-Ali, 2002: 258). Ultimately, as is true for other refugee communities, Bosnian women living in Britain often find themselves managing child care without the support of the extended family, which was usually relied upon, particularly in rural Yugoslavia (Al-Ali, 2002: 253–4). Likewise, men can find themselves without the networks of friends and relatives which sustained their social life and acted as a source of mutual support.

Coping strategies among refugees from former Eastern Bloc countries

Refugees from former Eastern Bloc countries also come to the United Kingdom with many skills and coping strategies. The huge bureaucracies and centrally planned economies of communist countries resulted in frequent shortages of basic goods, difficulty in obtaining some services and powerlessness to bring about corrective state action when there were clear inefficiencies or injustices. More recently, the political and economic dislocations caused by the collapse of communism have led to high inflation, the loss of state support and widespread poverty. The combination of communism and post-communist crises have made collective and mutual support critical mechanisms for meeting daily needs (Michael & Florica, 1998; Shevchenko, 2002: 844; Bühler, 2004: 264–5; Wallace & Latcheva, 2006). Families in both rural and urban areas are often productive units merging domestic and economic activities to meet household needs. For example, those living on the outskirts of towns and cities in many post-communist countries often grow fruit and vegetables, both for their own consumption and for sale. Other urban households have purchased or rented a plot of land within travelling distance of the city for the same purpose. In many instances, children's labour is crucial to sustaining this mix of domestic and commercial activity. This is particularly so where parents or guardians are having to juggle several different jobs in order to make ends meet.

Networks of friends and kin have also become vital as personal connections and trust have replaced the contractual relations of the formal economy (Pickup & White, 2003). This reliance is so pervasive that a survey conducted in Russia revealed that up to 90% of people depend on social networks to get things done rather than public institutions or civil-society organisations (Rose, 1998: 7). Known as *blat* exchanges in

Russia, these interactions depend on a system of 'functional friendships' which permit the trade of favours and are governed by strict social norms of reciprocity. Such networks attract considerable loyalty and are built on bonds of mutual interdependence. Among large numbers of people from former communist countries, this form of social organisation may continue to be of vital importance. For refugees in the United Kingdom, they can constitute essential support networks. However, this can create a paradoxical situation whereby recent refugees, who are themselves struggling to make ends meet, are assisting their even more impoverished compatriots (Sales, 2002: 466; Dwyer & Brown, 2005: 377–8).

Community-based refugee organisations also have a major role to play in 'overcoming isolation, providing material help to community members, defending the interests of the community and promoting the community's culture ... and assisting the adaptation of the community members to the host society' (Kelly, 2003: 38). These organisations can reduce culture shock for new arrivals alongside the persistent feelings of disorientation and loss which are often experienced by those forced from their homeland. Likewise, web-based communities are important contact points for isolated refugee families and communities within the United Kingdom and can act as vital sources of information and the sharing of experiences. Websites for refugees provide advice on accessing health care, education, vocational training, employment and cultural activities. In addition, some sites offer material assistance through information on welfare entitlements or the sale of second-hand items. Practical help is also made available through listings of telephone numbers and addresses for services, often provided by members of a refugee's own community living in Britain. The cumulative effect of these virtual communities is to validate the experiences of refugees and to act as a reference point in circumstances of uncertainty and confusion (Siapera, 2005: 513–14).

Economic Migrants and Refugees from Africa

Prior to the 1950s there were only around 10,000 people of African descent in the United Kingdom, mainly living in the port cities of Cardiff, Liverpool and London. The majority had been seafarers originating from the costal areas of Sierra Leone, Nigeria and Ghana, with a smaller number from British Somaliland. Once established with accommodation and employment, some were joined by family members. Thereafter, most Africans who settled in the United Kingdom came initially as university students and then decided to remain rather than return to their own countries. The deteriorating economic and political situation in many West African nations throughout the 1970s and 1980s meant that ever greater numbers of students opted to live permanently in England after attaining their academic or professional training. Inter-ethnic conflict and military coups, often connived at by the United States or the Soviet Union, resulted in many African nations being affected by ongoing regional wars. African students who left a peaceful country often found themselves unable to return because of a military takeover or a war-torn homeland. Due to the vested interest of the British government in retaining skilled labour, many students were able to obtain a work permit after their period of study and later gained the right to reside permanently in the United Kingdom.

Initially, the African student population was predominantly male, but increasingly progressive attitudes towards female education and employment across Africa meant that by the 1980s roughly as many men as women were coming to study (Daley, 1998: 1708). Violent upheavals in countries such as Ghana, Uganda, Nigeria, Ethiopia and Angola also led to a small number of Black African politicians and professionals, along with their families, seeking refuge in the United Kingdom. Between 1980 and 1991 there were 53,000 applications for asylum made by Africans although only 8,500 were granted (Daley, 1998: 1704–5). For those deciding to remain in Britain, many were joined by their spouse or children. Others were not reunited with their families but continued to send remittances back to their countries of origin. Some married fellow Africans in Britain or met partners from other ethnic groups. Due to this form of immigration, by 1991 Black Africans were the most highly qualified ethnic group living in the United Kingdom.

In the 2001 Census, 476,000 people identified as 'Black or Black British – African', consisting both of people born in the United Kingdom of African parentage and those who had been born in Africa, but were now resident in Britain (National Statistics, 2003). Taken altogether, they form one of the largest ethnic minorities in the United Kingdom. But in reality they come from 53 different countries and do not form a single community. Given the poly-ethnic nature of sub-Saharan countries, even individuals who share the same nationality are likely to identify with different ethnic groupings, religious beliefs and kinship systems. Out of those Black Africans who trace their family roots to the same country, the largest numbers are from Ghana, Nigeria and Somalia. The vast majority of them are concentrated in London and to a lesser extent other major cities such as Manchester. Although there has been a historic Somali community in the United Kingdom, most have arrived since 1980 as asylum seekers escaping persecution in their own country. While a large proportion of them live in London, the government's dispersal policy, introduced under the Immigration and Asylum Act 1999, means that many have been accommodated in the regions. Consequently, there are many cities and towns across the United Kingdom where there are small numbers of Somalis.

The settlement pattern of Africans also reflects their initial purpose for coming to the United Kingdom. As most of the country's universities are concentrated in Greater London, it was inevitable that it would become the nucleus of different African communities, with 80% of those identifying as Black African living there. Smaller numbers have gravitated to Cardiff and Liverpool, the cities hosting historical African centres of population (Daley, 1998: 1708–9). Concentration in certain inner-city wards is also a consequence of discrimination and Africans from different countries having to rely mainly on other compatriots to house them or assist with securing employment. As is the case among other ethnic minorities, many Black Africans find themselves living in over-crowded conditions, either in social housing or the private rented sector. Despite their high levels of qualification a large proportion are employed in unskilled and semi-skilled occupations. It is not uncommon for professionals from African countries to be working in Britain as taxi-drivers or cleaners, either as a consequence of direct discrimination, non-recognition of their qualifications or due to their lack of fluency in English (Daley, 1998: 1716–23). Others, despite the obstacles created by racial prejudice, have secured well-paid employment, bought their own homes and moved into the suburbs.

The 1990s witnessed a steep rise in asylum applications from Africans as civil war and economic collapse continued to ravage their countries. Out of all the regions of the world, Africa contains the highest number of people displaced by armed conflict, natural disaster (often precipitated or exacerbated by war) and the deprivations of absolute poverty. The total collapse of financial institutions, the industrial base and commercial enterprises in circumstances of perpetual armed conflict or political unrest, as in Sierra Leone, Somalia and more recently Zimbabwe, have generated successive waves of refugees. Many are forced to leave their homelands due to persecution on the grounds of their political opinions or ethnicity. Others flee in the wake of violence per-petrated against their family and community in the course of combat. Some of those granted asylum in the United Kingdom are the victims of torture, rape, brutalisation, abduction, public humiliation or injury by landmines, light-weapon fire and deliber-ate mutilation (Turshen, 1998: 6–8).

Problems Confronting African Refugees in the United Kingdom

The language barrier

Those who come to the United Kingdom as students or on work permits, and are then confronted with violent events in their homeland making a return impossible, are likely to be competent in written and spoken English. The majority of refugees from African nations which were formerly under British colonial rule, such as Ghana and Nigeria, will probably have fluency in English. This is because English is the official language of the country and usually the language of instruction in secondary and ter-tiary education. Those from Muslim countries such as Somalia may also understand and speak Arabic, as this is normally the language in which religious instruction is given. Although Qur'ānic Arabic is not exactly the same as modern-day Arabic, it can offer a point of contact with other Muslims in Britain.

In some refugee families, individuals may have different levels of competence in written and spoken English. These differences tend to exist between men and women, on the one hand, and older and younger family members on the other. For some refugee families this can mean children gaining competence in English due to formal schooling in the United Kingdom, while their parents (particularly mothers) either face a long wait to access adult language classes or cannot attend because of work or child-care commitments. Among some refugee families, young people may gain fluency in English while loosing competence in their heritage language. This is most likely to occur where families are isolated from fellow refugees from their country, with the result that there are few opportunities to use their heritage language. Where a heritage language follows an oral tradition, as is the case with many minority languages in Africa, it may be more susceptible to being lost (Arthur, 2004: 222–8).

Unemployment and poverty

Those granted asylum will have their right to assistance from the National Asylum Support Service (NASS) terminated with one month's notice, although in practice it can actually be shorter (Dwyer & Brown, 2005: 377). This gives them little time to arrange alternative accommodation or to access benefits. Indeed, take-up of benefits by refugees is particularly low as many are not aware of their entitlements. Consequently, the majority of refugees are dependent on favours from relatives, friends and acquaintances to put them up on a temporary basis. This often means living in over-crowded conditions or sleeping on a floor (Carey-Wood et al., 1995: 102). Unemployment among refugees is often very high as they may not have fluency in English or knowledge of the local job market. Many rely on personal contacts within their ethnic-minority group to find work or seek self-employment in the informal sector. If they have been prohibited from working over several years as a result of awaiting a decision, some of their skills may be redundant. Re-training or the up-dating of skills may be necessary. Their qualifications may not be recognised in the United Kingdom. These problems, combined with racial discrimination, can result in many refugees having to accept unskilled and semi-skilled jobs which do not reflect their educational or professional achievements. Poor mental or physical health as a result of their experiences both in their country of origin and since arriving in the United Kingdom may also diminish the employment prospects of refugees (Carey-Wood et al., 1995: 98–101; Sales, 2002: 466–7).

Gender roles

The whole process of seeking asylum, even when it ends in the granting of refugee status, can have a profound effect on gender relations. For those who migrated with their families, the experience of forced migration, unfamiliarity in another language or society, involuntary unemployment and the loss of self-determination created by the asylum process can change gender roles and power relationship between men and women (Sales, 2002: 467). Men may lose status as a result of both having to flee from their homeland and losing the social context which gave them that status. Secondly, as the acknowledged breadwinners in most societies, enforced unemployment under asylum legislation, together with provision by NASS and/or reliance on fellow nationals, is likely to undermine male authority where this has to some extent been based on economic power.

Women, on the contrary, may find their opportunities expand as they obtain benefits in their own right on being granted refugee status or are better able to find work than their male partners. On the other hand, the isolation of women from members of their own kin and ethnic community, combined with the considerable stress on both partners caused by forced migration and the restrictions imposed by immigration control, can lead to a rise in domestic violence. Refugee women can also find themselves more isolated than men from British society as they are less likely than their husbands or partners to have fluency in English, employable skills, or be in paid work (Sales, 2002: 467).

Child welfare

There is considerable diversity in the way that parents or guardians bring up their children across different societies. These include variations in parental responsibilities (some being assumed by other family members), age-related expectations of children and the norms relating to their care, supervision and discipline. For example, in many developing countries children may not be weaned until they are several years old, rather than several months after birth, as is common in Britain (Mares et al., 1985: 123). There is a high incidence of child labour in many African countries, which is closely associated with an inadequate education system, widespread household poverty and the demand for casual unskilled workers (Bequele & Boyden, 1995). Even where deprivation does not force children to miss school in order to contribute to family income, there may be strong expectations that they take on adult responsibilities at a much younger age than is usual in the United Kingdom. Among a number of societies it is normal to use an implement to physically discipline a child. Indeed, the judicious administering of corporal punishment may be seen as evidence of good parenting (Thoburn et al., 2005: 83).

In addition to the possible clash between childrearing practices in their country of origin and those generally accepted in the United Kingdom, parental capacity may be restricted by circumstances. Refugee parents or guardians, who are coping alone or only with the assistance of their partner, are not well placed to give the same standard of care to their children as they might have done in their homeland. The abrupt loss of support networks, exacerbated by culture shock, and often combined with unemployment and poor access to benefits or services, are likely to adversely affect standards of child care (Lau, 2004: 103). In other words, refugees in Britain face considerable obstacles in trying to support and care for their children.

Coping Strategies among African Refugees

People who have survived war and persecution are likely to have developed considerable resilience and effective survival strategies. They may use a range of coping strategies to manage the difficulties of a new life in an unfamiliar society.

Social support

Many refugees quickly link into established networks in the United Kingdom made up of other exiles from their country or of other individuals confronting similar difficulties. These contacts provide vital information about welfare entitlements, housing, health care, education and training opportunities, access to the labour market, and the informal exchange of goods and services. Often these networks revolve around outlets which provide specialist goods and services to people of different nationalities, for example a shop or restaurant which offers foods imported from Africa. For those who arrive in the United Kingdom with few possessions and no family, connecting with other refugees or the wider expatriate community from their country of origin is a vital first step to adjustment in the United Kingdom. This is especially the case where refugees are confronted by hostility from a section of the British population.

Due to the concentration of the African diaspora in London, many ethnic groups live in identifiable areas, which results in specialist shops and restaurants which cater to the needs of specific ethnic groups, while also selling produce to the wider community. For instance, Brixton market in the London Borough of Lambeth offers the greatest variety of African foodstuffs anywhere in Britain. Consequently, it has become both a shopping centre and a meeting place for many British citizens of African descent and for African refugees. An increasing number of specialist outlets are being run by Black African entrepreneurs who have identified a niche market for African goods among their fellow compatriots. Churches and mosques are also centres where refugees can meet and integrate with settled communities of the same ethnicity or original nationality (Daley, 1998: 1722–3). Large numbers of Somalis in London use informal economic networks to establish and promote commercial activity. Commonly internet cafés, specialist shops and the *hawilad* system (a low-cost method of sending remittances which bypass the formal banking system) act as hubs for making initial personal contacts (Griffiths et al., 2006: 894).

For a number of refugees, such networks may be regarded with suspicion and trepidation, particularly where they have experienced persecution or violence in their homeland. They may have well-founded fears of being identified by compatriots and their whereabouts being relayed to government officials or factions in their country of origin. This information could either threaten their own safety in the United Kingdom or that of family members remaining behind (Williams, 2006: 872). Some of the contacts in a refugee's network can be unreliable, with promises of support often left unfulfilled. Precisely because such networks are composed of people who may only have their language or nationality in common, these networks can also be relatively weak and ties easily broken. At times, accepted gender roles can make it more difficult for women than men to link into and develop contacts across a wide range of people. Social norms among some ethnic groups may make it awkward for a woman to approach a man directly, as opposed to doing it through a male relative (Williams, 2006: 875). Other women unexpectedly find themselves as heads of households and develop new skills and approaches to dealing with their circumstances. Making initial contacts and accessing such networks is greatly determined by a person's location. Those living in urban centres with established populations of fellow nationals are much more likely to be able to link into such networks.

Child care

Kinship fostering is common in many African societies. For households coping with severe deprivation, it has enabled children to be moved out of their parental home to live with more prosperous relatives who can better care for them. Alternatively, sending children to live with their grandparents or other relatives is used to strengthen family ties and kinship loyalties. But, at times, fostered children are exploited as cheap domestic labour or move to live with unknown kin or non-kin many miles away and without the protective input of immediate family (Lloyd & Desai, 1991; CAS & UNICEF, 1999: 35–7). A small, but significant, proportion of African families living in the United Kingdom organise private fostering arrangements for their children, either with relatives or friends. Though many availing of private fostering would prefer to use nursery schools, these are often not affordable for parents. The main reasons for substitute child care are that parents are studying or working full-time, parents are separated, parental illness, or their housing is unsuitable for children. For a number of children the private fostering arrangement means moving them to a different local council area and possibly less frequent visits from their natural parents (Olusanya & Hodes, 2000).

International networks

The dislocations caused by involuntary exile can lead to a strong desire to re-create social networks, re-establish connections to one's homeland and to participate in culturally significant activities. For these reasons, linking up with compatriots living in Britain is likely to be extremely important, as is obtaining access to satellite television and internet sites connected to a person's country of origin or broadcasting in their own language. The establishment of transnational networks of friends and relatives may also be an important aspect of assisting adjustment to life in the United Kingdom and restoring a sense of place and identity after the trauma of fleeing one's homeland and seeking asylum. For many refugees these transnational exchanges of news, support and information can be intensive and form an integral part of their social lives. Often these support networks work in both directions, with refugees already experiencing hardship in the United Kingdom still endeavouring to save sufficient monies to send back to relatives in worse straits in their homeland. On the other hand, even people remaining behind in their country of origin may have information which can help a recently arrived refugee in Britain make a new contact who can assist with accommodation and employment (Williams, 2006: 873–4).

Those relying on informal networks often adapt survival strategies used in their countries of origin to escape persecution or cope with deprivation. The use of social networks, linked by strong norms of reciprocity, is a widespread form of mutual support on the African continent (Davies, 1996: 36–7; Moser & Holland, 1997: 11–2; Anie et al., 2001). Longstanding patterns of internal migration in African countries have led to the setting up of ethnically based hometown associations wherever a sufficient number of people from that locality find themselves. For example, Yoruba migrants in Nigeria settling in another place maintain links with their village of origin and commonly create new social ties in relation to their birthplace. These associations involve strong loyalties both towards fellow members of the home-town association branch and to the home town itself. In other words, new social networks are established around 'a community of origin' (AFFORD, 1998: 21). These traditional forms of support are widespread in cities with large concentrations of expatriate African communities. For example, in South London, Ugandans, Ghanaians and Nigerians have formed welfare associations which provide mutual financial support in times of hardship. Some are based around regional, village or even clan loyalties (Daley, 1998: 1722–3). Social-housing tenancies may also be passed backwards and forwards between kin or other members of a person's ethnic group (Daley, 1998: 1723).

Most African countries are poly-ethnic. For example, in Ghana there are 17 major ethnicities and 60 different languages, while in Nigeria there are approximately 250 tribal groups speaking almost as many languages. These differences are further cross-cut by religious faith, with large proportions of the population in both countries practising Islam, Christianity or traditional African religions. These distinctions can be of greater or lesser importance for Africans involved in welfare associations in the United Kingdom. Who is permitted to join and benefit will depend on the views of members and what they regard as the purpose of the welfare association. Consequently, a welfare organisation may serve a broad range of people of African origin or restrict its activities to those of a particular country, ethnicity or religion. In other words, such welfare associations can be inclusive or exclusive in the assistance they offer.

Refugee organisations

Within the community charitable organisations and social networks have developed to cater for the growing asylum and refugee populations in the regions. These are dependent on a large number of unpaid and untrained workers who devote their time out of humanitarian concern. Many former asylum seekers have also formed community groups which offer assistance to both those making an application and those whose claims for asylum have been successful. Voluntary-sector and community-based organisations usually offer a mixture of legal advice, advocacy, material assistance, referral to other agencies, arranged cultural events and organised leisure activities (Dwyer & Brown, 2005: 372). However, the informal nature of such organisations, combined with their dependence on voluntary support and unpredictable funding, means that many are short-lived or cannot cater to the needs of those making demands on them (Dwyer & Brown, 2005: 376).

Other community-based organisations in Birmingham and elsewhere can have quite a restrictive definition of who they are willing to assist. For instance, the factionalism in Somalia, which has lead to decades of violence between warring clans, is reflected among some refugee groups, which only assist fellow clansmen and women. It is understandable that where civil strife has caused many to flee their homeland, the resentments and tensions will often continue between different groupings, even in their country of adoption. What is more, the divisions within an apparently homogeneous community can be disguised by the preference of local and central government to work with umbrella organisations as 'representatives' of ethnic-minority populations. This can have the effect of marginalising those refugees who for many reasons operate within informal social networks and are reluctant to engage with state agencies (Griffiths et al., 2006: 891–4). Moreover, power relationships between older and younger people and between men and women may be reproduced in community-based organisations. The result can be to sideline the opinions and needs of young Africans growing up in British society and of women who may be restricted in their participation (AFFORD, 1998: 24–5, 30–2). In short, African community-based organisations can be representative or unrepresentative of local populations. They can either act to unify or further fragment the diversity of ethnicity which already exists in African communities across the United Kingdom.

Case Study 8.1

Yuri and his wife Natasha, along with their son Dimitry aged 10 years, and daughters Olga aged 9 and Alina aged 3 years, sought asylum in Britain a year ago after leaving the Russian Federation. They were recently granted refugee status. Due to the government's dispersal policy, Yuri's family has been re-located to a town where there are no other Russian-speaking refugees, although there are other refugees living in the area. Natasha speaks very little English and Yuri has only a limited knowledge of the language, which he picked up since arriving in the United Kingdom. Neither Yuri nor Natasha know anyone in Britain. They are presently living in a fourth-floor, two-bedroom flat in an apartment block owned by a housing association.

Yuri was a trained and experienced electrician in Russia. He is not permitted to work under immigration rules, pending the outcome of his asylum application. Now that he has been granted refugee status, he cannot obtain work as an electrician, partly because he lacks fluency in English and partly because his qualifications are not recognised in the United Kingdom. As a result, Yuri is presently stacking shelves and working at a checkout in a large supermarket in the town centre. Natasha owned and managed a grocery shop in a small town in Russia and presently undertakes casual work whenever she can get it. Natasha has also enrolled to learn English at the local college of further education, but is really struggling to stay on the course because of the costs. Yuri approached a grass-roots refugee organisation in the locality that is known to provide help to people from the former Eastern Bloc, but they refused to assist on the grounds that the family are native Russians.

An anonymous letter is received by Children's Services alleging that two very young children are being left alone together in their home for extended periods of time and appear to be locked in. The address given is that of Yuri and Natasha's flat.

There has also been telephone contact with the duty social worker from the head teacher of the school attended by Dimitry and Olga to voice concern over their continued absences and the failure of their parents to respond to a series of letters. The school principal also relates that one teacher has observed what seems to be an untreated and infected wound on Dimitry's forearm.

OUTLINE OF INTERVENTION

Identify and address child-protection issues.

Explore the reasons for the children's absence from school.

Identify Yuri and Natasha's needs as parents.

Identify the assistance required to meet any additional needs of family members and negotiate with providers.

Points for Practice

You visit Yuri and Natasha's flat during the day on several occasions and establish that two young children are being locked in and left on their own. Neither of the children will communicate with you. From a neighbour you find out that Yuri and Natasha are normally at home in the evenings. Due to the shortage of Russian interpreters in the area, you are met by a woman who has no experience of child-protection situations. Yuri and Natasha are evidently very frightened by your presence in their home and you experience great difficulty explaining to them through the interpreter why you are there and what your responsibilities are. They do not at all seem to understand the points you are trying to make about leaving the children unsupervised and the concern over Dimitry's and Olga's absenteeism from school. You point to what appears to be the untreated injury to Dimitry's arm and ask why he has not been taken to the doctor. Natasha says she will take Dimitry to the hospital the next day.

Over the next few days you discover that the family are not registered with a general practitioner. You contact the Accident and Emergency Units of the two local hospitals who report that no child answering to Dimitry's description has been admitted. Another telephone call is received by Children's Services from a neighbour who gives her name and informs the duty social worker that Olga and her sister are still being regularly locked in the flat together during the day. Further contact with the school reveals that neither of the children have attended over the last few days. You and your line manager decide to call a strategy meeting where it is agreed that you will make another home visit to the parents with an interpreter and commence a Section 47 inquiry under the Children Act 1989. This situation has very quickly spiralled into a child-protection investigation.

Cultural encounter means coming with an open mind as to what is happening and exploring the influence of a person's cultural background in terms of their attitudes, beliefs and behaviour. In this case, a couple have relatively recently arrived in the United Kingdom from a former Eastern Bloc country. They have been granted asylum, so they will have experienced persecution by their own government, possibly torture and imprisonment, and certainly discrimination or harassment. For over a year they have been subject to the rigours of the British immigration system, including detailed interrogation of their private lives, imposed unemployment and total dependence on NASS for assistance. It is quite probable that Yuri and Natasha, like many other refugees, will have little grasp of dominant social norms and legal rules in the United Kingdom or what their entitlements are or how to negotiate the public sector to obtain them. In view of this, they are likely to be suspicious and frightened of official-dom and intent on keeping a low profile.

How might a culturally competent practitioner approach such a situation? The safety of children always comes first and sometimes those who have recently entered the United Kingdom do abuse their children. However, in many instances what appears to be neglect or cruelty may be the outcome of misunderstanding, poverty and a lack of social support. In this instance, both Yuri and Natasha are trying to earn a liv-ing. Both of them have been reluctant to bring themselves to the attention of the authorities by trying to claim benefits, and in any case neither of them know what their entitlements are. In these circumstances and without recourse to assistance from family members or community based groups, Yuri and his wife had to leave their children at home while they went out to work. As for Dimitry's wound, he was bitten by a dog when out with his father making home deliveries.

In the small Russian town and surrounding countryside where Yuri and Natasha lived, it is common for parents to withdraw older children from school to look after younger siblings or assist family members with their work to ensure a minimum household income. Cultural practices and customary coping strategies have com-bined with poverty in the United Kingdom to result in Yuri and Natasha withdrawing their children from school. Furthermore, Dimitry's wound remained untreated because Yuri and his wife, despite being quite worried, assumed they had to pay a doctor to treat him. This is because it has become the norm in parts of Russia, since the collapse of communism, for patients to be charged for access to treatment. The culturally competent practitioner will not assume that an individual's every behav-iour is attributable to custom. Instead, he or she will remain open-minded and explore the social and economic circumstances and forms of oppression, which influence the choices and actions of service-users and carers.

Obviously you would need to ensure that the couple receive information in Russian outlining all their entitlements and that they receive any necessary support that is available to them. You will need to act as a cultural broker to explore the different expectations of children in some parts of Russia and Britain. This might include exploring the different social and economic circumstances in the two countries and the consequences for the children in later life of not attending school regularly. Apart from focusing on their parental responsibilities, it is obvious that Yuri and Natasha are extremely isolated. You do not know of any Russian welfare associations or com-munity groups in the local-authority area, but you make an internet search. You turn up several groups and use contact with these to identify two further organisations which cater for a broad range of ethnic-minority needs. You also contact a number of mainstream bodies, such as the city council, and several national voluntary agen-cies working with migrants and refugees to get any listings they have of Russian-based organisations in the local area. You also identify websites which might be useful to Yuri and Natasha in networking with other compatriots and discover free access to the internet at the local library. You bring all this information to Yuri and Natasha to let them decide which contacts they wish to pursue. Cultural competence often involves a proactive approach to identifying resources on behalf of service-users in order to meet their cultural needs.

Further Reading

Dwyer, P. & Brown, D. (2005) 'Meeting basic needs? Forced migrants and welfare', *Social Policy and Society* 4(4), pp. 369–380. Drawing on interviews with forced migrants and the professionals who work with them, this article explores the difficulties they encounter. Their lack of entitlement to public support and the problems this creates for forced migrants are explored in some detail.

Harris, J. (2003) 'All doors are closed to us: a social model analysis of the experiences of disabled refugees and asylum seekers in Britain', *Disability and Society* 18(4), pp. 395–410. This article uses excerpts from interviews conducted with asylum seekers and refugees with disabilities to explore the barriers which prevent them from gaining access to services.

Hayes, D. & Humphries, B. (eds) (2004) *Social Work, Immigration and Asylum.* London: Jessica Kingsley. This collection of papers critically examines different aspects of asylum law, policy and practice from a social-work perspective. It considers the dilemmas posed for social workers when offering assistance to people who are subject to immigration control.

Wade, J., Mitchell, F. & Graeme, B. (2005) *Unaccompanied Asylum Seeking Children: The Response of Social Work Services.* London: British Association for Adoption and Fostering. This book describes the backgrounds of unaccompanied children and critically explores the response of Social Services to their needs. The coping strategies of refugee children are also detailed.

Conclusion: Developing Cultural Awareness

Cultural Awareness

Chapters Four to Eight of this book have focused on the importance of cultural knowledge. They have explored some of the areas of difference and similarity between members of various ethnic groups and between people within a given ethnic group. A number of key areas of variation have emerged and all of these will be explored by a culturally competent social worker as they assess and arrange services.

Differences between and within ethnic groups

- Values and aspirations
- Family structure
- The use of space
- Interpersonal space and eye contact
- Relations between the genders
- Relations between the generations
- Sex-role expectations
- Age-related expectations
- Decision-making responsibilities
- Caring responsibilities
- Types of coping strategiy
- Health beliefs and health care
- Food preparation and diet
- Literacy in and use of heritage languages
- Wearing of traditional garments and religious symbols
- Spirituality and religious observance
- The relationship between the individual, the family and the community
- The nature of local, national and transnational networks
- Ethnic and cultural identification
- Socio-economic circumstances
- Experience of racism and other forms of oppression

Cultural knowledge is only one aspect of cultural competence. To be able to effectively collect information about the cultural background of other people a social worker needs to be aware of their own cultural heritage. For those practitioners who are members of the white-majority community it can be particularly difficult to recognise and respect the diversity of beliefs, values, attitudes and social norms which are part and parcel of the everyday lives of people from minority communities. Dominelli (1997) and Thompson (2006) have attributed this to a white supremacist ideology at the cultural level in British society which assumes the superiority of Anglo-centric norms and devalues those of black people. Undoubtedly this does influence the outlook of people belonging to the white-majority population.

Equally, it is simply immensely difficult to reflect upon one's own cultural context if it is the dominant worldview. Such dominance naturalises one's own cultural heritage and acts as an obstacle to achieving objective distance. It is only by gaining cultural knowledge, that is learning to appreciate the variety of ways in which people with different heritages organise their lives, that practitioners from the white-majority community (or those from other backgrounds who have become very acculturated to Anglo-centric norms) can gain cultural awareness. This is because cultural knowledge is the accumulation of information about contrasting forms of living and offers practitioners a comparative analytical tool with which to examine the cultural influences upon their own lives. These influences are embedded in family relationships, lifestyle choices, beliefs and outlook. To get at the elements which make up their own cultural heritage, social workers need to ask themselves the following kinds of questions.

Social organisation

- How is my family organised?
- What are the important relationships in my family?
- What are the expectations of different family members?
- Who makes what kind of decisions in my family?
- What is considered proper or improper behaviour?
- Who is expected to take on caring responsibilities?
- What sort of relationship does my family have with other people in the neighbourhood?

Values and beliefs

- What are important values in my life?
- What are important aspirations for members of my family?
- Do I have spiritual beliefs and if so what are they?
- How do my spiritual beliefs influence other aspects of my life?
- What are the common health beliefs among members of my family and how do these influence my behaviour?

Lifestyle

- What sort of foods or beverages do I consume and why do I make these choices?
- What sort of clothes do I choose to wear and why?
- What choices do I make in relation to social and leisure activities and why?

Coping mechanisms

- What coping strategies do I typically adopt and where did I learn these?
- What social networks do I call upon for assistance?

Confronting Prejudice

Cultural awareness requires ongoing self-examination and reflection upon one's own heritage and the way in which it shapes perceptions and judgements about people from ethnic minorities. Cultural awareness is not about a passive absorption of cultural knowledge, such as that contained in this book. Nor is it about identifying the similarities or differences between one's own norms and those of others for the sake of it. Cultural awareness necessitates a painful recognition of the prejudices, presumptions and stereotypes one holds about people from other ethnic backgrounds. It means for example, asking yourself why you perhaps think that cohabitation of a heterosexual couple is superior to an arranged marriage or a visiting relationship by a male partner. In others words, the supremacy of Anglo-centric perspectives in British society and within the social-work profession itself have created a ranking of cultures whereby the dominant norms of the white-majority community are considered superior to those of others. It is this pre-programming that many social workers belonging to the white-majority community will have to grapple with.

Challenging Stereotypes

The cultural knowledge set out in this book uses research findings to challenge many of the dominant stereotypes about people from different ethnic groups. It also highlights a variety of values, beliefs and perspectives which are influential in the lives of people from the principal minority communities in the United Kingdom. At the same time, returning to Sue's (2001) Multidimensional Model of Cultural Competence (Chapter Three), it is important to remember that while 'all individuals are, in some respects, like some other individuals' they are also 'in some respects like no other individual'. In other words, there is always a danger of misusing cultural knowledge to stereotype people from different ethnic groups and to assume that everyone from the same minority has the same values and outlook. Just consider for a moment the sheer range of family forms, religious beliefs, lifestyle choices and outlooks which exist among people of the majority-white population. An equally diverse range exists within minority communities. Cultural knowledge should be used to inform cultural encounter with the uniqueness of each individual and not as a substitute for it.

The United Kingdom is a multicultural society and people are influenced not just by the values and perspectives which are handed down to them through their families, but also by their interactions with people from other ethnic communities at school, work and leisure. The mass media and the internet have also exposed people to many more sources of influence than has been true in the past. Many families are now themselves multicultural, as increasingly people inter-marry or cohabit from different ethnic backgrounds. Consequently, cultures are not pure monolithic structures which exert definable influences over people's values, beliefs and behaviours. Often influences are subtle, go unrecognised or exist as a composite of cultural and spiritual values drawn from a variety of sources. This multicultural context should inform cultural encounter.

Avoiding Cultural Relativity

Social workers are often caught in a dilemma when it comes to culture. On the one hand (as this book argues), they *must* understand, respect and accommodate the cultural and spiritual needs of service-users and their carers. On the other hand, practitioners *must not* adopt positions of cultural relativity which make no distinction between values or behaviours on the grounds that these are cultural expressions which automatically demand respect. Behaviours which are oppressive or abusive cannot be tolerated regardless of whether or not their perpetrators cite culture as a justification. Such practices include female genital mutilation, the marriage of under-age children and violence against women. This is far from an exhaustive list, but it should at least illustrate that there is a clear distinction to be made between practices which are simply different from those of the majority-white community and others which violate basic human rights, prejudice the safety of vulnerable people or are against the law.

This is not to deny that there are grey areas where it may not be so clear-cut as to whether a particular practice is directly harmful. But in the past, misunderstanding, misinformation and racial prejudice on the part of professionals has meant that many alternative social practices were pathologised, when in fact they were just different from those common among the white majority. What matters is to bring to bear cultural awareness and cultural knowledge in an open-minded encounter and to make an objective and unprejudiced judgement about the effects of a particular practice. Conversely, social workers need to be alert to the fact that some perpetrators of abuse use culture and religion as a pretext for violent and self-serving actions. For example, there is evidence to suggest that a particular interpretation of Islam is being deployed by some men to justify violence against women whose conduct is alleged to be un-Islamic (Mama, 1989: 67; Shaw, 2000: 162; Archer, 2003: 80–1). These sorts of interpretations are only subscribed to by a small number of people among the 1.5 million Muslims living in Britain. So what counts as culture or religious observance, and who decides it, is subject to constant dispute and contestation.

Cultural Competence

The journey towards cultural competence is difficult and fraught with hazard. It also promises personal enrichment and self-discovery for those prepared to put in the effort. To anxious practitioners working with people from ethnic minorities who are simply trying to get it right, cultural competence offers a sound basis for good practice. For service-users and carers it holds out the possibility of culturally appropriate provision, which better meets their needs. Cultural competence is now one of the greatest challenges for the social work profession.

Bibliography

Abd al'Atī, H. (1977) *The Family Structure in Islam*. Indianapolis: American Trust Publications

AFFORD (1998) *Survey of African Organisations in London*. London: African Foundation for Development

Ahmad, W.I.U. (1996) 'Family obligations and social change among Asian communities'. In W.I.U. Ahmad & K. Atkin (eds), *'Race' and Community Care*. Buckingham: Open University Press, pp. 51–72.

Ahmad, W.I.U. & Atkin, K. (eds) (1996) *'Race' and Community Care*. Buckingham: Open University Press

Ahmad, W.I.U., Darr, A. & Jones, L. (2000) '"I send my child to school and he comes back an Englishman": minority ethnic deaf people, identity politics and services'. In W.I.U. Ahmad (ed.), *Ethnicity, Disability and Chronic Illness*. Buckingham: Open University Press, pp. 67–84

Ahmad, W., Darr, A., Jones, L. & Nisar, G. (1998) *Deafness and Ethnicity: Services, Policy and Politics*. Bristol: Policy Press

Ahmed, A.A. (2000) 'Health and disease: an Islamic framework'. In A. Sheikh & A.R. Gatrad (eds), *Caring for Muslim Patients*. Abingdon: Radcliffe Medical Press, pp. 29–41

Al-Ali, N. (2002) 'Gender relations, transnational ties and rituals among Bosnian refugees', *Global Networks* 2(3), pp. 249–262

al-'Azmed, A. (1993) *Islams and Modernities*. London: Verso

Alexander, C. (2001) *The Art of Being Black: The Creation of Black British Youth Identities*. Oxford: Oxford University Press

Alexander, C. (2002) 'Beyond black: re-thinking the colour/culture divide', *Ethnic and Racial Studies* 25(4), pp. 552–571

Alexander, C. (2004) 'Imagining the Asian gang: ethnicity, masculinity and youth after "the riots"', *Critical Social Policy* 24(4), pp. 526–549

Ali, Z., Fazil, Q., Bywaters, P., Wallace, L. & Singh, G. (2001) 'Disability, ethnicity and childhood: a critical review of research', *Disability and Society* 16(7), pp. 949–968

Alleyne, M.C. (1989) *Roots of Jamaican Culture*. London: Pluto Press

Amin, A. (2002) *Ethnicity and the Multicultural City*, Report for the Department of Transport, Local Government and the Regions.

Amin, S. (1998) 'Family structure and change in rural Bangladesh', *Population Studies* 52, pp. 201–213

Anie, S.J., Kyeremeh, G. & Anarwat, S.G. (2001) *Mutual Health Organisations: A Quality Information Survey in Ghana* Bethesda, MD: Partners for Health Reformplus

Anthias, F. & Yuval-Davis, N. (1992) *Racialized Boundaries: Ethnic, Gender, Colour and Class Divisions and the Anti-Racist Struggle*. London: Routledge

Archer, L. (2001) 'Muslim brothers, black lads, traditional Asians: British Muslim young men's constructions of race, religion and masculinity', *Feminism and Psychology* 11(1), pp. 79–105

Archer, L. (2003) *Race, Masculinity and Schooling: Muslim Boys and Education*. Maidenhead: Open University Press

Archer, L. & Francis, B. (2005) 'Constructions of racism by British Chinese pupils and parents', *Race Ethnicity and Education* 8(4), pp. 387–407

Arthur, J. (2004) 'Language at the margins: the case of Somali in Liverpool', *Language Problems and Language Planning* 28(3), pp. 217–240

Back, L. (2002) *New Ethnicities and Urban Culture*. London: Routledge

Balk, D. (1994) 'Individual and community aspects of women's status and fertility in rural Bangladesh', *Population Studies* 48, pp. 21–45

Balk, D. (1997) 'Defying gender norms in rural Bangladesh: a social demographic analysis', *Population Studies* 51, pp. 153–172

Ballard, C. (1979) 'Conflict, continuity and change: second-generation South Asians'. In V.S. Khan (ed.), *Minority Families in Britain: Support and Stress*. London: Macmillan, pp. 109–130

Ballard, R. (1979) 'Ethnic minorities and the Social Services'. In V.S. Khan (ed.), *Minority Families in Britain: Support and Stress*. London: Macmillan, pp. 147–166

Ballard, R. (1994) 'Differentiation and disjunction among the Sikhs'. In R. Ballard (ed.), *Desh Pardesh: The South Asian Presence in Britain*. London: Hurst & Company, pp. 88–116

Ballard, R. & Ballard, C. (1977) 'The Sikhs: the development of South Asian settlements in Britain'. In J.L. Watson (ed.), *Between Two Cultures: Migrants and Minorities in Britain*. Oxford: Basil Blackwell, pp. 21–58

Banton, M. (1983) *Racial and Ethnic Competition*. Cambridge: Cambridge University Press

Barker, M. (1981) *The New Racism*. London: Junction Books

Barn, R. (1993) *Black Children in the Public Care System*. London: Batsford & British Agencies for Adoption and Fostering

Barn, R., Andrew, L. & Mantovani, N. (2005) *Life after Care: The Experiences of Young People from Different Ethnic Groups*. York: Joseph Rowntree Foundation

Barn, R., Sinclair, R. & Ferdinand, D. (1997) *Acting on Principle: An Examination of Race and Ethnicity in Social Services Provision for Children and Families*. London: British Agencies for Adoption and Fostering

Barnard, H. & Pettigrew, N. (2003) *Delivering Benefits and Services for Black and Minority Ethnic Older People*, Research Report No. 201. London: Department for Work and Pensions

Barot, R. (1998) 'Dowry and hypergamy among the Gujaratis in Britain'. In W. Menski (ed.), *South Asians and the Dowry Problem*. Stoke on Trent: Trentham Books, pp. 163–174

Barth, F. (1969) 'Introduction'. In F. Barth (ed.), *Ethnic Groups and Boundaries: The Social Organisation of Cultural Difference*. Oslo: Universitesforlaget, pp. 9–38

Basit, T.N. (1997) *Eastern Values, Western Milieu: Identities and Aspirations of Adolescent British Muslim Girls*. Aldershot: Ashgate

Baumann, G. (1997) 'Dominant and demotic discourses of culture: their relevance to multi-ethnic alliances'. In P. Werbner & T. Modood (eds), *Debating Cultural Hybridity*. London: Zed Books, pp. 209–225

BBC (2001) 'Charities unite against domestic violence', *BBC News*, 25 November, http://news.bbc.co.uk/1/hi/england/1674970.stm (accessed 18/06/07)

BBC (2005a) 'Hate crimes rise after UK bombs', *BBC News*, 28 July, http://news.bbc.co.uk/1/hi/uk/4723339.stm (accessed 30/07/05)

BBC (2005b) 'Born abroad: what's changed', BBC News, 7 September, http://news.bbc.co.uk/go/pr/fr/-/1/hi/uk/4220024.stm (accessed 23/09/06)

BBC (2006) '1,425,000 migrants in two years?', *BBC News*, 23 August, http://news.bbc.co.uk/go/pr/fr/-/hi/uk_politics/5274476.stm (accessed 23/09/06)

Begum, N. (1992) '...Something to be Proud of...': The Lives of Asian Disabled People and Carers in Waltham Forest. London: London Borough of Waltham Forest, Race Relations Unit and Disability Unit

Bequele, A. & Boyden, J. (eds) (1995) *Combating Child Labour*. Geneva: International Labour Office

Bhat, A.K. & Dhruvarajan, R. (2001) 'Ageing in India: drifting intergenerational relations, challenges and options', *Ageing and Society* 21, pp. 621–640

Bhugra, D. (1997) 'Coming out by South Asian gay men in the United Kingdom', *Archives of Social Behavior* 26(5), pp. 547–557

Bhui, K., Lawrence, A., Klineberg, E., Woodley-Jones, D., Taylor, S., Stansfeld, S. Viner, R. & Booy, R. (2005) 'Acculturation and health status among African-Caribbean, Banglasdeshi and White British adolescents', *Social Psychiatry and Psychiatric Epidemiology* 40, pp. 259–266

Blackledge, A. (1999) 'Language, literacy and social justice: the experiences of Bangladeshi women in Birmingham, UK', *Journal of Multilingual and Multicultural Development* 20(3), pp. 179–193

Blakey, D. & Crompton, D. (2000) *Policing London – Winning Consent*. London: Her Majesty's Inspectorate of Constabulary, Home Office

Böhm, A., Follari, M., Hewett, A., Jones, S., Kemp, N., Meares, D. et al. (2004) *Forecasting International Student Mobility – A UK Perspective*. London: British Council, Universities UK and IDP Education

Bonnett, A. (2000) *White Identities: Historical and International Perspectives*. Harlow: Pearson Education

Bowes, A.N. & Dar, N.S. (2000) 'Researching social care for minority ethnic older people: implications of some Scottish research', *British Journal of Social Work* 30(3), pp. 305–321

Bowes, A.N. & Wilkinson, H. (2003) 'We didn't know it would get that bad: South Asian experiences of dementia and service response', *Health and Social Care in the Community* 11(5), pp. 387–396

Bowling, B. (1993) 'Helping the community to care: four innovatory projects'. In J. Morton (ed.), *Recent Research on Services for Black and Minority Ethnic Elderly People*. London: Age Concern Institute of Gerontology, Kings College London, pp. 5–8

Brophy, J., Jhutti-Johal, J. & Owen, C. (2003) *Significant Harm: Child Protection Litigation in a Multi-cultural Setting*. London: Department of Constitutional Affairs

Brown, C. & Gray, P. (1985) *Racial Discrimination: 17 Years after the Act*. London: Policy Studies Institute

Brown, J., Newland, A., Anderson, P. & Chevannes, B. (1997) 'Caribbean fatherhood: under-researched, misunderstood'. In J.L. Roopnarine & J. Brown (eds), *Caribbean Families: Diversity among Ethnic Groups*. Greenwich, CT: Ablex Publishing, pp. 85–114

Bühler, C. (2004) 'Additional work, family agriculture, and the birth of a first or a second child in Russia at the beginning of the 1990s', *Population Research and Policy Review* 23, pp. 259–289

Burholt, V. (2004a) 'The settlement patterns and residential histories of older Gujaratis, Punjabis and Sylhetis in Birmingham, England', *Ageing and Society* 24, pp. 383–409

Burholt, V. (2004b) 'Transnationalism, economic transfers and families' ties: intercontinental contacts of older Gujaratis, Punjabis and Sylhetis in Birmingham with families abroad', *Ethnic and Racial Studies* 27(5), pp. 800–829

Burman, E., Smailers, S.L. & Chantler, K. (2004) '"Culture" as a barrier to service provision and delivery: domestic violence service for minoritized women', *Critical Social Policy* 24(3), pp. 332–357

Butt, J. & Mirza, K. (1996) *Social Care and Black Communities*. London: HMSO

Bywaters, P., Ali, Z., Fazil, Q., Wallace, L.M. & Singh, G. (2003) 'Attitudes towards disability amongst Pakistani and Bangladeshi parents of disabled children in the UK: considerations for service providers and the disability movement', *Health and Social Care in the Community* 11(6), pp. 502–509

Campbell, C., Cornish, F. and Mclean, C. (2004) 'Social capital, participation and the perpetuation of health inequalities: obstacles to African-Caribbean participation in "partnerships" to improve mental health', *Ethnicity and Health* 9(4), pp. 313–335

Campinha-Bacote, J. (2002) 'The process of cultural competence in the delivery of health-care services: a model of care', *Journal of Transcultural Nursing Care* 13(3), pp. 181–184

Carballeira, N. (1996) 'The LIVE and LEARN Model for culturally competent family services', *The Source* 6(2), pp. 4–12

Cardy, H.V. (1997) 'White women listen! Black feminism and the boundaries of sisterhood'. In H.S. Mirza (ed.), *Black British Feminism: A Reader*. London: Routledge, pp. 45–53

Carey-Wood, J., Duke, K., Karn, V. & Marshall, T. (1995) *The Settlement of Refugees in Britain*. London: HMSO

CAS & UNICEF (1999) *The Exodus*. Accra: Catholic Action For Street Children

Cawson, P., Wattam, C., Brooker, S. & Kelly, G. (2000) *Child Maltreatment in the United Kingdom: A Study of the Prevalence of Child Abuse and Neglect*. London: NSPCC

CCETSW (1991) *One Small Step Towards Racial Justice: The Teaching of Antiracism in Diploma in Social Work Programmes*. London: Central Council for the Education and Training of Social Workers

Chahal, K. (1999) *Minority Ethnic Homelessness in London: Findings from a Rapid Review*, Report for NHS Executive (London). Preston: Federation of Black Housing Organisations and University of Central Lancashire

Chamba, R., Ahmad, W., Hirst, M., Lawton, D. & Beresford, B. (1999) *On the Edge: Minority Ethnic Families Caring for a Severely Disabled Child*. Bristol: Policy Press

Chan, H. & Lee, R.P.L. (1995) 'Hong Kong families at the crossroads of modernism and traditionalism', *Journal of Comparative Family Studies* 26, pp. 83–99

Chana, P.J. (2005) *Domestic Violence: Impact of Culture on Experiences of Asian (Indian Subcontinent) Women*, Social Work Monographs. University of East Anglia, Norwich

Chand, A. (2000) 'The over-representation of Black children in the child protection system: possible causes, consequences and solutions', *Child and Family Social Work* 5, pp. 67–77

Charsley, K. (2005) 'Vulnerable brides and transnational *ghar damads*; gender, risk and "adjustment" among Pakistani marriage migrants to Britain', *Indian Journal of Gender Studies* 12(2&3), pp. 381–406

Chau, R.C.M. & Yu, S.W.K. (2001) 'Social exclusion of Chinese people in Britain', *Critical Social Policy* 21(1), pp. 103–125

Cheng, Y. (1994) *Education and Class: Chinese in Britain and the United States*. Aldershot: Avebury

Chinese Community Network (2006) *Information Digest*, Spring Issue. London: Chinese Community Network

Chiu, S. (1989) 'Chinese elderly people: no longer a treasure to take home', *Social Work Today* 2(48), pp. 15–17

Chiu, S. & Yu, S. (2001) 'An excess of culture: the myth of shared care in the Chinese community in Britain', *Ageing and Society* 21, pp. 681–699

CIH (2003) *Providing a Safe Haven: Housing Asylum Seekers and Refugees*. Coventry: Chartered Institute of Housing

Cinnirella, M. & Loewenthal, K.M. (1999) 'Religious and ethnic group influences on beliefs about mental illness: a qualitative interview study', *British Journal of Medical Psychology* 72, pp. 505–524

CJS (2006) *Race and the Criminal Justice System: An Overview to the Complete Statistics 2004–2005*. London: Criminal Justice System Race Unit

Clayton, G. (2004) *Textbook on Immigration and Asylum Law*. Oxford: Oxford University Press

Community Care (2006) 'Forced marriage: whose shame?', *Community Care* 16 (22 November), pp. 28–29

Council of Europe (2002) *The Protection of Women against Violence: Recommendation Rec (2002)5 of the Committee of Ministers to Member States on the Protection of Women against Violence*. Brussels: Council of Europe

Craig, G. & Rai, D.K. (1996) 'Social security, community care – and "race": the marginal dimension'. In W.I.U. Ahmad & K. Atkin (eds), *'Race' and Community Care*. Buckingham: Open University Press, pp. 124–143

CRE (1997) *Employment and Unemployment: Factsheet*. London: Commission for Racial Equality

Cross, M., Wrench, J. & Barnett, S. (1990) *Ethnic Minorities and the Careers Service: An Investigation into Processes of Assessment and Placement*, Research Paper Series No. 73. London: Employment Department

CSCI (2005) *Race Equality Scheme*. London: Commission for Social Care Inspection

Dadzie, S. (1993) *Older and Wiser: A Study of Educational Provision for Black and Ethnic Minority Elders*. Leicester: National Institute of Adult Continuing Education

Dale, A., Shaheen, J., Kalra, V. & Fieldhouse, E. (2002) 'Routes into education and employment for young Pakistani and Bangladeshi women in the UK', *Ethnic and Racial Studies* 25(6), pp. 942–968

Daley, P.O. (1998) 'Black Africans in Great Britain: spatial concentration and segregation', *Urban Studies* 35(10), pp. 1703–1724

Dalglish, C. (1989) *Refugees from Vietnam*. Basingstoke: Macmillan

Davies, S. (1996) *Adaptable Livelihoods*. Basingstoke: Macmillan

Daye, S.J. (1994) *Middle-class Blacks in Britain*. Basingstoke: Macmillan

Dein, S. & Sembhi, S. (2001) 'The use of traditional healing in South Asian psychiatric patients in the UK: interactions between professionals and folk psychiatrists', *Transcultural Psychiatry* 38(2), pp. 243–257

Dench, G., Gavron, K. & Young, M. (2006) *The New East End: Kinship, Race and Conflict*. London: Profile Books

Dengate, S. & Ruben, A. (2002) 'Controlled trial of cumulative behavioural effects of a common bread preservative', *Journal of Paediatrics and Child Health* 38, pp. 373–376

Department for Education and Skills (2005a) *National Curriculum Assessment, GCSE and Equivalent Attainment and Post-16 Attainment by Pupil Characteristics in England 2004*. London: Department for Education and Skills

Department for Education and Skills (2005b) *The Level of Highest Qualification Held by Young People and Adults: England 2004*. London: Department for Education and Skills

Department of Health (1991) *Care Management and Assessment: Practitioners' Guide*. London: HMSO

Department of Health (1999a) *The Government's Objectives for Children's Social Services*. London: Department of Health Publications

Department of Health (1999b) *The National Service Framework for Mental Health*. London: HMSO

Department of Health (1999c) *National Strategy for Carers*. London: HMSO

Department of Health (2000) *Assessing Children in Need and Their Families: Practice Guidance*. London: HMSO

Department of Health (2001a) *Health Survey for England 1999: The Health of Minority Ethnic Groups*. London: HMSO

Department of Health (2001b) *National Service Framework for Older People*. London: HMSO

Department of Health (2004) *National Service Framework for Children, Young People and Maternity Services*. London: Department for Education and Skills & Department of Health

Department of Health (2005) *Delivering Race Equality in Mental Health Care*. London: HMSO

Department of Health & Social Services Inspectorate (1998) *'They Look After Their Own, Don't They?': Inspection of Community Care Services for Black and Ethnic Minority Older People*. London: HMSO

Devore, W. & Schlesinger, E.G. (1999) *Ethnic-sensitive Social Work Practice*. New York: Allyn & Bacon

Dominelli, L. (1997) *Anti-racist Social Work*. Basingstoke: Macmillan

Dominelli, L. (2002) *Anti-Oppressive Social Work Theory and Practice*. Basingstoke: Palgrave Macmillan

Drumm, R., Pittman, S. & Perry, S. (2001) 'Women of war: emotional needs of ethnic Albanians in refugee camps', *Affilia* 16(4), pp. 467–487

Duke, K. & Marshall, T. (1995) *Vietnamese Refugees since 1982*. London: HMSO

Dwivedi, K.N. (2004a) 'Introduction'. In K.N. Dwivedi (ed.), *Meeting the Needs of Ethnic Minority Children*. London: Jessica Kingsley, pp. 17–41

Dwivedi, K.N. (2004b) 'Culture and Personality'. In K.N. Dwivedi (ed.), *Meeting the Needs of Ethnic Minority Children*. London: Jessica Kingsley, pp. 42–65

Dwyer, P. & Brown, D. (2005) 'Meeting basic needs? Forced migrants and welfare', *Social Policy and Society* 4(4), pp. 369–380

Eastern Eye (1994) 'Battered wife killed in-laws', *Eastern Eye*, 17 May, p. 5

Ekblad, S., Prochazka, H. & Roth, G. (2002) 'Psychological impact of torture: a 3-month follow-up of mass-evacuated Kosovan adults in Sweden: lessons learnt for Prevention', *Acta Psychiatrica Scandinavica* 106(412), pp. 30–36

Evandrou, M. (2000) 'Social inequalities in later life: the socio-economic position of older people from ethnic minority groups in Britain', *Population Trends* 101, pp. 11–18

Exploring Parenthood (1997) *Moyenda: Black Families Talking – Family Survival Strategies*. London: Exploring Parenthood

Flynn, R.M. (2002) *Short Breaks: Providing Better Access and More Choice for Black Disabled Children and their Parents*. Bristol: Policy Press

Foner, N. (1977) 'The Jamaicans: cultural and social change among migrants in Britain'. In J.L. Watson (ed.), *Between Two Cultures: Migrants and Minorities in Britain*. Oxford: Basil Blackwell, pp. 120–150

Gatrad, A.R. & Sheikh, A. (2000) 'Birth customs: meaning and significance'. In A. Sheikh & A.R. Gatrad (eds), *Caring for Muslim Patients*. Abingdon: Radcliffe Medical Press, pp. 57–71

Gervais, M. & Jovchelovitch, S. (1998) *The Health Beliefs of the Chinese Community in England: A Qualitative Research Study*. London: Health Education Authority

GHS (2003) *General Household Survey*. London: HMSO

Gibbons, J., Convoy, S. & Bell, C. (1995) *Operating the Child Protection System*. London: HMSO

Gibbons, J. & Wilding, J. (1995) *Needs, Risks and Family Support Plans: Social Services Departments' Responses to Neglected Children*, Interim report to Department of Health. Norwich: University of East Anglia

Gill, A. (2004) 'Voicing the silent fear: South Asian women's experiences of domestic violence', *The Howard Journal* 43(5), pp. 465–483

Gillborn, D. (1990) *'Race', Ethnicity and Education*. London: Unwin Hyman

Gillespie, M. (1995) *Television, Ethnicity and Cultural Change*. London: Routledge

Gilligan, P. & Akhtar, S. (2006) 'Cultural barriers to the disclosure of child sexual abuse in Asian communities: listening to what women say', *British Journal of Social Work* 36(8), pp. 1361–1377

Gilroy, P. (1987) *There Ain't No Black in the Union Jack: The Cultural Politics of Race and Nation*. London: Hutchinson

Gilroy, P. (1993) *The Black Atlantic: Modernity and Double Consciousness*. London: Verso

Ginn, J. & Arber, S. (2001) 'Pension prospects of minority ethnic groups: inequalities by gender and ethnicity', *British Journal of Sociology* 52(3), pp. 519–539

GLAD (1987) *Disability and Ethnic Minority Communities – A Study in Three London Boroughs*. London: Greater London Association for Disabled People

Goldstein, B.P. (1999) 'Black, with a white parent, a positive and achievable identity', *British Journal of Social Work* 29(2), pp. 285–301

Goldstein, B.P. (2002) '"Catch 22" – Black workers' role in equal opportunities for black service users', *British Journal of Social Work* 32(6), pp. 765–778

Goulborne, H. (2004) 'The transnational character of Caribbean kinship in Britain'. In S. McRae (ed.), *Changing Britain: Families and Households in the 1990s*. Oxford: Oxford University Press, pp. 176–197

Graham, M. (2002) *Social Work and African-centred Worldviews*. London: Venture Press

Gray, P., Elgar, J. & Bally, S. (1993) *Access to Training and Employment for Asian Women in Coventry*, Research Paper. Coventry: Coventry City Council, Economic Development Unit

Green, J.W. (1995) *Cultural Awareness in the Human Services*. Englewood Cliffs, NJ: Prentice-Hall

Griffiths, D., Sigona, N. & Zetter, R. (2006) 'Integrative paradigms, marginal reality: refugee community organisations and dispersal in Britain', *Journal of Ethnic and Migration Studies* 32(5), pp. 881–898

Guardian (2005) 'Two-thirds of Muslims consider leaving UK', *Guardian*, 26 July, http: //www.guardian.co.uk/print/0..5247604–117079.00.html (accessed 21/06/07)

Guardian (2006) 'By mutual agreement', *Guardian*, 3 October, p. 25

Gunaratnam, Y. (1997) 'Culture is not enough: a critique of multi-culturalism in palliative care'. In D. Field, J. Hockey & N. Small (eds), *Death, Gender and Ethnicity*. London: Routledge, pp. 167–186

Gupta, R. (2003a) 'Some recurring themes: Southall black Sisters, 1979–2003 – and still going strong'. In R. Gupta (ed.), *From Homebreakers to Jailbreakers: Southall Black Sisters*. London: Zed Books, pp. 1–27

Gupta, R. (2003b) 'Walls into bridges: the losses and gains of making alliances'. In R. Gupta (ed.), *From Homebreakers to Jailbreakers: Southall Black Sisters*. London: Zed Books, pp. 261–278

Hackett, L. & Hackett, R. (1994) 'Child-rearing practices and psychiatric disorder in Gujarati and British children', *British Journal of Social Work* 24(2), pp. 191–202

Hahlo, K. (1998) *Communities, Networks and Ethnic Politics*. Aldershot: Ashgate

Hall, S. (1992a) 'The question of cultural identity'. In S. Hall, D. Held & T. McGrew (eds), *Modernity and its Futures*. Cambridge: Polity Press, pp. 273–325

Hall, S. (1992b) 'New ethnicities'. In J. Donald & A. Rattansi (eds), *'Race' Culture and Difference*. London: Sage, pp. 252–259

Harris, J. (2003) 'All doors are closed to us: a social model analysis of the experiences of disabled refugees and asylum seekers in Britain', *Disability and Society* 18(4), pp. 395–410

Harris, P. & Rees, R. (2000) 'The prevalence of complementary and alternative medicine use among the general population: a systematic review of the literature', *Complementary Therapies in Medicene* 8, pp. 88–96

Hatton, C., Akram, Y., Shah, R., Robertson, J. & Emerson, E. (2004) *Supporting South Asian Families with a Child with Severe Disabilities*. London: Jessica Kingsley

Hatton, T.J. (2005) 'Explaining trends in UK immigration', *Journal of Population Economics* 18, pp. 719–740

Hayes, D. & Humphries, B. (eds) (2004) *Social Work, Immigration and Asylum*. London: Jessica Kingsley

Healy, M. & Aslam, M. (1990) *The Asian Community: Medicines and Traditions*. Huddersfield: Amadeus Press

Heath, A. & Cheung, S.Y. (2006) *Ethnic Penalties in the Labour Market: Employers and Discrimination*. London: Department for Work and Pensions

Heath, A and McMahon, D. (1997) 'Education and occupational attainments the impact of ethnic origins'. In V. Karn (ed.) *Ethnicity in the 1991 Census: Education, employment and housing among ethnic minorities in Britain*, vol. 4. London: HMSO, pp. 91–113.

Hélie, A. (2000) 'Holy hatred', *New Internationalist* 12(23), pp. 120–124

Helweg, A.W. (1986) *Sikhs in England*. Delhi: Oxford University Press

Henley, A. (1979) *Asian Patients in Hospital and at Home*. London: King's Fund

Henley, A. (1982) *Caring for Muslims and Their Families: Religious Aspects of Care*. London: Department of Health and Social Services/King Edward's Hospital Fund for London

Henley, A. (1983a) *Caring for Sikhs and Their Families: Religious Aspects of Care*. London: Department of Health and Social Services/King Edward's Hospital Fund for London

Henley, A. (1983b) *Caring for Hindus and Their Families: Religious Aspects of Care*. London: Department of Health and Social Services/King Edward's Hospital Fund for London

Hennink, M., Diamond, I. & Cooper, P. (1999) 'Young Asian women and relationships: traditional or transitional?', *Ethnic and Racial Studies* 22(5), pp. 867–891

Holland, K. & Hogg, C. (2001) *Cultural Awareness in Nursing and Health Care*. London: Arnold

Home Office (1965) *Immigration from the Commonwealth*, Cmnd. No. 2739. London: HMSO

Home Office (2000) *A Choice by Right: The Report of the Working Group on Forced Marriage*. London: Home Office, Communications Directorate

Home Office (2001a) *Building Cohesive Communities* (The Denham Report). London: HMSO

Home Office (2001b) *Secure Borders, Safe Haven; Integration with Diversity in Modern Britain*, Cm 5387. London: HMSO

Home Office (2004) *Home Office Statistical Bulletin: Asylum Statistics United Kingdom 2003*, November. London: Home Office

Howard, V. (1987) *A Report on Afro-Caribbean Christianity in Britain*. Leeds: University of Leeds

HRSA (2001) *Health Resources and Services Administration Study on Measuring Cultural Competence in Health Care Delivery Settings*. Washington, DC: US Department of Health and Human SERVICES, http://www.hrsa.gov/culturalcompetence/measures/default.htm (accessed 07/05/07)

Hughes, E.C. (1994) *On Work, Race and the Sociological Imagination*, ed. L.A. Coser. Chicago: University of Chicago Press

Hunt, J. & Macleod, A. (1999) *The Best-Laid Plans: Outcomes in Judicial Decisions in Child Protection Proceedings*. London: HMSO

Huque, A.S., Tao, J. & Wilding, P. (1997) 'Understanding Hong Kong'. In P. Wilding, A.S. Huque & J. Tao (eds), *Social Policy in Hong Kong*. Cheltenham: Edward Elgar, pp. 1–22

Hussain, Y., Atkin, K. & Ahmad, W. (2002) *South Asian Disabled Young People and their Families*. Bristol: Policy Press

Hutnik, N. (1991) *Ethnic Minority Identity: A Social Psychological Perspective*. Oxford: Clarendon Press

Hylton, C. (1999) *African-Caribbean Community Organisations: The Search for Individual and Group Identity*. Stoke on Trent: Trentham Books

Ifekwunigwe, J.O. (1997) 'Diaspora's daughters, Africa's Orphans? On lineage, authenticity and "mixed race"'. In H.S. Mirza (ed.) *Black British Feminist*. London: Routledge, pp. 127–152

Ifekwunigwe, J.O. (2002) '(An)other English city: multiethnicities, (post)modern moments and strategic identifications', *Ethnicities* 2(3), pp. 321–348

Ismail, H., Wright, J., Rhodes, P., Small, N. & Jacoby, A. (2005) 'South Asians and epilepsy: exploring health experiences, needs and beliefs of communities in the north of England', *Seizure* 14, pp. 497–503

Jackson, R. & Nesbitt, E. (1992) *Hindu Children in Britain*. Stoke on Trent: Trentham Books

Jacobson, J. (1997) 'Religion and ethnicity: dual and alternative sources of identity among young British Pakistanis', *Ethnic and Racial Studies* 20(2), pp. 238–256

Jawad, H. (2003) 'Historical and contemporary perspectives of Muslim women living in the West: experiences and images'. In H. Jawad & Benn, T. (eds), *Muslim Women in the United Kingdom and Beyond*. Leiden: Brill, pp. 1–18

Jenkins, R. (1997) *Rethinking Ethnicity: Arguments and Explorations*. London: Sage

Jewell, J.A. (1983) 'Theoretical basis of Chinese traditional medicine'. In S.M. Hillier & J.A. Jewell (eds), *Health Care and Traditional Medicine in China 1800–1982*. London: Routledge & Kegan Paul, pp. 221–241

Jhutti, J. (1998) 'Dowry among Sikhs in Britain'. In W. Menski (ed.), *South Asians and the Dowry Problem*. Stoke on Trent: Trentham Books, pp. 175–198

Jobanputra, R. & Furnham, A. (2005) 'British Gujarati Indian immigrants' and British Caucasians' beliefs about health and illness', *International Journal of Social Psychiatry* 51(4), pp. 350–364

Johal, A. (2003) 'Struggle not submission: domestic violence in the 1990s'. In R. Gupta (ed.), *From Homebreakers to Jailbreakers: Southall Black Sisters*. London: Zed Books, pp. 28–50

Jones, A., Jeyasingham, D. & Rajasooriya, S. (2002) *Invisible Families: The Strengths and Needs of Black Families in which Young People have Caring Responsibilities*. Bristol: Policy Press

Jones, L., Atkin, K. & Ahmad, W.I.U. (2001) 'Supporting Asian deaf young people and their families: the role of professionals and services', *Disability and Society* 16(1), pp. 51–70

Jones, S. (1988) *Black Culture, White Youth*. Basingstoke: Macmillan Education

Jones, T. (1993) *Britain's Ethnic Minorities*. London: Policy Studies Institute

Jones, T. & Ram, M. (2003) 'South Asian businesses in retreat? The case of the UK', *Journal of Ethnic and Migration Studies* 29(3), pp. 485–500

Kai, J. & Hedges, C. (1999) 'Minority ethnic community participation in needs assessment and service development in primary care: perceptions of Pakistani and Bangladeshi people about psychological distress', *Health Expectations* 2, pp. 7–20

Kalilombe, P. (1998) 'Black Christianity in Britain'. In G. ter Harr (ed.), *Strangers and Sojourners: Religious Communities in the Diaspora*. Leuven: Peeters, pp. 173–194

Karmi, G. (1996) *The Ethnic Health Handbook: A Factfile for Health Care Professionals*. Oxford: Blackwell Science

Karseras, P. & Hopkins, E. (1987) *British Asians – Health in the Community*. Chichester: John Wiley and Sons

Kassam-Khamis, T., Judd, P.A. & Thomas, J.E. (2000) 'Frequency of consumption and nutrient composition of composite dishes commonly consumed in the UK by South Asian Muslims originating from Bangladesh, Pakistan and East Africa (Ismailis)', *Journal of Hum Nutr Dietet* 13, pp. 185–196

Katbamna, S., Ahmad, W., Bhakta, P., Baker, R. & Parker, G. (2004) 'Do they look after their own? Informal support for South Asian Carers', *Health and Social Care in the Community* 12(5), pp. 398–406

Keating, F. & Robertson, D. (2004) 'Fear, black people and mental illness: a vicious circle?', *Health and Social Care in the Community* 12(5), pp. 439–447

Kelley, L.S. (2005a) 'Growing old in St Lucia: expectations and experiences in a Caribbean village', *Journal of Cross-cultural Gerontology* 20, pp. 67–78

Kelley, L.S. (2005b) 'Gendered elder care exchanges in a Caribbean village', *Western Journal of Nursing Research* 27(1), pp. 73–92

Kelly, L. (2003) 'Bosnian refugees in Britain: questioning community', *Sociology* 37(1), pp. 35–49

Khan, V.S. (1977) 'The Pakistanis: Mirpuri villagers at home and in Bradford'. In J.L. Watson (ed.), *Between Two Cultures: Migrants and Minorities in Britain*. Oxford: Basil Blackwell, pp. 57–89

Khanum, S.M. (2001) 'The household patterns of a "Bangladeshi village" in England', *Journal of Ethnic and Migration Studies* 27(3), pp. 489–504

Knott, K. (1994) 'The Gujarati Mochis in Leeds: from leather stockings to surgical boots and beyond'. In R. Ballard (ed.), *Desh Pardesh: The South Asian Presence in Britain*. London: Hurst & Company, pp. 213–230

Knott, K. & Khokher, S. (1993) 'Religious and ethnic identity among young Muslim women in Bradford', *New Community* 19(4), pp. 593–610

Knowles, C. (1991) 'Afro-Caribbeans and schizophrenia: how does psychiatry deal with issues of race, culture and ethnicity?', *Journal of Social Policy* 20(2), pp. 173–190

Kostovicova, D. & Prestreshi, A. (2003) 'Education, gender and religion: identity transformations among Kosovo Albanians in London', *Journal of Ethnic and Migration Studies* 29(6), pp. 1079–1096

Laguerre, M. (1987) *Afro-Caribbean Folk Medicine* South Hadley: Bergin & Garvey

Lau, A. (2004) 'Family therapy and ethnic minorities'. In K.N. Dwivedi (ed.), *Meeting the Needs of Ethnic Minority Children*. London: Jessica Kingsley, pp. 91–107

Law, I., Hylton, C., Kamani, A. & Deacon, A. (1994) *The Provision of Social Security Benefits to Minority Ethnic Communities: Findings*, Social Policy Research 59. York: Joseph Rowntree Foundation

Lawson, S. & Sachdev, I. (2004) 'Identity, language use, and attitudes: some Sylheti-Bangladeshi data from London, UK', *Journal of Language and Social Psychology* 23(1), pp. 49–69

Lees, S. (2002) 'Gender, ethnicity and vulnerability in young women in local authority care', *British Journal of Social Work* 32(7), pp. 907–922

Leininger, M. & McFarland, M.R. (2002) *Transcultural Nursing*. New York: McGraw-Hill

Leo-Rhynie, E.A. (1997) 'Class, race, and gender issues in child rearing in the Caribbean'. In J.L. Roopnarine & J. Brown (eds), *Caribbean Families: Diversity among Ethnic Groups*. Greenwich, CT: Ablex Publishing, pp. 25–56

Lewis, J. (1996) *Give Us a Voice*. London: Choice Press

Lloyd, C.B. & Desai, S. (1991) *Children's Living Arrangements in Developing Countries*, Working Paper No. 31. New York: The Population Council Research Division

Lloyd-Evans, S. & Potter, R.B. (2002) *Gender, Ethnicity and the Informal Sector in Trinidad*. Aldershot: Ashgate

Loewenthal, K.M. (1993) 'Religion, stress and distress', *Religion Today* 8, pp. 14–16

Lum, D. (1996) *Social Work Practice and People of Color: A Process Stage Approach*. Monterey, CA: Brooks/Cole

Luthra, M. (1997) *Britain's Black Population*. Aldershot: Arena

Lyle, S., Benyon, J., Garland, J. & McClure, A. (1996) *Education Matters: African Caribbean People and Schools in Leicestershire*. Leicester: Scarman Centre for the Study of Public Order, University of Leicester

Lynch, E.W. & Hanson, M.J. (1994) *Developing Cross-Cultural Competence: A Guide for Working with Young Children and Their Families*. Baltimore, MD: Paul H. Brooks Publishing

Macdonald, I., Bhavnani, R., Khan, L. & John, G. (1989) *Murder in the Playground: The Report of the Macdonald Inquiry into Racism and Racial Violence in Manchester Schools.* London: Longsight Press

Macpherson, W. (1999) *The Stephen Lawrence Inquiry: Report of an Inquiry by Sir William Macpherson of Cluny,* Cm 4262–I. London: Home Office

Maiter, S., Alaggia, R. & Trocmé, N. (2004) 'Perceptions of child maltreatment by parents from the Indian subcontinent: challenging myths about culturally based abusive parenting practices', *Child Maltreatment* 9(3), pp. 309–324

Maitra, B. & Miller, A. (2004) 'Children, families and therapists: clinical considerations and ethnic minority cultures'. In K.N. Dwivedi (ed.), *Meeting the Needs of Ethnic Minority Children.* London: Jessica Kingsley, pp. 108–129

Malek, M. & Joughin, C. (2004) *Mental Health Services for Minority Ethnic Children and Adolescents.* London: Jessica Kingsley

Mama, A. (1989) *The Hidden Struggle: Statutory and Voluntary Sector Responses to Violence against Black Women in the Home.* London: London Race and Housing Research Unit

Mares, P., Henley, A. & Baxter, C. (1985) *Health Care in Multiracial Britain.* Cambridge: Health Education Council/National Extension College

Marshall, A. (1996) 'From sexual denigration to self-respect: resisting images of Black female sexuality'. In D. Jarrett-Macauley (ed.), *Reconstructing Womanhood, Reconstructing Feminism: Writings on Black Women.* London: Routledge, pp. 5–35

Mason, D. (2000) *Race and Ethnicity in Modern Britain.* Oxford: Oxford University Press

Mclean, C., Campbell, C. & Cornish, F. (2003) 'African-Caribbean interactions with mental health services in the UK: experiences and expectations of exclusion as (re)productive of health inequalities', *Social Science and Medicine* 56, pp. 657–669

McLoughlin, S. (2005) 'Mosques and the public space: conflict and cooperation in Bradford', *Journal of Ethnic and Migration Studies* 31(6), pp. 1045–1066

Merrell, J., Kinsella, F., Murphy, F., Philpin, S. & Ali, A. (2005) 'Support needs of carers of dependent adults from a Bangladeshi community', *Journal of Advanced Nursing* 51(6), pp. 549–557

Messent, P., Saleh, H. & Solomon, X. (2005) 'Asian families "back home": an unexplored resource', *Contemporary Family Therapy* 27(3), pp. 329–344

Michael, S. & Florica, B. (1998) 'Opportunities, constraints and pluriactivity in rural Romania during the transition period: preliminary observations', *GeoJournal* 44(4), pp. 783–796

Michailova, S. & Worm, V. (2003) 'Personal networking in Russian and China: *Blat* and *Guanxi*', *European Management Journal* 21(4), pp. 509–519

Micklewright, J. (1999) 'Education, inequality and transition', *Economics of Transition* 7(2), pp. 343–376

Milanovic, B. (1998) *Income, Inequality, and Poverty during the Transition from Planned to Market Economy.* Washington, DC: World Bank

Miles, R. & Brown, M. (2004) *Racism.* London: Routledge

Miller, D. (1994) *Modernity: An Ethnographic Approach.* Oxford: Berg

Mir, G., Andrew, N., Ahmad, W. & Jones, L. (2001) *Learning Difficulties and Ethnicity.* London: Department of Health

Mir, G. & Tovey, P. (2003) 'Asian carers' experiences of medical and social care: the case of cerebral palsy', *British Journal of Social Work* 33(4), pp. 465–479

Mirza, H.S. (1992) *Young, Female and Black.* London: Routledge

Modood, T. (1988) '"Black" racial equality and Asian identity', *New Community* 14(3), pp. 397–404

Modood, T. (1992) *Not Easy Being British*. Stoke on Trent: Trentham Books

Modood, T. (2003) 'Ethnic differentials in educational performance'. In D. Mason (ed.), *Differences: Changing Patterns of Disadvantage in Britain*. Bristol: Policy Press, pp. 53–67

Modood, T., Beishon, S. & Virdee, S. (1994) *Changing Ethnic Identities*. London: Policy Studies Insitute

Modood, T., Berthoud, R., Lakey, J., Nazroo, J., Smith, P., Virdee, S. & Beishon, S. (eds) (1997) *Ethnic Minorities in Britain: Diversity and Disadvantage,* The Fourth National Survey of Ethnic Minorities. London: Policy Studies Institute

MOOA & CIBF (2004) *Needs of the Chinese Community in the North West Region*. Manchester: Manchester Oriental Organisations Alliance & Chinese in Britain Forum

Morris, J. (1998) *Still Missing? The Who Cares?* York: Joseph Rowntree Foundation

Moser, C. & Holland, J. (1997) *Household Responses to Poverty and Vulnerability*. Washington, DC: World Bank

NASW (2001) *Cultural Competence in Social Work Practice*. Washington, DC: National Association of Social Workers

National Black Carers Workers Network (2002) *We Care Too: A Good Practice Guide for People Working with Black Carers*. London: National Black Carers Workers Network/Afiya Trust

National Statistics (2003) *Census, April 2001*. London: HMSO

National Statistics Online (2005) *Labour Market*, http: //www.statistics.gov.uk/cci/ nugget.asp? id=271 (accessed 21/07/05)

Nazroo, J.Y. (1997) *The Health of Britain's Ethnic Minorities*. London: Policy Studies Institute

Nazroo, J.Y. (2003) 'Patterns of and explanations for ethnic inequalities in health'. In D. Mason (ed.), *Differences: Changing Patterns of Disadvantage in Britain*. Bristol: Policy Press, pp. 87–103

Nesbitt, E. (2005) *Sikhism: A Very Short Introduction*. Oxford: Oxford University Press

Nesbitt, S. & Neary, D. (2001) *Ethnic Minorities and their Pension Decisions: A Study of Pakistani, Bangladeshi and White Men in Oldham*. York: Joseph Rowntree Foundation

Nielsen, J.S. (1995) *Muslims in Western Europe*. Edinburgh: Edinburgh University Press

NIMHE (2003) *Inside Outside: Improving Mental Health Services for Black and Minority Ethnic Communities in England*. Leeds: National Institute for Mental Health in England

Nobes, G., Smith, M., Upton, P. & Heverin, A. (1999) 'Physical punishment by mothers and fathers in British homes', *Journal of Interpersonal Violence* 14(8), pp. 887–902

Observer (2005) 'Bombers, racists, the law: they're all out to get Muslims', *Observer*, 24 July, http: //www.guardian.co.uk/print/0,,5246407–117079,00.html (accessed 21/06/07)

O'Hagan, K. (2001) *Cultural Competence in the Caring Professions*. London: Jessica Kingsley

Office of the Registrar General (2001) *Census of India*. New Delhi: Office of the Registrar General

Okitikpi, T. (ed.) (2005) *Working with Children of Mixed Parentage*. Lyme Regis: Russell House Publishing

Olusanya, B. & Hodes, D. (2000) 'West African children in private foster care in City and Hackney', *Child: Care, Health and Development* 26(4), pp. 337–342

O'Neale, V. (2000) *Excellence Not Excuses: Inspection of Services for Ethnic Minority Children and Families*. London: Department of Health

Owusu-Bempah, K. (2005) 'Mulatto, marginal man, half-caste, mixed race: the one-drop rule in professional practice'. In T. Okitikpi (ed.), *Working with Children of Mixed Parentage*. Lyme Regis: Russell House Publishing, pp. 27–44

Parekh, B. (2000) *Report of the Commission on the Future of Multi-Ethnic Britain*. London: Profile Books

Parker, D. (1998) 'Chinese people in Britain: histories, futures and identities'. In G. Benton & F.N. Pieke (eds), *The Chinese in Europe*. Basingstoke: Macmillan, pp. 67–95

Parker, D. & Song, M. (2006) 'Ethnicity, social capital and the internet', *Ethnicities* 6(2), pp. 178–202

Payne, M. (2005) *Modern Social Work Theory*. Basingstoke: Palgrave Macmillan

Peach, C. (1998) 'South Asian and Caribbean ethnic minority housing choice in Britain', *Urban Studies* 35(10), pp. 1657–1680

Peach, C. (2006) 'Muslims in the 2001 Census of England and Wales: gender and economic disadvantage', *Ethnic and Racial Studies* 29(4), pp. 629–655

Pearson, V. (1997) 'Social care'. In P. Wilding, A.S. Huque & J. Tao (eds), *Social Policy in Hong Kong*. Cheltenham: Edward Elgar, pp. 95–111

Phillips, D. (1998) 'Black minority ethnic concentration, segregation and dispersal in Britain', *Urban Studies* 35(10), pp. 1681–1702

Phillips, A. and Dustin, M. (2004) 'UK initiatives on forced marriage: regulation, dialogue and exit'. *Political Studies* 52, pp. 531–551

Pickup, F. & White, A. (2003) 'Livelihoods in post-communist Russia', *Work, Employment and Society* 17(3), pp. 419–434

Plaza, D. (2000) 'Transnational grannies: the changing family responsibilities of elderly African Caribbean born women resident in Britain', *Social Indicators Research* 51, pp. 75–105

Prior, L., Chun, P.L. & Huat, S.B. (2000) 'Beliefs and accounts of illness: views from two Canonese-speaking communities in England', *Sociology of Health and Illness* 22(6), pp. 815–839

Pulsifer, M.B., Gordon, J.M., Brandt, J., Vining, E.P.G. & Freeman, J.M. (2001) 'Effects of ketogenic diet on development and behavior: preliminary report of a prospective study', *Developmental Medicine and Child Neurology* 43, pp. 301–306

Qureshi, K. & Moores, S. (1999) 'Tradition and translation in the lives of young Pakistani Scots', *European Journal of Cultural Studies* 2(3), pp. 311–330

Qureshi, T., Berridge, D. & Wenman, H. (2000) *Where to Turn: Family Support for South Asian Communities*. London: National Children's Bureau/Joseph Rowntree Foundation

Reynolds, T. (1997) '(Mis)representing the black (super)woman'. In H.S. Mirza (ed.), *Black British Feminism: A Reader*. London: Routledge, pp. 97–112

Reynolds, T. (2001) 'Black mothering, paid work and identity', *Ethnic and Racial Studies* 24(6), pp. 1046–1064

Robinson, L. (2005) 'South Asians in Britian: acculturation, identity and perceived discrimination', *Psychology and Developing Societies* 17(2), pp. 182–194

Rose, R. (1998) 'Getting things done in an anti-modern society: social capital networks in Russia', *Social Capital Initiative*, Working Paper No. 6. Washington, DC: World Bank

Rosenthal, D.A. (1987) 'Ethnic identity development in adolescence'. In J.S. Phinney & M.J. Rotheram (eds), *Children's Ethnic Socialisation: Pluralism and Development*. London: Sage, pp. 153–179

Runnymede Trust (1997) *Islamophobia: A Challenge for Us All.* London: The Runnymede
    Trust
Säävälä, M. (2001) *Fertility and Familial Power Relations.* Richmond: SURREY Curzon
Saeed, A., Blain, N. & Forbes, D. (1999) 'New ethnic and national questions in Scotland:
    post-British identities among Glasgow Pakistani teenagers', *Ethnic and Racial Studies*
    22(5), pp. 821–844
Sales, R. (2002) 'The deserving and the undeserving? Refugees, asylum seekers and welfare
    in Britain', *Critical Social Policy* 22(3), pp. 456–478
Salisbury, H. & Upson, A. (2004) *Ethnicity, Victimisation and Worry about Crime: Findings
    from the 2001/02 and 2002/03 British Crime Surveys.* London: Home Office
Samad, Y. & Eade, J. (2002) *Forced Marriage.* London: Community Liaison Unit, Foreign
    and Commonwealth Office
Sandu, A. (2005) 'Poverty, women and child health in rural Romania: uninformed choice
    or lack of services', *Journal of Comparative Policy Analysis* 7(1), pp. 5–28
Saraswathi, T.S. & Dutta, R. (1988) *Invisible Boundaries: Grooming for Adult Roles.* New
    Delhi: Northern Book Centre
Sashidharan, S.P. & Francis, E. (1993) 'Epidemiology, ethnicity and schizophrenia'. In
    W.I.U. Ahmad (ed.), *'Race' and Health in Contemporary Britain.* Buckingham: Open
    University Press, pp. 96–113
Schnoll, R., Burshtey, D. & Cea-Aravena, J. (2003) 'Nutrition in the treatment of atten-
    tion-deficit hyperactivity disorder: a neglected but important aspect', *Applied
    Psychophysiology and Biofeedback* 28(1), pp. 63–75
Schoen, D.E. (1977) *Enoch Powell and the Powellites.* London: Macmillan
Secker, J. & Harding, C. (2002) 'Users' perceptions of an African and Caribbean mental
    health resource centre', *Health and Social Care in the Community* 10(4), pp. 270–276
SEU (2000a) *Minority Ethnic Issues in Social Exclusion and Neighbourhood Renewal.*
    London: Social Exclusion Unit
SEU (2000b) *Report of Policy Action Team 12: Young People.* London: Social Exclusion Unit
Sewell, T. (1997) *Black Masculinities and Schooling: How Black Boys Survive Modern
    Schooling.* Stoke on Trent: Trentham Books
Shah, R. & Hatton, C. (1999) *Caring Alone: Young Carers in South Asian Communities.*
    London: Barnardo's
Shain, F. (2003) *The Schooling and Identity of Asian Girls.* Stoke on Trent: Trentham Books
Shang, A. (1988) *The Chinese in Britain.* London: Batsford Academic and Educational
Shaw, A. (2000) *Kinship and Continuity: Pakistani Families in Britain.* Amsterdam: Hardwood
Shaw, A. (2001) 'Kinship, cultural preference and immigration: consanguineous marriage
    among British Pakistanis', *Journal of Royal Anthropological Institute* 7, pp. 315–334
Sheikh, A. & Gatrad, A.R. (eds) (2000) *Caring for Muslim Patients.* Abingdon: Radcliffe
    Medical Press
Shen, Z. (2004) 'Cultural competence modules in nursing: a selected annotated bibliogra-
    phy', *Journal of Transcultural Nursing* 15(4), pp. 317–322
Shevchenko, O. (2002) '"Between the holes": emerging identities and hybrid patterns of
    consumption in Post-socialist Russia', *Europe-Asia Studies* 54(6), pp. 841–866
Siapera, E. (2005) 'Minority activism on the web: between deliberative democracy and
    multiculturalism', *Journal of Ethnic and Migration Studies* 31(3), pp. 499–519
Siddiqui, H. (2003) '"It was written in her kismet": forced marriage'. In R. Gupta (ed.),
    From Homebreakers to Jailbreakers: Southall Black Sisters. London: Zed Books, pp. 67–91

Simpson, A. & Stevenson, J. (1994) *Half a Chance, Still?* Nottingham: Nottingham and District Racial Equality Council

Sims, J.M. (2007) *The Vietnamese Community in Great Britain – Thirty Years On.* London: The Runnymede Trust

Siu, H.F. (1993) 'Reconstituting dowry and brideprice in South China'. In D. Davis & S. Harrell (eds), *Chinese Families in the Post-Mao Era.* Berkeley: University of California Press, pp. 165–188

Smaje, C. (1995) *Health, 'Race' and Ethnicity: Making Sense of the Evidence.* London: King's Fund Institute

Smaje, C. & Le Grand, J. (1997) 'Ethnicity, equity and use of health services in the British NHS', *Social Science and Medicine* 45(3), pp. 485–496

Smith, M.G. (1986) 'Pluralism, race and ethnicity in selected African countries'. In J. Rex & D. Mason (eds), *Theories of Race and Ethnic Relations.* Cambridge: Cambridge University Press, pp. 187–225

Song, M. (1995) 'Between "the front" and "the back": Chinese women's work in family business', *Women's Studies International Forum* 18(3), pp. 285–298

Sproston, K. & Nazroo, J. (eds) (2002) *Ethnic Minority Psychiatric Illness Rates in the Community (EMPIRIC).* London: HMSO

Srinivasan, S. (1995) *The South Asian Petty Bourgeoisie in Britain.* Aldershot: Avebury

Sue, D.W. (2001) 'Multidimensional facets of cultural competence', *The Counselling Psychologist* 29(6), pp. 790–821

Sue, D.W. (2005) *Multicultural Social Work Practice.* Indianapolis: Wiley

Sutton, C.R. (2004) 'Celebrating ourselves: the family reunion rituals of African-Caribbean transnational families', *Global Networks* 4(3), pp. 243–257

Taylor, M.J. (1987) *Chinese Pupils in Britain.* Windsor: Nfer-Nelson

Thelle, H. (2004) *Better to Rely on Ourselves: Changing Social Rights in Urban China since 1979.* Copenhagen: Nordic Institute of Asian Studies

Thoburn, J., Chand, A. & Proctor, J. (2005) *Child Welfare Services for Minority Ethnic Families.* London: Jessica Kingsley

Thoburn, J., Wilding, J. & Watson, J. (2000) *Family Support in Cases of Emotional Maltreatment and Neglect.* London: HMSO

Thomas, G. (1990) *Afro-Caribbean Elderly People: Coping with Aging.* Coventry: University of Warwick

Thompson, N. (1998) *Promoting Equality: Challenging Discrimination and Oppression in the Human Services.* Basingstoke: Macmillan

Thompson, N. (2006) *Anti-Discriminatory Practice.* Basingstoke: Palgrave Macmillan

Toulis, N.R. (1997) *Believing Identity: Pentecostalism and the Mediation of Jamaican Ethnicity and Gender in England.* Oxford: Berg

Troyna, B. & Carrington, B. (1990) *Education, Racism and Reform.* London: Routledge

Turshen, M. (1998) 'Women's war stories'. In M. Turshen & C. Twagiramariya (eds), *What Women do in Wartime: Gender and Conflict in Africa.* London: Zed Books, pp. 1–26

UNDP (2004) *Human Development Report: Cultural Liberty in Today's Diverse World.* New York: United Nations Development Programme

Vernon, A. (2002) *Users' Views of Community Care for Asian Disabled People.* Bristol: Policy Press/Joseph Rowntree Foundation

Wade, J., Mitchell, F. & Graeme, B. (2005) *Unaccompanied Asylum Seeking Children: The Response of Social Work Services.* London: British Association for Adoption and Fostering

Wadley, S.S. (1995) 'No longer a wife: widows in rural north India'. In L. Harlan & P.B. Courtright (eds), *From the Margins of Hindu Marriage*. Oxford: Oxford University Press, pp. 92–118

Wah, Y.Y., Avari, B. & Buckley, S. (1996) *British Soil Chinese Roots*. Liverpool: Countrywise

Wallace, C. & Latcheva, R. (2006) 'Economic transformation outside the law: corruption, trust in public institutions and the informal economy in transition countries of Central and Eastern Europe', *Europe–Asia Studies* 58(1), pp. 81–102

Wallman, S. (1979) 'Introduction: the scope for ethnicity'. In S. Wallman (ed.), *Ethnicity at Work*. London: Macmillan, pp. 1–14

Wanigaratne, S., Dar, K., Abdulrahim, D. & Strang, J. (2003) 'Ethnicity and drug use: exploring the nature of particular relationships among diverse populations in the United Kingdom', *Drugs: Education, Prevention and Policy* 10(1), pp. 39–55

Wardak, A. (2000) *Social Control and Deviance: A South Asian Community in Scotland*. Aldershot: Ashgate

Warrier, S. (1994) 'Gujarati Prajapatis in London: family roles and sociability networks'. In R. Ballard (ed.), *Desh Pardesh: The South Asian Presence in Britain*. London: Hurst & Company, pp. 191–212

Watson, J.L. (1977) 'The Chinese: Hong Kong villagers in the British catering trade'. In J.L. Watson (ed.), *Between Two Cultures: Migrants and Minorities in Britain*. Oxford: Basil Blackwell, pp. 181–213

Wei, L. (1994) *Three Generations, Two Languages and One Family: Language Choice and Language Shift in a Chinese Community in Britain*. Clevedon: Multilingual Matters

Weine, S.M., Ware, N. & Klebic, A. (2004) 'Converting cultural capital among teen refugees and their families from Bosnia-Herzegovina', *Psychiatric Services* 55(8), pp. 923–927

Werbner, P. (1997) 'Essentialising essentialism, essentialising silence: ambivalence and multiplicity in the constructions of racism and ethnicity'. In P. Werbner & T. Modood (eds), *Debating Cultural Hybridity*. London: Zed Books, pp. 226–256

Werbner, P. (2004) 'Theorising complex diasporas: purity and hybridity in the South Asian public sphere in Britain', *Journal of Ethnic and Migration Studies* 30(5), pp. 895–911

White, P. (1998) 'The settlement pattern of developed world migrants in London', *Urban Studies* 35(10), pp. 1725–1744

Whiteley, P., Rodgers, J., Savery, D. & Shattock, P. (1999) 'A gluten-free diet as intervention for autism and associated disorders: preliminary findings', *Autism* 3(1), pp. 45–65

Wilding, P. (1997) 'Social policy and social development in Hong Kong', *Asian Journal of Public Administration* 19, pp. 244–275

Williams, L. (2006) 'Social networks of refugees in the United Kingdom: tradition, tactics and new community spaces', *Journal of Ethnic and Migration Studies* 32(5), pp. 865–879

Wilson, M. (2001) 'Black women and mental health: working towards inclusive mental health services', *Feminist Review* 68, pp. 34–51

Wrench, J. & Hassan, E. (1996) *Ambition and Marginalisation: A Qualitative Study of Underachieving Young Men of Afro-Caribbean Origin*. London: HMSO

Wrench, J. & Qureshi, T. (1996) *Higher Horizons: A Qualitative Study of Young Men of Bangladeshi Origin*. London: HMSO

Wyss, B. (2001) 'Gender and cash child support in Jamaica', *Review of Radical Political Economics* 33, pp. 415–439

Yamey, G. & Greenwood, R. (2004) 'Religious views of the "medical" rehabilitation model: a pilot qualitative study', *Disability and Rehabilitation* 26(8), pp. 455–462

Yip, A.K.T. (2004) 'Negotiating space with family and kin in identity construction: the narratives of British non-heterosexual Muslims', *The Sociological Review* 52(3), pp. 336–350

Yip, A.K.T. (2005) 'Queering religious texts: an exploration of British non-heterosexual Christians' and Muslims' strategy of constructing sexuality affirming hermeneutics', *Sociology* 39(1), pp. 47–65

Yu, W.K. (2000) *Chinese Older People: A Need for Social Inclusion in Two Communities.* Bristol: Policy Press

Index